SYST
WAR AND PEACE

SECOND EDITION

Theodore Caplow
Louis Hicks

University Press of America,® Inc.
Lanham · Boulder · New York · Toronto · Plymouth, UK

Copyright © 2002 by
University Press of America,® Inc.
4501 Forbes Boulevard
Suite 200
Lanham, Maryland 20706
UPA Acquisitions Department (301) 459-3366

Estover Road
Plymouth PL6 7PY
United Kingdom

ISBN-13: 978-0-7618-2198-4 (paperback : alk. paper)
ISBN-10: 0-7618-2198-8 (paperback : alk. paper)

Contents

Part Two - *Military Systems*

v

Part Three - *Peacekeeping Systems*

Preface to the Second Edition

In the seven years since the first edition of this book went to press, the ground has shifted under the international system. During that interval, there was not a single armed clash between sovereign nations but innumerable armed conflicts within nations, while the secure, technologically advanced societies were repeatedly shocked by the ability of miniscule terrorist groups to sow havoc and fear in their midst.

Within that brief period—somewhere between the massacres in Rwanda and the massacres in East Timor—the poorly organized international community acquired the right and duty to intervene in internecine conflicts that become sufficiently bloody to attract its wavering attention. Because the international community is poorly organized, each intervention—in Bosnia, Haiti, Somalia, Colombia, Sierra Leone, Kosovo, Macedonia, Congo, East Timor, and Afghanistan—had to be improvised in haste and the results were not uniformly favorable. But the long-standing principle that every nation-state was exclusively responsible for maintaining order within its territory was irretrievably breached.

"You may not be interested in war," wrote one of the twentieth century's most successful generals, "but war is interested in you."

That came home to most Americans as the towers of the World Trade Center collapsed on September 11, 2001, although the terrorist campaign against the U.S. had been expanding ever since Islamic fundamentalists attacked that same structure in 1993. Meanwhile, in Israel, northern Ireland, Japan and western Europe, the vulnerability of technologically advanced societies and the difficulty of defending them against determined fanatics was demonstrated again and again.

The immediate future is, as ever, unknowable but it surely holds more war than peace. The systematic investigation of war and peace by the social sciences has never been more urgently needed.

Many thanks are due to our students whose comments over the years have led us to numerous improvements in the text. We are very grateful to Pamela Hicks for her significant efforts in the editing and formatting of this edition.

Preface to the First Edition

This book is an introduction to the sociological study of what Charles Sumner in a more eloquent age called, "the War System of the Commonwealth of Nations,"—really two systems if we include peace along with war. It views the national governments and would-be national governments which participate in these systems as social actors and the commonwealth of nations as a giant social group that in many ways resembles social groups composed of mere individuals. This perspective differs somewhat from that of the historian or the political scientist and it leads us to consider questions that are seldom raised in their disciplines, for instance about the connections between systems of war and peace and other major social institutions.

With a few notable exceptions, contemporary sociologists have not given systems of war and peace their rightful place as institutions no less consequential than the family, religion, industry, politics and science—all of which have been shaped as much by war and peace as by each other. It is misleading to describe the national societies of the twentieth century without recognizing the pervasive effects of war and peace but that is what many sociology textbooks try to do. This huge sphere of social action is somehow made to disappear from the realm of normality.

Very few courses in the sociology of war and peace are currently taught in American colleges and universities and most of those fall into two specialized categories: military sociology and peace studies. These are interesting topics but they fall far short of representing the range and complexity of systems of war and peace. Until now, there has been no suitable textbook for courses concerned with that larger subject matter. It is our hope that the publication of this volume will stimulate the development of new courses to fill a conspicuous gap in the sociological curriculum.

Thanks are due to St. Mary's College of Maryland for a faculty development grant that enabled Hicks to work on the manuscript during the academic year 1994–1995, to Kathleen Delaney and Stephanie Lake for cheerful and competent editorial assistance, to Curt Raney for design assistance, and to some hundreds of University of Virginia undergraduates whose intelligent interest in the sociology of war and peace inspired this project.

§

Part One

Institutional Patterns

1

War as a Social Institution

Conflict is the central problem of human society, and the problem is especially acute today because of the destructiveness of modern weapons. In this chapter we define social conflict, distinguishing it from other forms of social interaction; identify the principal types of social conflict; mention some clues from animal behavior; survey the evolution of war; and identify the principal types of modern war.

The Nature of Social Conflict

Social conflict is an interaction between two or more human groups seeking to benefit themselves by injuring others. The minimum elements of social conflict are: two or more antagonistic groups, one or more scarce things for which they contend, and means of inflicting injury. Social conflict should not be confused with impersonal competition, one-sided aggression, systems of exploitation, conflicts between humans and animals, differences of taste, psychological indecision, or the opposition of abstract ideas.

War may be defined as social conflict between organizations that possess trained and disciplined combat forces equipped with deadly weapons. This sociological definition should be contrasted with the legal definition of war as a formally defined situation that permits and encourages violent and hostile actions that are otherwise prohibited by law (Grotius [1625] 1901).

The standard attributes of social conflict include implicit cooperation, boundary maintenance, emotional arousal, perceptual distortions, spontaneous mythmaking and an eventual redistribution of
resources.

The idea of *implicit cooperation* is neatly expressed by the
common parental admonition to quarreling children: "It takes two
to fight." When one side of an armed conflict refuses to fight there
may be a slaughter, but there cannot be a war. Mass exterminations
have often occurred during wartime, but they are not war. Most
armed forces are reluctant to fight defenseless civilians, manage
internment camps, or execute prisoners in secret. A general officer
who became involved in the criminal investigation of "termina-
tions with extreme prejudice" by the U.S. Army—working in
a partnership with the Central Intelligence Agency (CIA)—in
Vietnam turned aside requests to drop the inquiry saying, "Murder
doesn't fit in my book anywhere . . . I was not raised that way"
(Stein 1992, 306). Failures to observe the norms hidden in the idea
of implicit cooperation between belligerents, such as executing
prisoners of war, are termed "war crimes." The "Laws of War,"
though not enacted by a world legislature, apply to every international war, though the content of the laws may vary with local
circumstances (Axinn 1989, 112). We return to this subject in
Chapter 4.

Boundary maintenance during social conflict refers to the
heightened sense of organizational, institutional, and territorial
distinctiveness and the special steps taken to enhance the differences between opposing forces. The Union wore blue; the Confed-
erates, gray. Each small unit of the armed forces has a special
insignia to identify its members. Armed forces in conflict restrict
communication with the opposing side to very limited formal
channels—unauthorized communication across the boundary is
an offense punishable by court-martial. Nations at war commonly
seal their borders to normal traffic and may expel or intern suspect
populations inside the country, as the United States did to citizens
of Japanese ancestry during World War II.

Emotional arousal is a standard feature of social conflict.
Individuals engaging in conflict may be frightened, exhilarated,

appalled, satisfied, embittered or saddened by it, but they are seldom indifferent. Those few members of military organizations who approach combat with equanimity are regarded as freaks by their comrades. It is generally believed that a commander who is not emotionally stirred by combat cannot exercise effective leadership. The experience of emotional arousal during wartime can be long-lasting: even veterans of prisoner-of-war camps have been known to report that they "were never more alive" than during their imprisonment.

Perceptual distortion is the warping of reality that occurs under the emotional pressure generated by social conflict. In mild conflicts this distortion may be minor and self-evident. Team sports commonly lead to mild distortions of reality that must be corrected by coaches, umpires, and calmer players. During intense conflicts, like civil wars, reality can be twisted beyond recognition. Enemies become alien fiends, capable of inhuman strength and brutality. Armor becomes impenetrable—or unnecessary as in the case of Native Americans going into battle after the Ghost Dance. Transport aircraft are expected to supply entire ground armies (the Luftwaffe promised to provision the surrounded German Sixth Army after the Soviets surrounded it at Stalingrad). After the conflict is over, participants are often shocked to discover how distorted their perceptions were.

Mythmaking is the creation and dissemination of ideologies that explain and justify the conflict for participants. Myths appear spontaneously and spread rapidly through an engaged force. Preposterous accounts of enemy behavior are widely accepted. Heroic feats on one's own side are celebrated without regard to plausibility.

The Typical Sequence of Social Conflict

The typical sequence of social conflict begins with a hostile contact and runs through threats, mobilization, confrontation, further mobilization, hostile action, escalation, counterescalation, retreat, assessment of outcome, suspension of hostilities, and finally to the reorganization of one or both parties.

Hostile contact involves the mutual recognition of potentially damaging intent. Each side recognizes the other as an adversary and identifies one or more objects of contention. *Threats* routinely follow hostile contact. They may be secret or open; explicit or vague; authoritative or merely rumored. Threats have two distinct purposes: (1) warning, and, if possible intimidating, the adversary; (2) alerting one's own forces to the impending conflict.

Mobilization is preparation for hostile action. It may be brief or protracted. The cowboy who unsnaps his holster is adequately mobilized. In tribal societies, mobilization involves no more than the assembly of combatants, weapons, and supplies and the suspension of normal routines. In technologically advanced societies, mobilization becomes much more complicated. Elaborate military and civilian bureaucracies operate sophisticated programs intended to design, produce, store, and deploy the materiel[1] required for the conflict. Other elaborate bureaucracies arrange for the transfer of millions of citizens from peacetime to wartime roles.

At the same time, the whole population must be initiated into new ways of thinking and behaving.

Hostile action is the actual employment of weapons against the enemy. Even if successful, the action will be resisted. Almost invariably resistance results in a resort to further hostilities with weapons of greater destructiveness, or to the widening of the conflict in other ways. This is called *escalation*. The adversary must match or beat the escalation. The enemy may respond in kind, or by opening up a new front, or by introducing a novel weapon. A cycle of escalation and *counter-escalation* may ensue, broadening and deepening the conflict. This may continue far beyond the intentions of anyone initially involved in the conflict. Evenly matched adversaries may escalate to their ultimate limits and fight at that level until the total exhaustion of one or both sides.

Eventually, one side will *retreat* from the field, either by actually fleeing or by arranging some type of truce.

The end of hostile action permits an *assessment* of the outcome of the conflict. Normally, some formal understanding of what has taken place and its meaning for the future of the parties will be negotiated and attested. The objects of contention—land, money, honor, religious allegiance, trading privileges, or whatever—are redistributed.

Finally, the loser, and often also the winner, *reorganizes* to adapt to the new situation created by the conflict.

Relatively simple conflicts, even simple wars, fall neatly into this scheme. The Falklands War saw hostile contact take place as Argentina and Great Britain squabbled for years over the sovereignty of the tiny sheep-covered islands. Threats were issued, especially by Argentina, stating what conditions would provoke hostilities. The Argentine army mobilized and seized the islands. British mobilization took longer because of the vast distance their forces needed to cover. As British forces arrived, escalation and counter-escalation ensued. What had begun as a small infantry action now involved Argentine air-to-ship missiles, a much larger invasion of the islands by British naval and land forces, and the sinking of ships on both sides. Because the two parties were so unevenly matched—recent Argentine military experience consisted mostly of murdering leftist students, while the British fielded many of the assets with which they had prepared to fight the Soviet Union in the air and at sea—the conflict was brief and decisive. Argentine units that could retreat did so; the others surrendered. The outcome was assessed by both as a return to the previous dispute over sovereignty of the islands, with promises to negotiate the issue in the future. Reorganization in Britain included a swift rise in the Prime Minister's political fortunes. In Argentina, the military government responsible for the war was overthrown and civilian rule was restored.

The typical sequence of social conflict is quite stable, but some phases may be omitted in a particular conflict that terminates quickly. Numerous conflicts between NATO and the Warsaw Pact bloc during the Cold War barely reached the mobilization stage before an assessment was agreed upon. Conversely, long-running conflicts can see an occlusion of phases, so that eventually, many phases can be running concurrently. In the ongoing Israeli-Palestinian conflict, the parties are sometimes engaged in all the phases—threats, mobilization, hostile action, escalation, counter-escalation, retreat, assessment and re-organization—almost simultaneously.

Basic Types of Social Conflict

Episodic conflicts are recurrent events regulated by rules of engagement that are respected by the parties. The episodes of conflict occur at scheduled times and places under prescribed conditions. The weapons and tactics that may be used are specified in advance, together with very detailed procedures for regulating and terminating hostile actions. A superior authority or mutual agreement of the contestants controls the conflict and oversees the distribution of rewards at its end. Episodic conflict is intensely gratifying both to participants and to spectators. It arouses strong but transient emotions. Group boundaries are maintained and usually reinforced.

European wars in the century prior to Napoleon (the so-called "parlor wars") were essentially episodic.

Chronic conflict occurs between parties in permanent contact in situations where the gains of one group are losses for another. Chronic conflicts are neither planned nor scheduled. They appear spontaneously. The weapons and tactics of each side are regarded as illegitimate by the other. The parties seek rewards within an established situation, but the conflict is without specified means. There are often distinct offensive and defensive roles; the object of the offensive side is to shift an existing boundary that the defenders are struggling to maintain. One side seeks to subjugate, the other to avoid subjugation. In any set of interacting organizations, up to and including national states, there is sure to be a chronic conflict between the two leading members of the set as they contend for dominance. The balances of power that develop under conditions of chronic conflict may be quite stable under certain conditions (Wright 1965) but generally break down in the long run. Chronic conflict is more often troubling than gratifying to participants and spectators.

International relations in peacetime are an example of chronic conflict. As we discuss in Chapter 3, states routinely seek to dominate other states and to avoid domination by other states. They defend their geographic boundaries with walls and legal sanctions, and their economic boundaries with fiscal policy, tariffs, and export subsidies, but the ultimate guarantor of national boundaries is armed force. All the world's large states and most smaller ones maintain military forces in permanent confrontation with their neighbors.

Terminal conflicts involve the effort of one organized group to destroy another. The object is to eliminate boundaries by destroying whatever is beyond them. There is no agreement and no possibility of agreement about the rules of engagement, since mutual trust is unimaginable. The means of conflict are unlimited; escalation is routine. Terminal conflict readily escalates to extraordinary levels of cruelty. The people on each side come to see the people on the other side as inhuman because they inflict or endure treatment that falls outside the normal range of human behavior. Terminal conflict arouses strong but predominantly unpleasant emotions in both participants and spectators. It often involves severe perceptual distortion and a spiral of ferocity.

World War II illustrates the nature of terminal conflict. Battlefield tactics at the start of the war included some conformity to international law regarding the status of noncombatants and open cities, but both sides were eventually caught up in a spiral of ferocity that seemed to justify any and all uses of military means against noncombatants. In the later stages of the war, the legitimacy of attacks on non-military targets was taken for granted, culminating in the atomic bombing of two Japanese cities that had no significant military installations.

Similar sentiments animated the North during the American Civil War. At the beginning of the conflict, Northerners expected the South to seek peace after a short, decisive war. After numerous Union victories, however, Southern resolve was unshaken. General Grant realized after the slaughter at Shiloh that only "complete conquest" would terminate the conflict. Union generals were thereupon instructed to leave the rebels "with nothing but their miserable lives and eyes with which to view their ruin (Murray 1992, 185)."

Clues from Animal Behavior

The study of animal behavior (technically known as *ethology*) has made great progress in recent decades as new methods of observation have enabled investigators to follow and record the behavior of animals in the wild over long periods of time.

Conflict appears to be virtually universal among mammals, birds and fish, and it is usually intraspecific—that is, between animals of the same species (Huntingford and Turner 1987). Interspecific conflict is rare and should not be confused with predatory relationships where the infliction of harm is largely one-sided; the salmon does nothing to the bear. In conflict, both parties are capable of inflicting harm.

Intraspecific conflict occurs routinely in mammalian species, although with varying frequency. In some species, fighting occurs only between adult males or adult females in the breeding season. In other species, any encounter is likely to turn into a fight.

Almost all mammals live in groups that occupy and defend a territory, like wolves and chimpanzees, or that roam together as a pack and resist the intrusion of strangers, like rats and elephants. Humans seem to combine territorial and pack solidarity to an exceptional degree, establishing individual and group territories whose boundaries are fiercely defended, but also showing a high degree of group solidarity and spontaneous hostility to outsiders.

Besides resisting the intrusion of strangers, apes and other mammals fight with members of their own groups about dominance, sexual access and food. In most mammalian species, males are more contentious about these matters than females.

The observation of conflict in numerous mammalian species has turned up some curious findings:

- In the defense of established territories against intruders of the same species, the defenders almost always prevail, even if they are smaller and weaker.

- Animals that carry potentially lethal weapons—claws, fangs, sharp horns—often refrain from using them in intraspecific conflict or use them in non-lethal ways.

- Mammals in conflict generally exhibit a mixture of anger and fear and contradictory impulses to fight or flee. Patterns of animal conflict involve much more posturing and threatening than actual fighting and the emotional machinery that is activated by a hostile encounter includes a number of bodily changes that give the animal a threatening appearance as well as others that prepare it for action.[2]

We humans inherit that emotional machinery and our objects of contention are similar to those that provoke other mammals to fight each other. But we differ from other mammals in using lethal weapons freely against members of our own species, in organizing conflicts of much larger scale and in interpreting them symbolically. The effort to explain aspects of human warfare by reference to studies of animal behavior has now been largely abandoned, but it produced some interesting speculations in its time.[3]

Is War Instinctive?

Anger is not removable from human nature; efforts to suppress anger altogether have been generally futile, but modes of expressing anger need not be lethal.

Sociologists do not generally rely on instincts as explanations. If an explanatory factor does not vary, then it is impossible for it to account for variation. In other words, if war is instinctive, why is there so much more of it at certain times and places? Moreover, an unvarying instinct for war can hardly account for the wide variety of forms that it takes. But it is not unreasonable to view aggressiveness as primordial. As Sigmund Freud wrote,

> Aggressiveness was not created by property. It reigned almost without limit in primitive times, when property was very still very scanty,

and it already shows itself in the nursery . . . it forms the basis of
every relation of affection and love among people . . . ([1930] 1961,
113)

But this need not, he thought, lead to war:

The fateful question for the human species seems to me to be
whether and to what extent their cultural development will succeed
in mastering the disturbance of their communal life by the human
instinct of aggression and self-destruction (145).

An ingenious, if unprovable, variant of the theory that war is
instinctive is proposed by Ehrenreich (1998) who attributes the
impulse to war to the blood rites that early humans performed
to inoculate themselves against the fear inspired by the stronger
carnivores who preyed upon them.

The idea of developing moral equivalents of war, introduced by
William James in a famous essay (1912) finds a contemporary
echo in the often-expressed hope that the Olympic Games, World
Cup soccer, and similar events can act as surrogates for war,
discharging the animosities that otherwise would lead to armed
conflict. There may be some basis for this hope but the murderous
frenzy of soccer fans in Europe and Latin America suggests that
such displacement mechanisms are not entirely reliable.

The Evolution of War

War is absent only in a few isolated human groups without tribal
organization, like the Eskimos, although they too display socially
patterned violence (Riches 1987). Some anthropologists speculate
that war was unknown to matriarchal Neolithic peoples (Eisler
1987) but the hypothesis cannot be proved or disproved.

The ubiquity of war among existing tribal societies is undeniable.
The ethnographic literature emphasizes the episodic character of
most tribal warfare, as in this example from the Philippines:

Kalinga warfare . . . includes all of a region's available manpower
pitted against another such group from an enemy region . . . Encoun-
ters of this kind are always announced; the challengers move up to
the regional boundary and from a hill or slope overlooking one of

the settlements, shout a challenge . . . The challenged group has the option to make peace by agreeing to pay indemnities or make other reparations. However, since a life taken can only be satisfied by substituting another life, a group which has been challenged to war over a killing or series of killings usually decides to fight it out. Such pitched battles could usually take a large number of lives if fought to the last man, but Kalinga usually stop after a few men from each side have been mortally wounded and others injured. The side that has fared worst initiates the truce . . . (Dozier 1967, 69)

But not all tribal warfare is episodic. Some of it is continuous. Much of it is terminal. And even episodic warfare can take a severe toll on the manpower of a simple society.

Keeley (1996) presents a mass of cross-cultural evidence to show that tribal societies on average mobilize a larger proportion of their male populations as warriors than state societies, are more frequently involved in combat than state societies, and suffer far more casualties in proportion to their populations. He concludes that:

There is simply no proof that warfare in small-scale societies was a rarer or less serious undertaking than among civilized societies. In general, warfare in pre-state societies was both frequent and important. If anything peace was a scarcer commodity for members of bands, tribes and chiefdoms than for the average citizen of a civilized state (39).

The rise of civilization created new patterns of warfare. Ancient Egypt, Sumer, Assyria, Babylon, Persia, Japan, India, China, and Mexico were all empires built on wars of conquest, undertaken first against neighboring cities and eventually, against competing empires.

The western tradition of war begins with the wars of the Greeks and of the Hebrews before 1000 B.C. and increases greatly in scale with the conquests of Alexander of Macedon in the fourth century B.C. Quincy Wright (1965) identified eight great ancient and medieval wars in this tradition.[4]

1.   The campaigns of Alexander of Macedon, the temporary conquest of Greece, the Near East, and India. The key

innovation was the phalanx, a heavily armed and well-disciplined infantry formation.

2.   The Roman wars of conquest that extended the empire from Britain to Armenia under Julius Caesar and his immediate successors. The key innovation was the legion, a heavily armed and well-disciplined infantry formation like the phalanx, but with a more flexible organization, plus auxiliary cavalry, artillery, and support services.

3.   The invasion of the Roman empire by Attila and the Huns in the middle of the fifth century and the subsequent Germanic invasions that led to the fall of the western part of the Roman empire in A.D. 476. The key innovation was the fast-moving cavalry horde.

4.   The Muslim conquest of Arabia, Persia, North Africa, and Spain between A.D. 622 and 711. The key innovation was a set of religious beliefs that induced fanatical resolve.

5.   Charlemagne's conquest of western Europe in the eighth century. The key innovation was the armored horseman, supported by a troop of unarmored helpers.

6.   The Viking invasions of northern and southern Europe from the ninth to the eleventh centuries. The key innovation was the unpredictable amphibious landing. Viking raiders landed on the coast, plundered the surrounding area, and escaped back to the sea before the slow moving feudal forces could react. In time, they used their mobility to establish permanent strong points in coastal areas.

7.   The Hundred Years' War, 1337 to 1453, followed in England by the War of the Roses. The key innovation was the cannon.

8.   The war of the Seljuk Turks against the Byzantine empire until 1453 and then against Europe until their unsuccessful siege of Vienna in 1683. The key innovation was the Turkish system of military fiefs.[5]

In six of these eight instances, the key innovation was an organizational form, not a technological advance. The wars in which technology played as important a part as organization were the wars of Charlemagne, whose success has been attributed by one authority to the introduction of the stirrup, and the Hundred Years' War, where the new artillery was used on both sides, and the outcome was indecisive.

If we were to extend Wright's list of the great wars that changed the world into the modern era, we might include the following:

9.   The European conquest of the world, beginning with the fifteenth century voyages to Africa, India and America and ending around 1914. The key innovation was the cannon-carrying ship and the navigational devices that enabled it to reach any port in the world and return home.

10. The American Revolutionary War of 1775–1781, and the French Revolution and its associated wars, 1789–1795. These two events were closely linked in personnel, ideology, and military style, although differing greatly in detail. The key innovation was the patriot army, whose soldiers conceived themselves as fighting on their own behalf for a state whose authority derived from themselves.

11. The Napoleonic Wars, 1796–1815. This was the first modern war to involve all major military powers and the first to threaten an end to the existing international system. The key innovation was an increase of scale: armies were numbered in millions instead of thousands and military organization became more intricate than ever before.

12. The Great War, 1914–1945. This usage conflates World War I and World War II into a single war between Germany and Austria on one side and Britain, France, Russia and the United States on the other, with shifting constellations of lesser allies and with two active phases separated by an uneasy truce. The key innovation was the mechanization of war. Huge quantities of tanks, guns, shells, planes, bombs and ships were consumed in battle, and victory eventually went to the side that could sustain the greater volume of industrial production.

13. The Cold War, 1947–1989. In this unprecedented event, the United States and the Soviet Union fully mobilized for a decisive conflict, confronted each other for more than forty years without firing a shot in anger. Each side continuously fielded an army of more than a million men on a battle line running through Germany, and backed them up with huge air and naval fleets and thousands of nuclear missiles.

But this massive confrontation was not harmless: directly or indirectly, it fueled more than a hundred smaller wars all around the globe, with uncounted millions of casualties. The key innovation was the nuclear weapon, which rendered the states that possessed it immune from direct attack.

The Increasing Lethality of War

The destructiveness of warfare has been growing for centuries at an accelerating rate. According to Sorokin ([1937] 1962), four European powers (France, Britain, Austria-Hungary, and Russia) together mobilized 10 million men in the sixteenth century and around 20 million in each of next three centuries. In the first 25 years of the twentieth century, however, these four powers raised armies containing over 41 million men. During the same period, war was becoming more dangerous to the participants. Only 6 percent of mobilized men were casualties in the sixteenth century, as compared to 15 percent during the next three centuries. Of the 41 million soldiers from 1900 to 1925, almost 40 percent became casualties. More soldiers were killed or wounded in that quarter century than in the previous 400 years.

Sorokin's figures covered only four countries. Dupuy and Dupuy (1986, 990) estimated that, for all countries in World War I, 65 million men were mobilized, more than 50 percent became casualties of one kind or another; eight million combatants and almost seven million non-combatants were killed by hostile action. Some 13 million men died in World War I, while Napoleon in the war against Russia, the bloodiest campaign before that time, lost

400,000 men—some 600,000 fewer than fell in the inconclusive battle of the Somme in 1916 (Mosse 1990, 3–4). Total mobilization in World War II was over 100 million men, with about 15 million military dead but somewhere around 30 million civilian dead. Untold numbers were wounded or made homeless (Dupuy and Dupuy 1986, 1198).

These figures take no account of other human costs—more than a million soldiers were permanently impaired by poison gas in World War I, many millions of soldiers and civilians in both wars suffered permanent psychic damage (Gabriel 1987), and millions more lived on with severe physical disabilities.

Types of War

The common varieties of war include private wars, insurrections, guerrilla wars, civil wars, religious wars, international wars and world wars. All were well represented in the twentieth century.

Private wars occur between powerful individuals, supported by their respective retainers. The turf battles fought by drug traffickers in modern American cities and in the hinterlands of Thailand and Colombia involve all the elements of war: two or more organizations that contend for a scarce thing by deploying forces that use lethal weapons. Private wars are likely to occur where contracts are not enforceable by a political authority.

Insurrection is the armed revolt of a people or some segment of it against an existing government. The military engagements are often very one-sided, either a massacre of demonstrators and street fighters as in Tiananmen Square, or a sudden triumph of the populace when the armed forces refuse to support the regime, as in the Russian Revolution of 1917.

Guerrilla war is the mode adopted by organizations that seek to change the political structure but are too weak to challenge the government's forces in open combat. Although guerrilla war is an ancient phenomenon, its widespread appearance in the twentieth century as part of the decolonization of the world makes it appear novel. Like the Viking raiders, guerrilla fighters strike quickly and make good their escape before the slower-moving government forces can respond. The tactics of guerrilla warfare include symbolic violence to attract supporters, attacks against the government's high-value targets, such as oil refineries, and random violence calculated to create resentment against the government both for the inconvenient measures employed to prevent it and for their failure to do so. "Terrorism" is a synonym for guerrilla warfare.

Civil wars involve the fracturing of a society along ethnic, economic, or political lines and the subsequent armed combat between the fragments. These wars tend to be deadly and expensive. A civil war may lead either to a partition of the state or the re-establishment of state authority. As this is written, civil wars are active in Somalia, Sudan, Sierra Leone, Liberia, Angola, Congo, Rwanda, Sri Lanka, Myanmar, the Philippines, Afghanistan, Turkey, Macedonia, Colombia, and several of the successor states of the Soviet Union.

Religious wars are motivated by doctrines that encourage the defense or recapture of sacred symbols or places, war itself as a sacred duty, the conversion of infidels or the gathering of victims for ritual sacrifice. Both the Christian and Muslim conquests of vast areas at various times in the past were partly motivated by religious exhortations to spread the faith among the heathen. The Crusades had the object of securing Christian control over Jerusalem and the Holy Land while Muslims today fight to wrest control of Jerusalem from the Jewish state of Israel.

International wars occur between sovereign states and are fought by regular military forces. The motives may be political, economic or cultural. The Gulf War, in the early 1990s, was a straightforward example.

World wars are a more recent innovation. Before 1900, the technological means for warfare on a global scale were unavailable. The Great War that ranged over the world between 1914 and 1945 was unprecedented in the scope of its operations and destructiveness, and in the complexity of its political consequences. Since 1945, a future world war has been envisaged as a nuclear Armageddon. Another *conventional* war on a global scale seems unlikely.[6]

Nevertheless, there are competent observers (see especially Orme 1998) who regard another world war as possible, arguing that the application of information technology to the battlefield, coupled with the enormous pressure of the world's growing population on land, water and energy resources, may revive the attraction of wars of conquest, while the wider proliferation of nuclear weapons might continue to deter their use.

For Further Reading

John Keegan, *A History of Warfare,* New York: Knopf, 1993.

Lawrence H. Keeley, *War Before Civilization*, New York: Oxford University Press, 1996.

Notes

[1] *Materiel* is not to be confused with *material. Materiel* is a word used by armed forces to refer to weapons and supplies of all kinds.

[2] ". . . adrenaline pours into the blood and the whole circulatory system is profoundly affected. The heart beats faster and blood is transferred from the skin and viscera to the muscles and brain. There is an increase of blood pressure. The rate of production of red blood corpuscles is rapidly stepped up. There is a reduction of the time taken for blood to coagulate . . . Stored carbohydrate is rushed out of the liver and floods the blood with sugar. There is a massive increase in respiratory activity. Breathing becomes quicker and deeper. The temperature-regulating mechanisms are activated. The hair stands on end and there is profuse sweating" (Morris 1967, 149).

[3] See especially Ardrey 1966, Morris 1967, Tiger and Fox 1971, Johnson 1972. A fascinating example is Goodall's (1986, 503–514) account of the annihilation of a group of chimpanzees by another group over a period of three years.

[4] We have copied the list of wars from Quincy Wright but the identification of a key innovation in each case is our own.

[5] Wright's list is not exhaustive, of course. A case could be made for including the Athenian wars of conquest a century before Alexander, or

the eight crusades that pitted the Christian world against Islam in the twelfth and thirteenth centuries.

⁶ Conventional war is the nuclear-age term for large-scale military conflicts without nuclear weapons. The Gulf War was a conventional war.

2

Peace as a Social Institution

Peace is best visualized as an interim condition between wars. There is no such thing as a large, peaceful state and never has been, although two small, heavily armed, and once warlike states, Sweden and Switzerland, were able to avoid the wars of the twentieth century, and a few small states like Costa Rica and Jamaica remain unarmed under the protection of the United States. Permanent peace, as distinct from an interim between wars, is normally established when two formerly warring groups come under a common authority and lose their independent war-making capacity.

The King's Peace

All polities develop by the suppression of private war, which was endemic in earlier societies. Around the year 1200 for example, the groups with warmaking capacity were quite small: feudal baronies, armed monasteries, fortified cities, robber bands, mountain clans, merchant leagues, and so forth. This made it possible for a slightly more powerful war-maker to extend his reach gradually until he could prohibit war in his own neighborhood. Beginning with the medieval condition of weak central authority and widespread private war, the king was eventually able to enforce a ban on fighting in his presence, in his castle, in the area immediately adjacent, then on the highways and eventually in the entire domain. In the course of this transition, the right of retribution for injury was transferred from the victim to the sovereign. The extension of the king's peace and the broadening of state power were two aspects of the same phenomenon.[1] But private war revives from time to time in places where the king's peace is not supported by the general population, as, for example, in the cattle towns of the Great Plains in the nineteenth century, Chicago in the Prohibition Era, Beirut in the 1970s and 1980s, and Brazil and Russia in the 1990s.

Religious Peace

Christianity was originally pacifist: "But I say unto you, That ye resist not evil: but whosoever shall smite thee on thy right cheek, turn to him the other also" (Matthew 5:39). Early Christians could not be soldiers. This changed after Christianity became the state religion of Rome in the fourth century. St. Ambrose and St. Augustine elaborated Cicero's doctrine of the just war: it must be declared by legitimate authority, have a just cause, right intention, be a last resort, have a high probability of success, provide immunity for noncombatants, and be proportional to the ends.[2]

This doctrine has enabled Christians to shed each other's blood in good conscience ever since, because most wars appear just to the attackers and all wars appear just to the defenders. But, though it did little to oppose public wars, the Church did play an active role in the de-legitimation of private war in the medieval and early modern era.

Immunity and Sanctuary

The medieval Church's insistence on immunity from armed attack for its buildings and personnel developed into the Truce of God, limiting private warfare to certain times and places,[3] and led also to a degree of religious immunity for women, children, and non-combatants.

The sanctuary privilege has survived largely intact in modern embassies. Manuel Noriega, sought by the U.S. Army on drug-trafficking charges, was granted temporary sanctuary at the home of the Pope's representative in Panama. Much longer sanctuary in Western embassies was granted to dissident notables in Eastern Europe during the Cold War.

The idea of immunity for non-combatants has withered in contemporary warfare. A sad and strange consequence of Western democratic theory was the idea that, since leaders depended on popular support, bombing the civilian population would cause the government to fall or sue for peace. On this basis, Hitler directed attacks against the civilians of London. Even more curiously, democratically elected leaders applied similar logic to justify the saturation bombing of such German cities as Dresden and Hamburg and such Japanese cities as Tokyo and, eventually, Hiroshima and Nagasaki.[4] Today, attempts to manipulate public opinion by the intentional slaughter of innocents have become routine in war.[5]

National Fusion and Fission

Historically the most reliable method of achieving durable peace is the fusion of potential adversaries into a single polity. All of today's large states represent the consolidation of many smaller states by conquest, dynastic inheritance and marriage, purchase or cession. The growth of Britain began with the absorption of Kent, Surrey, Essex and Sussex by the kingdom of Wessex around A.D. 825, with numerous later accretions until the British empire reached its maximum extension around 1900. France grew by similar accretions, mostly achieved by war but some by marriage, purchase, or donation. The U.S. grew by purchase and war, Spain by a marriage. Germany and Italy were not unified until the middle of the nineteenth century. Russia began with the seizure of Novgorod by the Muscovites in 1471 and grew steadily until it was the largest polity on earth. Every act of political consolidation is an attempt to establish a durable peace between two entities that were formerly at war, or capable of going to war, with each other.

But not all mergers work. The necessary conditions for a durable consolidation appear to be: (1) contiguous borders; (2) a shared mythology; (3) some degree of cultural unity; (4) a single, dominant ethnic group in the consolidated entity; (5) compatible status orders; (6) common enemies. Mergers do not always endure when these conditions are present but seem always to fail when one or more of them are absent. For example, the United Arab Republic lacked common borders, the Federation of the West Indies lacked common enemies, and the various Scandinavian unions lacked compatible status orders. Most mergers begin with a war and are maintained by subsequent wars. The element of forcible subjection may linger for centuries.

In the nineteenth century, the fusion of states appeared to knowledgeable observers as an inevitable evolutionary trend. In 1850, Charles Sumner (later chairman of the U.S. Senate Committee on Foreign Relations) put it as follows:

> It is in the order of Providence that individuals, families, tribes and nations should tend, by means of association to a final Unity. History bears ample testimony to the potency of this attraction (1850, 381–382).

From the remote past, as Sumner saw it, nations had been merged by conquest and purchase, by inheritance and marriage, on battlefields and in peace conferences, always in the direction of fewer and larger units. The end-point of this process would be the abolition of war. In Sumner's view, the evolutionary advantage of these mergers was that they put an end to the war-making potential of the fused states. What Sumner thought he saw was a tendency for each fusion to facilitate the next so that a universal state would eventually form and war would then cease.

He wrote this some years before the piecemeal fusion of more than twenty sovereign entities with Piedmont between 1859 and 1870 created the kingdom of Italy, and the more rapid fusion of 4 kingdoms, 18 duchies and principalities and 3 city-states in 1871 brought a new German Reich into existence, and also before the defeat, which Sumner helped to bring about, of the nineteenth century's most conspicuous attempt at fission, the secession of the Confederate States of America.

At the beginning of the twentieth century, the faith in national fusion was still strong.

If it is profitable and consistent with progress to put down the primitive struggle for life among individuals with one another . . . and to enlarge the area of social internal peace until it covers a whole nation, may we not go farther and seek, with hope, to substitute international peace and co-operation, first among the more civilized and more nearly related nations, and finally through the complete society of the human race? If progress is helped by substituting rational selection for the struggle for life within small groups, and afterwards, within the larger national groups, why may we not extend the same mode of progress to a federation of European states and finally to a world-federation? (Hobson [1902] 1993)

The predominance of fusion over fission between 1814 and 1914 was unmistakable. More than 300 European sovereigns were represented at the Congress of Vienna in 1814, but at the first Hague Peace Conference in 1899, intended to be universal, only 26 states appeared and six of those were non-European. Despite the achievement of independence by fragments of the decaying Ottoman empire (Greece in 1829; Rumania, Serbia and Montenegro in 1878, Bulgaria in 1909) and the separation of Sweden and Norway in 1905, Sumner's view of an inevitable trend towards the fusion of states remained plausible until World War I. Then the tide turned. Out of the wreck of the Romanov and Hapsburg empires came independent Lithuania, Latvia, Estonia, Poland, Finland, Yugoslavia, Czechoslovakia, Hungary, and Austria, while in the old territories of the Ottoman empire, the victorious allies conceded independence to Yemen (1918), Albania (1920), Egypt (1922), Saudi Arabia (1927), Iraq (1932), and Lebanon (1941).

The trend was briefly reversed in the 1930s by the fusion of Germany and Austria, the partition of Poland by Germany and the Soviet Union, and the annexation of the three Baltic republics by the Soviet Union.

Systems of War and Peace

Table 1. Fusions of Sovereign States, 1944–2000

1.	1951	China-Tibet
2.	1953–1963	Federation of Rhodesia and Nyasaland (Northern Rhodesia, Southern Rhodesia, Nyasaland). Dissolved into Malawi, Zambia, Rhodesia (later Zimbabwe).
3.	1958	Iraq-Jordan
4.	1958–1961	United Arab Republic (Egypt, Syria)
5.	1958–1961	United Arab States (Egypt, Syria, Yemen)
6.	1958–1963	United States of Africa (Ghana, Guinea, Congo, Mali)
7.	1962–1967	Federation of South Arabia
8.	1962–1969	Ethiopia and Eritrea
9.	1963	Malaysia (Malay States, Sabah, Sarawak)
10.	1964	Tanzania (Tanganyika, Zanzibar, Pemba)
11.	1958	United Arab Emirates
12.	1972	Vietnam (North Vietnam-South Vietnam)
13.	1979	Federated States of Micronesia (Yap, Truk, Ponape)
14.	1989	Germany (FRG-GDR)
15.	1990	Republic of Yemen (Yemen Arab Republic-People's Democratic Republic of Yemen)
16.	1990–1991	Greater Iraq (Iraq-Kuwait)

Thereafter, the trend towards fission resumed. Between 1944 and 2000, there were 16 fusions of two or more existing states into a single state as shown in Table 1, and 17 fissions of existing states into two or more independent states, as shown in Table 2.

There were 16 episodes of fusion from 1944 to 1999. Six of these were successful (China-Tibet, Vietnam, Germany, Tanzania, Yemen, Micronesia), but five of these represent restorations of past entities. There were ten failures. There were three attempted military fusions (China-Tibet, Vietnam, Greater Iraq), of which two succeeded.

Table 2. Fissions of Sovereign States, 1944–1999

1.	1944	Iceland-Denmark
2.	1945	Germany-Austria
3.	1947	India-Pakistan
4.	1948	North Korea-South Korea
5.	1949	Taiwan-China
6.	1949	FRG-GDR
7.	1954	North Vietnam-South Vietnam
8.	1965	Singapore-Malaysia
9.	1967	North Yemen-South Yemen
10.	1971	Bangladesh-Pakistan
11.	1983	Republic of Cyprus-Turkish Republic of Northern Cyprus
12.	1991	Ukraine, Turkmenistan, Armenia, Moldova, Belarus, Tajikistan, Georgia, Kyrgyzstan, Azerbaijan, Uzbekistan, Kazakhstan, Lithuania, Estonia, Latvia, Russia
13.	1992	Yugoslavia, Croatia, Slovenia, Bosnia, Macedonia
14.	1993	Ethiopia-Eritrea
15.	1993	Czech Republic-Slovakia
16.	1999	Yugoslavia-Kosovo
17.	2000	Indonesia-East Timor

There were 17 episodes of fission of which 14 were successful. The only failures were Vietnam, Germany and Yemen. All nine military attempts succeeded. The success rate was 35 percent for fusion and 83 percent for fission—success being measured by the persistence of the fused or fissioned units as independent sovereign states in 2000.

On closer inspection of these tables, the predominance of fission becomes even clearer. Five of the six successful fusions (Germany, Vietnam, Tanzania, China's acquisition of Tibet, Yemen) purported to be restorations of earlier boundaries. All three failures of fission preceded restorations.

The principal advantages of fusion for the initiating state, which is almost invariably the stronger, is an increase of military potential by the enlargement of the population, the addition of natural resources, and the acquisition of strategic positions. The sole advantage of fusion for third parties is the reduction of the possibility of armed conflict among the fused states and that is the motive which activated the grand designs for world government advanced from time to time by political philosophers and by ambitious tyrants. Take away the military factor and the preference for fission would be almost universal. To the political class, fission offers more honorifics and more influence. To the people at large, the fissioned state appears more friendly and more responsive.

The tendency to political fragmentation that developed in the aftermath of World War I and the reinforcement of that tendency after World War II was not limited to the fission of sovereign states. It is reflected also in Strang's set of decolonization events (1991). Between 1831 and 1923, not a single colonial dependency became independent; but 17 colonial dependencies achieved independence between 1923 and 1945, and 113 of them did so between 1945 and 1987, profoundly changing the international system. The factors related to decolonization cannot be assumed to account for the fission of independent states, but both series of events were strongly affected by the ideal of national self-determination.

One of the few things on which the U.S. and the Soviet Union agreed during the Cold War was the desirability of liberating the British, French, Dutch, and Portuguese colonies. But fragmentation was also created by their disagreements, as in the partitions of Germany, Palestine, Korea, Vietnam, and Yemen. Separations sometimes occurred in stages, as in the splitting of Pakistan from India and of Bangladesh from Pakistan.

If the European Union should eventually convert itself into a federal state, with a single armed force, a common currency, and an enforceable body of domestic law, as envisaged in the Maastricht Treaty of 1991, it might signal the beginning of a reversal of the trend towards fission. But European progress toward unification has not been rapid and the outcome remains in doubt.

Historically, political consolidation has taken many different forms including empires established by conquest, spheres of influence, protectorates, and even a few permanent alliances. Some social scientists have detected the recent emergence of supra-national civilizations in the disorder following the end of the bipolar superpower rivalry. Each of these emerging civilizations is united by a common culture spread by mass media. According to Huntington (1993), there appear to be seven or eight of these culturally defined civilizations: (1) Western; (2) Confucian; (3) Islamic; (4) Slavic-Orthodox; (5) Latin American; (6) Japanese; (7) Hindu; and possibly, (8) African. Some of these civilizations are themselves conveniently sub-divided into divisions that do not necessarily correspond to national states. Western civilization has European and North American variants and Islamic civilization is divided into Arab, Turkic, and Malay variants. The future includes the unpleasant possibility of intercivilizational wars.

Balances of Power

A balance of power among contending states is relied on for peacekeeping in the absence of political consolidation. It is the traditional way of maintaining peace. A balance of power arises from the formation of a coalition intended to prevent a given state and its satellites from dominating a region or the world. Thus, the underlying logic of a balance of power is defensive. The political history of Western Europe during the nineteenth century involved successive alliances aimed at preventing domination of the Continent by a single power. In the balance of power that emerged from the Congress of Vienna, a considerable degree of stability was maintained for 99 years. Britain and France were opposed to Prussia and Austria-Hungary, with Russia and Italy sometimes on one side and sometimes on the other. Balances of power are likely to explode into war when peaceful containment of the potentially dominant power fails or threatens to fail. The balance of power that prevailed in the world from the San Francisco conference in 1945 to the disintegration of the Soviet Union in 1989–90 involved two blocs led respectively by the

United States and the Soviet Union. The remainder of the world's states moved in and out of the periphery of these great alliances.

Peace through Deterrence

A credible threat of disproportionate response to aggression discourages potential aggressors. A simpler political formula can hardly be imagined: states are mutually restrained by their mutual fear. The validity of its rationale continues to be debated, along with the much older theory embodied in the maxim, *vis pacem, pare bellum,*[6] but as a practical matter, nuclear deterrence has been a powerful factor in international relations since 1945.

There was a curious twist to the military confrontation at the heart of the Cold War. For more than forty years, two great armies faced each other on the central front in Germany, armed to the teeth and prepared to do battle at a moment's notice. But since it was known that actual shooting might lead in a few hours to the obliteration of each side's cities, no shots were fired. The tactical frame of reference that animated the planners on both sides excluded this uncomfortable fact and permitted them to develop complicated scenarios for invasions in both directions. But the only rational strategy was to avoid combat altogether.

Since nuclear weapons systems include semi-automatic responses to attack, there has never been much doubt about the willingness of nuclear states to use their nuclear weapons reactively. The point has been demonstrated repeatedly in situations in which U.S. nuclear forces have been put on full alert, ready to fire if the appropriate provocation occurred (Bracken 1983).

It would be premature to assert that conventional war is impossible between nuclear-armed states, since there are at least two situations in which it might conceivably occur: (1) if one side was convinced that the other side lacked the political will to respond in kind; (2) if the disparity in nuclear weapons was very great and the war did not threaten the survival of the state with the nuclear advantage. Even in those circumstances, the risks would probably be perceived as excessive. Since the dawn of the nuclear age, nuclear-armed states have meticulously abstained from shooting directly at each other, preferring to conduct their wars by proxy and to engage directly only with the forces of non-nuclear states.[7]

An attack on a nuclear-weapons state by a non-nuclear state or coalition is strategically absurd, as Israel's neighbors have reluctantly come to recognize. The magnitude of the potential reprisal is out of proportion to any possible gain.

The multiple paradoxes of the Cold War are still with us. Nuclear weapons can only be safely used against a non-nuclear adversary with no nuclear allies—like Japan in 1945. Since the use of nuclear weapons against any state, even an outlaw state, might be construed as threatening by nuclear-armed third parties, the only situation that is now likely to provoke the use of nuclear weapons is one in which the survival of a nuclear-weapons state is put in jeopardy by the conventional forces of another state. But no state, nuclear or non-nuclear, is likely to attack a nuclear state directly. Thus, conventional military forces are usable only against non-nuclear states and against domestic insurgents. This principle, resolutely ignored in the strategic plans of nuclear weapons states, has been respected in practice since 1945.

Under the ground rules of the Cold War, the danger of armed conflict between the conventional forces of nuclear-weapons states was averted by a tacit understanding that the active engagement of one superpower's forces in a theater of operations limited the other superpower to passive involvement. With the Cold War ended, a new set of ground rules seems to be evolving, under which a nuclear-weapons state may not attack a non-nuclear state with its conventional forces if other nuclear-weapons states might be drawn into the conflict on the other side. It was necessary for the United States to obtain the reluctant consent of the Soviet Union for its war against Iraq and its even more reluctant consent for NATO intervention in the former Yugoslavia. Similarly, it is taken for granted that military action by the United States against North Korea would require at least the tacit agreement of China.

The new rules of engagement are still being worked out; they may be even more restrictive than the old ones. The use of Russian forces in the smaller countries of the Commonwealth of Indepen-

dent States (CIS) seems to be subject in some degree to international oversight, while the United States, in 1994, sought and
obtained the approval of the UN Security Council, i.e., of Russia
and China, for proposed military actions in the Caribbean—a
region in which we had acted unilaterally since the presidency of
Thomas Jefferson.

To sum up, in the existing international system it is unsafe for
a non-nuclear state to attack a nuclear-weapons state under any
conditions. It is likewise unsafe for one nuclear-weapons state
to attack another, even if there is great disparity in their nuclear
forces. And it is also unsafe for a nuclear-weapons state to attack a
non-nuclear state that enjoys the protection of a nuclear-weapons
state. Calculations of expected utility by national decision-makers
are monotonously negative in all of these cases. There is always,
of course, the possibility that one of these unsafe wars might be
initiated by accident or error, but so far, no political leader has
volunteered to test the efficacy of nuclear deterrence.

Peacekeeping Organizations

These range from simple treaties of friendship and non-aggression to protectorates and spheres of influence, regional blocs like
the North Atlantic Treaty Organization (NATO),[8] and world-wide
organizations like the League of Nations and the United Nations.
Peacekeeping organizations are occasionally but not consistently
successful in repressing conflict. Bueno de Mesquita (1981)
presented evidence that war had been more frequent between allies
than non-allies during the previous two centuries. The Monroe
Doctrine has protected Western Hemisphere states from outsiders
but not from each other, and it has been spectacularly ineffective
in preventing civil wars. The existence of the Arab League seems
to have encouraged both international and internecine wars. The
peacekeeping efforts of the League of Nations and the United
Nations are analyzed at length in Chapter 13.

The Diplomatic Network

The peaceful interaction of modern nations is conducted through a diplomatic network. Every sovereign state, however small, has a Ministry of Foreign Affairs or equivalent, sends diplomatic envoys to foreign capitals, to international conferences, and to international organizations, and appoints consuls to represent its interests in certain foreign cities. The larger and more powerful a state, the more extensive its diplomatic network (Barbera 1973). A special body of international law, based on custom and treaties, gives special rights and immunities to diplomats and their staffs. They are immune from the local law of the countries to which they are accredited, and cannot be arrested, prosecuted, punished or taxed by foreign authorities. The foreign diplomats in any capital city form an intensely sociable circle called the Diplomatic Corps. Collectively, they represent world opinion to the host government and may exert considerable influence when that government is weak.

The functions of diplomats and embassies in a foreign capital are: (1) to transmit and receive intergovernmental communications; (2) to conduct espionage, both overt and covert; (3) to provide logistic support for official visitors from the home country; (4) to protect home country nationals and national interests; (5) to encourage cultural, military and trade exchanges; (6) to intervene discreetly in local politics.

The transitions from peace to war and from war to peace are marked by the suspension or rupture of diplomatic relations. The outcomes of revolutions and coups d'état are often decided by the diplomatic recognition or non-recognition of a new regime. For example, rapid recognition by the United States was important to Israel's early survival; the withholding of European, especially British, recognition, helped to doom the Confederacy in the American Civil War; and Germany's quick recognition of Slovenia and Croatia as Yugoslavia fell apart in the early 1990s limited the expansionist aims of Serbia, which had inherited most of the Yugoslav army. Conversely, tardy diplomatic recognition of successful revolutions has been blamed for the isolation and belligerence of numerous countries, such as the Soviet Union in the 1920s and Cuba under Fidel Castro. The diplomatic recognition of communist China was delayed for decades after Mao's revolution.

Two governments without formal diplomatic relations communicate through signals in their respective media, strategic rumors at international diplomatic gatherings and permanent forums such as the United Nations, and through special "interests sections" in the embassies of neutral states. States with reputations for neutrality do a brisk business in maintaining such sections for states that cannot communicate officially but nevertheless have business to conduct.

The acceleration of communication and transportation technology has modified the functions of embassies and diplomats without diminishing their importance. The radio and the airplane, and more recently satellite television, the fax machine, and the Internet, have diminished the autonomy of diplomats in foreign capitals. Face-to-face meetings of heads of state (called summit meetings) are now very frequent and important negotiations are personally conducted by foreign ministers or their deputies. But the general expansion of international contacts has preserved the diplomatic network from obsolescence and given it the new function of providing logistical support for summit and near-summit meetings.

At the same time, the number of international organizations to which governments send permanent or semi-permanent missions and the number of international conferences requiring similar representation, have greatly increased. Each of these develops a diplomatic corps of its own.

Diplomatic protocol has two aspects: the etiquette of communication between governments and the etiquette of sociability among diplomats. Both are based on the absolute, ceremonial equality of sovereign states, regardless of how they differ in size and resources. Thus, the dean of the diplomatic corps in a foreign capital is the ambassador who has been posted there for the longest time, whether from a superpower or a mini-state.

The Financial and Commercial Network

The development of a banking and credit network for international loans, the long-distance transmission of funds, and the international exchange of currencies and debt obligations began in the early Renaissance and grew up side by side with the diplomatic network. The volume and velocity of transactions increased greatly after 1815 and again after 1918, but the most spectacular expansion has occurred since 1960. The present network is multipolar, with Tokyo, New York, Frankfurt, and London as the major centers. The ratio of international transactions to domestic transactions and the ratio of electronic transactions to actual foreign trade are both much higher than at any time in the past and they increase from year to year.

Multinational Institutions

The period since 1945 has been marked by the exuberant growth of multinational institutions, all of which tend to increase the density of interaction between nations and the number of cross-connections among their citizens. These include: (1) a large and ever-increasing number of intergovernmental organizations concerned with terms of trade, environmental issues, scientific exchange, patents, fisheries, communications, public health, migration, energy, etc.; (2) the private and public banks, exchanges, brokerages and trading associations that are active in the world-wide financial market; (3) multinational corporations and conglomerates with branches in many countries; (4) non-governmental organizations (NGOs) active in international affairs. They include the representatives of religious denominations, social movements, interest groups, and voluntary associations that cross or disregard national boundaries.

International trade is now the subject of permanent negotiations in several forums. Most of the world falls under the General Agreement on Trade and Tariffs (GATT) which has periodic marathon negotiating sessions (called "rounds" and named for the host country, as in the "Uruguay Round") and the World

Trade Organization created to enforce the resulting agreements and to handle the grievances they produce. Much of the world is also dividing into regional trading blocs such as the European Community and the North American Free Trade Association (NAFTA) of the United States, Mexico and Canada and the recently formed East Asian free trade zone. The names notwithstanding, these are not "free" trade agreements, but *managed* trade agreements. The terms and conditions of international trade are negotiated in great detail by specialists in these organizations.

Conflict Resolution

Research on conflict resolution in family, industrial and commercial settings has produced a considerable body of information about the effectiveness of third party intervention under variable conditions. One persuasive theory holds that the authoritativeness (and by implication, the effectiveness) of third party intervention depends on the relational distance between the settlement agent and the contending parties (Black 1998, 16). The greater the relational distance from the settlement agent to the principal actors, the more authoritative the settlement. The continuum of settlement styles ranges from friendly pacification (as when an adult deals with the disputes of children playing in a sandbox), through mediation, arbitration, and adjudication, to repressive pacification. Repressive pacification was the original style of the King's Peace, whereby a fight between subjects came to be treated as an offense against the sovereign.

For nearly two centuries, the international community has labored to improvise effective modes of conflict resolution, including:

- mediation by a neutral state, as in the settlement of the Russo-Japanese War by the good offices of the United States;
- active intervention by a neutral state, as in the U.S. naval intervention on behalf of Iraq in the Iran-Iraq War;
- mediation by a consortium of states; the Concert of Europe functioned this way throughout the nineteenth century;

- mediation by a peacekeeping organization, as on the one occasion when the League of Nations managed to halt a small war between Greece and Bulgaria in 1925;
- armed intervention by a peacekeeping organization, as when the United Nations joined in the Katanga War;
- armed intervention by outside powers, as in the NATO air war in Kosovo;
- legal process, as in the settlement of disputes about fisheries and other minor matters by the World Court or the Permanent Court of International Justice; and
- diplomatic intervention by third party states, as in innumerable crises from the secession of the Spanish colonies in 1821 to the Balkan wars of the 1990s.

Although these methods have occasionally succeeded in preventing or ending a war when the configuration of great power relationships was favorable, they have more often failed, and sometimes disastrously. The intervention of third party states in a conflict between Austria and Serbia provoked World War I; the League of Nations' futile efforts to halt the Japanese invasion of Manchuria and the Italian invasion of Ethiopia helped to bring on World War II.

For Further Reading

Donald Black, *The Social Structure of Right and Wrong*, revised edition, San Diego: Academic Press, 1998.

Theodore Caplow, *Peace Games*, Middletown, Conn.: Wesleyan University Press, 1989.

Notes

[1] The usage survives today in the criminal offense of "disturbing the peace," the magistrate's title "Justice of the Peace," and the term "peace officers" for policemen.

[2] For a comprehensive account of the origin and development of the *just war* doctrine, see Christopher 1994, Chapters 1–4.

[3] The Truce of God flourished in medieval France—at one point prohibiting war on most days of the year.

[4] Another motivation, that of halting civilian production of war material, was also cited.

[5] The latest catastrophe being the destruction of the World Trade Center on September 11, 2001.

[6] "If you want peace, prepare for war."

[7] The small engagements between Russian and Chinese troops on the island of Damansky in 1969 constitute an apparent exception, but it is notable that the affair was wound up quickly and that it had the immediate effect of stimulating a rapprochement between the United States and China (Brogan 1990, 171).

[8] NATO as a peacekeeping organization refers to its role in preventing war between NATO members, such as Greece and Turkey, not its role in deterring the Soviet Union.

3

Theoretical Models of War and Peace

Systems of war and peace are far too complex to be understood without theoretical models, but also too complex to be satisfactorily contained within any single model. In this chapter, we look at several different theoretical approaches with which social theorists have attempted to clarify the causes and consequences of these vast phenomena.

A Simplified Model of the Interaction of States

Three hundred years ago, in his "Essay Towards the Present and Future Peace of Europe by the Establishment of an European Dyet, Parliament or Estates," ([1693] 1983) William Penn, better known as the founder of Pennsylvania, suggested that the relations among sovereign states were very similar to the relations among lawless individuals. The modern theory of conflict that began with Georg Simmel ([1908] 1955) takes for granted the virtual equivalence of conflict processes at every level from the interaction of individuals to the interaction of huge collectivities. The modern theory of social control also can be applied to interactions among sovereign states (Borg 1992). Insofar as states maintain continuous relations, interact both amicably and aggressively, acknowledge superiority and enforce subordination, return favors and requite injuries, it is analytically useful to view the "commonwealth of nations" as a giant social group.

The constant motive of each national government within this giant social group is to avoid subjugation, or if subjugation is unavoidable, to minimize it and obtain as much freedom of action as possible. Those who can do so attempt to dominate others—neighbors, allies, a region, the entire world system. The attempt to dominate usually provokes the formation of a resistant coalition. The great wars of the past two centuries have occurred when a national government was able to threaten world domination and the design was frustrated by a broad coalition: France was the ambitious power in 1812, Russia in 1815, Germany in 1914 and again in 1939, the United States and the Soviet Union posed competing threats of world domination after 1945. In this oversimplified model, military strength and the willingness to use it, are the most important variables. It is anticipated that ideological commitments will be abandoned when they interfere with the objectives of dominating or avoiding domination. As Winston Churchill wrote:

> The policy of England takes no account of which nation it is that seeks the overlordship of Europe. It is concerned solely with whoever is the strongest or the potentially dominating tyrant. It is a law of public policy which we are following and not a mere expedient dictated by accidental circumstances or likes and dislikes . . . (*Washington Post*, 2/26/91, A21)

Attempts at regional domination are likely to provoke the formation of a coalition that extends beyond the region, since regional states threatened with subjugation enlist outside states as coalition partners, as illustrated by the close dependence of Taiwan on the United States.

A Simplified Model of Internecine War

Another constant motive of national governments is to maintain or increase their domestic authority. This is measured by the effectiveness of a government's commands on the population to which they apply. Governments resist any attempt to reduce their authority, whether it takes the form of a refusal of its commands, the secession of a population or territory, or an insurrection.

Insurrections occur when part of a nation—a formerly independent state, or a region with a separate identity, or a popular movement—refuses further obedience to the commands of a national government. If the armed forces remain obedient to the government and there is no foreign military support for the insurrection, it fails (as in China in 1989) and the government reasserts its authority, often with bloodshed. If the armed forces join the insurrection (as in the Philippines in 1986) the government falls and a new regime takes its place. If the armed forces split (as in Sri Lanka in 1990) the outcome is decided by a civil war. Civil wars often attract outside military support, and that support may decide the eventual winner (as in India's intervention in the Pakistani civil war of 1971).

Objections to the Simplified Models

The principal objection to the simplified models presented above is that they seem to ignore the ideological, psychological, biological and economic factors that are commonly thought to account for wars and revolutions.

That objection is half-founded. The simplified model of international war does assert that national governments react to threats of domination in a uniform manner, regardless of their constitutions and ideologies. Whether a government is capitalist or communist, democratic or despotic, secular or religious, it can be counted on to resist domination by other national governments regardless of other circumstances. The initial responses of national governments to insurrections are equally consistent.

But while nearly all governments react forcefully nearly all the time to the threat of military domination by external or internal forces, only some governments some of the time attempt to expand their spheres of domination by military means. And although every sizable nation includes a large assortment of dissident factions and separatist movements, armed insurrections are relatively rare in strong modern states.

It takes a strong ideological base to support an aggressive state or a serious insurrection. The three overt bids for universal domination in the past two centuries have been ideologically based; Napoleon's France, Hitler's Germany, and Stalin's Soviet Union were inextricably associated with theories of history, biology, and human destiny. Armed insurrections, likewise, nearly always have a strong ideological base; emotionally potent themes are essential for the mass recruitment of volunteers.

Although we can observe that most states most of the time behave in a remarkably uniform manner, seeking to avoid subjugation by other states, and to dominate other states when opportunities appear, that observation does not carry us very far towards explaining the outbreak of a particular war or a particular insurrection, and we must resort to other theories.

The Geometry of Coalitions

The geometry of coalitions is one of the best theoretical tools for understanding the international system and for analyzing the causes and outcomes of particular wars. A *coalition* is a combination of two or more social actors who adopt a common strategy in a situation of continuous, episodic, or terminal conflict. (A social actor may be as small as a single individual or as large as a state. The geometry of coalitions does not seem to be affected by the scale of the social system in which coalitions occur.)

Many studies in this field deal with the coalitions that occur in triads. A *triad* is a group of three social actors contending for advantage. Most conflict situations can be reduced to the triad of two principal adversaries and an audience. More complicated situations can be described as a cluster of related triads.

Triads have some interesting, non-obvious properties. They routinely change weakness into strength and strength into weakness by splitting into coalitions of two against one that transform their initial distributions of power (Caplow 1968).

We can start the analysis with a triad of three social actors, whom we will call A, B, and C (Figure 1). B and C are equal in power. A is a little stronger but not as strong as B and C combined.

In this common situation, the formation of a B–C coalition is almost inevitable, and that coalition will dominate A. A's strength has been transformed into weakness.

Figure 1.

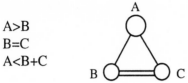

A>B
B=C
A<B+C

Or we can examine another triad in which B and C are equal in power, but A is weaker than either of them (Figure 2). Under these circumstances, a B–C coalition offers no particular advantage to B or C. Each of them will try to form a coalition with A and one of them will presumably succeed in doing so. The triad will be dominated either by an A–B or an A–C coalition. In either event, A will be part of the winning coalition. Its weakness has been transformed into strength.

Figure 2.

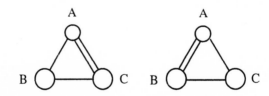

A<B
B=C

At the founding of the United Nations in San Francisco in 1945, it was already apparent that the determinative interstate conflicts of the postwar era would take this form, in which A<B, B=C, B and C being the United States and the Soviet Union. In triads of this type, any coalition is a winning coalition, and both of the strong players, B and C, seek to form a coalition with the

weak player, A, who then becomes what Georg Simmel called the "*tertium gaudens*," the "enjoying third." By virtue of its weakness, A is almost certain to be included in a winning coalition. By virtue of their strength, both B and C are at risk of being dominated.

A great many of these triads would be activated during the forty-odd years of the Cold War. Each superpower would win in some of them and lose in others. But it was obviously prudent for each superpower to keep the national states and combinations of states that enacted the role of A as weak as possible, both to assure their own control of the winning coalitions they succeeded in forming and to limit their losses when winning coalitions were formed against them.

Similar transformations of weakness into strength and strength into weakness occur in triads with other distributions of power, when, for example, the three actors are unequal but any two of them can dominate the third.

Balances of power ordinarily involve a pattern of shifting coalitions intended to prevent the domination of an international system by its strongest state.

More complicated systems—with more than three members— can be analyzed as clusters of linked triads. Triads are linked when they have one or more members in common. The selection of coalition partners in linked triads is likely to follow two self-enforcing rules:

Rule A. An adversary in one triad may not be chosen as a coalition partner in a linked triad. Those coalitions would be incompatible.

Rule B. An actor invited to join incompatible coalitions in linked triads should select the one in the more powerful triad.

Rule A leads to a set of universally recognized political principles. My friend's enemy is my enemy. My enemy's friend is my enemy. My enemy's enemy is my friend.

Rule B leads to an apparent exception to Rule A. When a triad is involved in an external conflict of larger scale, coalitions within the triad may be suspended. An Arab proverb runs: "I against my brother, I and my brother against my cousin, I, my brother and my cousin against the next village. All of us against the stranger."

The relationship among the world's major military powers from the middle of the seventeenth to the middle of the twentieth century was vulnerable to a transformation of its leading triads from the form in which A>B>C but A<(B+C), and no player can dominate the system by itself, to one in which A became stronger than any possible opposing coalition, and the game would be over. This structural flaw was responsible for the European wars of the eighteenth century, the Napoleonic wars, and World Wars I and II.

The balance of power that emerged from World War II had a different flaw—the possibility that one of the A's in one of the numerous triads that made up the system would grow strong enough to form a coalition with B or with C that might inflict a serious defeat on the excluded superpower. There was a reasonable fear that the defeated superpower might then prefer a nuclear Armageddon to peaceful submission.

Given the enormous military power of the United States and the Soviet Union and their continuous mobilization during the Cold War, there were only a few candidates for the role of a destabilizing A. In the heyday of the Non-Aligned movement, it seemed possible that the Soviet Union might be able to organize the world's weak states into an effective anti-American bloc, but the plan soon failed. The U.S. opening to China in the early 1970s held a similar promise, but it was soon apparent that China's considerable military assets, like those of Switzerland, were not useful at a distance. In the early 1980s, the most likely candidate was the European Community, which, as a sovereign state, could field more soldiers than the Soviet Union and produce as many weapons as the United States. But the west Europeans, after decades of economic progress and light defense budgets, and still subject to an American occupation, showed no inclination to reenter the arena of military politics in a serious way.

Expected Utility Theory

Bruce Bueno de Mesquita (1981) studied 251 wars and threats of war between 1800 and 1974, and found that most of them were initiated by an identifiable decision-maker who had estimated the costs and benefits, found the cost-benefit ratio favorable, and eventually proved to be correct. In 86 percent of the wars in the sample, the expected utility of the initiator exceeded that of the defender. In other words, wars are usually begun by the side that seems to have the advantage and that side usually wins. The theory emphasizes the role of the individual decision-maker, since, in nearly every instance, the decision whether and when a state goes to war is made by a single, identifiable person. Even if the calculation gives a positive expected utility, the decision-maker may not elect to start a war. But the theory insists that war is unlikely if the decision-maker's calculations give a negative expected utility.

The calculation of expected utility involves much more than a simple comparison of the military strength of the parties, since most wars are ultimately decided by the intervention or non-intervention of third parties. Third party states play a large and paradoxical part in the calculation of expected utility. States often enter wars on what appears to be the wrong side in order to prevent some shift in a wider alignment of power, e.g., Britain and France in the Crimean War, and the Hitler-Stalin alliance of 1939.

Belonging to an alliance does not necessarily improve the initiator's chances. About a fifth of the wars in the sample were begun by a state attacking its own ally and states without allies were as likely to prevail as those with several allies.

The cost of wars was much higher when both sides had positive expected utilities. That is, when both sides were confident of winning, the number of casualties and the extent of destruction was much greater than when one side was prepared to lose.

The fact that most of the wars of the past two centuries were initiated by states that expected to win, and did win, contradicts the common view of war as a form of collective insanity. The governments that initiated most of these wars calculated that they had more to gain than to lose, and in most cases, their calculations were correct. Another study by Starr (1972) investigated the distribution of gains and losses in coalitions that won or lost wars between 1818 and 1960 and concluded that wars were generally profitable for the states that initiated them.

The concept of expected utility implies short, cheap wars, which most wars are. The exceptions to the theory are the big wars in which the initial calculations turn out to be abysmally wrong—Napoleon's Russian campaign, the American Civil War, Paraguay's Lopez War, World Wars I and II, the Vietnam War, the Iran-Iraq War. The few exceptional wars in which the initiators' calculations of expected utility are totally wrong probably have more durable consequences than the "normal" wars that conform to the theory.

The Behavior of National Governments

While individuals generally make the decision for war or peace, the behavior of national governments before and after that decision is composed of a myriad of bureaucratic and individual responses. In a notable analysis of the Cuban missile crisis, Allison (1971) pointed out that analysts of international affairs, as well as ordinary newspaper readers, visualize interacting governments as unitary actors who make rational decisions and attempt to carry them out. He calls this the Rational Actor Model.

But he suggests that a careful examination of how governments actually perform in a crisis leads us to two alternative conceptions, somewhat awkwardly labeled as the Organizational Process Model and the Governmental Politics Model.

He was able to show that the Rational Actor Model left the important features of the Cuban missile crisis unexplained, including the original Soviet decision to emplace missiles in Cuba, their failure to conceal the missile sites and their initial disregard of U.S. warnings. On the U.S. side, the Rational Actor Model did not seem to explain why the U.S. reacted so slowly, why a naval blockade was chosen over other options, or how the blockade was carried out.

The Organizational Process Model builds on an existing body of knowledge about how government bureaucracies operate. They are designed to accomplish particular tasks in particular ways by following standard procedures. Tasks that cannot be accomplished with standard procedures are performed slowly, ineffectively, or not at all. Assignments that threaten the agency's parochial interests are actively resisted. For these reasons, projects that require the rapid coordination of several agencies are not likely to be executed as intended by the decision-makers, and the information fed back to the decision-makers is not likely to be accurate.

In the Cuban missile crisis, Soviet missiles were transported to Cuba and unloaded in great secrecy but no attempt was made to camouflage the missile sites under construction. Analysts who used the Rational Actor Model developed extraordinarily ingenious theories about why the Soviet planners wanted the missile sites to be identified before they became operational, but the Organizational Process Model provides a much simpler explanation. The shipments were handled by the security-conscious Soviet intelligence services, but on-site construction was managed by their Strategic Rocket Forces, whose standard operating procedures made no provision for camouflage or concealment.

On the American side, Allison found that the ten-day delay in checking the original reports that missiles were being installed in Cuba was the time required to resolve a jurisdictional dispute between the Air Force and the CIA about who should take the aerial photographs. The study provided many other illustrations to show the inflexibility of U.S. agencies in the missile crisis. For example, the President's order for a blockade line close to Cuba did not prevail over the Navy's preference for a line five hundred miles away.

The Governmental Politics Model examines how the personal motives of the principal officials in a government affect their views of the situation and the decisions they make. President Kennedy, with a failed invasion of Cuba close behind him, believed that he could not take any of the softer options in the missile crisis without risking impeachment and Khrushchev's actions were partly dictated by his reluctance to provoke a Republican landslide in the approaching Congressional elections.

The effect of the two latter models is to diminish the rationality and effectiveness of the actions of national governments in crises, as Allison shows with abundant examples. The same models can be fitted to Clark's (1985) account of the decision to bomb Hiroshima and Nagasaki, and to the controversial decision that ended the Gulf War short of a complete victory.

National Governments as Social Actors

As the simplified models presented earlier suggest, national governments interacting with their peers have interests—resisting subjugation, achieving domination—that are peculiar to themselves and should not be confused with the private interests of their citizens. A government's decision to go to war or to make peace is normally based on that *government's* expected utility, which may be roughly related to the pooled utilities of its population, or, as quite commonly happens, not related at all.

This distinction is usually masked by patriotic rhetoric, but occasionally becomes overt. Discussing Israel's restless restraint under Iraqi missile attacks, the *Washington Post* (6 February 1991) quoted an aide to the Prime Minister:

> This has nothing to do with the Israeli public. This is something that the leadership of the Israeli army and the government resent and feel very, very deeply.

The lack of congruence between the interests of governments and of their peoples shows most clearly in the later stages of desperate wars when, as a matter of course, governments seek to preserve themselves at the cost of destroying large numbers of their citizens.

Long ago, Jean-Jacques Rousseau ([1756] 1962) observed that the real purposes of kings and ministers are always the same, to increase their power inside and outside their realms, and that the happiness and prosperity of their subjects concern them only as means to their own aggrandizement. The replacement of absolute monarchs by elected officials in the following century was supposed to create a closer identity of interest between government and people, but seems not to have done so. In matters of war and peace, the calculations of expected utility by elected heads of state do not differ radically from the calculations of autocrats in the same circumstances, although domestic political factors may carry more weight. Socialist doctrines, too, promised to create an identity of interest between rulers and ruled, but the policies of socialist governments in international relations have followed the usual pattern.

Other Approaches to Explaining War

War is viewed by some theorists as the collective expression of individual aggression against individuals or against civilization *per se*. This theory is most commonly associated with the writings of Sigmund Freud, especially his *Civilization and Its Discontents* ([1930] 1961). A more recent version of the psychoanalytic explanation of war describes it as an expression of a male flight from femininity (Theweleit 1987). Other psychological explanations for war attribute it to frustrated expectations or relative deprivation.

The theory that war is caused by population pressure was first enunciated by Thomas Malthus at the end of the eighteenth century. His *Essay on Population* describes society as trapped between the arithmetic growth of the food supply and the exponential growth of human numbers.

> One of [war's] first causes and most powerful impulses was undoubtedly an insufficiency of room and food; and greatly as the circumstances of mankind have changed since it first began, the same cause continues to operate and to produce, though in a smaller degree, the same effects . . . A recruiting sergeant always prays for a bad harvest and a want of employment, or in other words, a redundant population . . . rapid procreation [is] partly the effect and partly the cause of incessant war. The vacancies occasioned by former desolations make room for the rearing of fresh supplies; and the overflowing rapidity with which these supplies followed constantly

furnished fresh incitements and fresh instruments for renewed hostilities (Malthus [1798] 1973, 165).

A society that successfully restricted child-bearing would have no reason to invade its neighbors and, Malthus thought, would be better able to defend itself against more profligate enemies.

McNeill (1982) draws an analogy between disease parasitism and early war:

> . . . it is worth pointing out the parallels between the microparasitism of infectious disease and the macroparasitism of military operations. Only when civilized communities had built up a certain level of wealth and skill did war and raiding become an economically viable enterprise. But seizing the harvest by force, if it led to speedy death of the agricultural work force from starvation, was an unstable form of macroparasitism . . . The shift from acute to chronic infection of society is the dawn of what we recognize as history and civilization . . . Very early in civilized history, successful raiders became conquerors, i.e., learned how to rob agriculturalists in such a way as to take from them some but not all of the harvest (53–54).

Taking some, but not all, of the harvest became a regular, predictable activity undertaken by an organization with specialized functionaries such as clerks, soldiers, armorers, tax collectors, storehouse guards—in short, a government.

A successful government immunizes those who pay rent and taxes against catastrophic raids and foreign invasion in the same way that a low-grade infection can immunize its host against a lethal disease. Immunity arises by stimulating the formation of antibodies and raising other physiological defenses to a heightened level of activity; governments develop immunity to foreign macroparasitism by stimulating surplus production of food and raw materials sufficient to support specialists in violence in suitably large numbers. Both defense reactions constitute burdens on the host populations, but a burden less onerous than periodic exposure to lethal disaster.

A society with a government that extracts a surplus and diverts it to military purposes is, of course, far more powerful than its unarmed counterparts. Such a society can be expected to conquer or destroy everything in its path, except for other armed societies. To switch metaphors, this theory views government as the original protection racket, founded on internal threats of violence. However, by stimulating the creation of counterparts in other societies, the external threat is made real.

Other observers have viewed war as the inevitable outcome of existing economic arrangements. Lenin ([1916] 1929), following an earlier socialist tradition, ascribed all the international wars of the nineteenth and twentieth centuries to the internal exhaustion of capitalism, which drove it to imperialism. Wallerstein (1974), the originator of what is called world system theory, revised and extended this explanation of international war, with particular attention to the exploitation of peripheral states by core states in the international system.

Given the complexity of intergovernmental relations and the reciprocal interplay between war-and-peace and other domestic institutions, no single explanatory scheme seems to account satisfactorily for particular wars. A model that emphasizes economic factors, like world system theory, can give a coherent account of any given war, without being able to refute contrary accounts, as does a model that attributes war to cultural and ideological differences.

For Further Reading

William H. McNeill, *The Pursuit of Power: Technology, Armed Force and Society Since A.D. 1000,* Chicago: University of Chicago Press, 1982.

Michael E. Brown, ed., *Theories of War and Peace: An International Security Reader*, Cambridge: MIT Press, 1998.

4

International Law

Corbett (1968, 347) quotes Brierly's ([1928] 1963) definition of *international law* as "the body of rules and principles of action which are binding on civilized states in their relations with one another," and then challenges it with the following comment:

> We move nearer to the facts when we describe international law as the complex of rules, principles, standards, and procedures more or less observed by governments in their business with one another. Governments habitually observe that they are scrupulously observing internationally approved norms of official conduct in such business. They even acknowledge a legal obligation so to act. But they also claim the right to determine for themselves what the rules are . . . We have not yet reached in the international sphere that basic rule of modern legal systems which requires universal submission to impartial determination of what the law is in any given situation.

Public International Law

Public international law deals with two large categories of governmental action: (1) the rules and customs of peaceful interaction among states, such as recognition and non-recognition, diplomatic and consular representation, treaties, protocol, flags, passports, borders, coastal rights, air rights, and commercial relations, and (2) rules of international war concerning interaction between belligerents and neutrals, between opposing military forces and between military forces and non-combatants. Each of these categories is extensively subdivided. Interaction between belligerents and neutrals includes such historically sensitive issues as impressment, internment, safe havens, search and seizure, contraband carried by neutrals, and the effect of blockades on neutral commerce. The rules of interaction between belligerent forces cover such matters as insignia, ruses and stratagems, truces, cease-fires, safe-conducts, capitulations, and most important, the treatment of enemy wounded and prisoners. The rules of interaction between belligerents and non-combatants specify the responsibilities of occupying forces in hostile territory, enjoin the protection of civilian lives and property in battle zones, and prohibit rape and pillage, the murder of civilians, the bombardment of undefended settlements, the taking of hostages, the torture of informants, the destruction of historic monuments, and many other commonly practiced barbarities.

Sources of International Law

International law is not enacted by legislative bodies. Its sources are: (1) custom; (2) juristic theory; (3) treaties, especially multilateral treaties; and (4) international organizations.

War has been regulated for thousands of years. The ancient Hittites, Sumerians, Hindus, Chinese, Hebrews, Greeks and Romans all had rules about the immunity of priests and heralds, the observance of truces and the treatment of prisoners. Much of international law is based on customs so old that their origins have been forgotten—like the extraterritorial status of embassies and the immunity of diplomats and their servants from arrest.

But international law as we know it is largely the creation of volunteer, private theorists, who based their proposals for government conduct on what they understood to be divine law, or natural law, or customary practices. The most influential of these writers was Hugo Grotius (1583–1645), who advocated the subordination of all private rights to the rights of a sovereign engaged in public war, an argument that the expanding national states of the seventeenth century found very congenial.

The rules of war proposed by Grotius look amazingly cruel to modern eyes. For example:

- The right to inflict injury extends even to infants and children.
- The right to inflict injury extends to prisoners who have surrendered unconditionally.
- Even enemy property of a sacred nature may be destroyed and pillaged.
- All persons captured in a war become slaves, and their descendants become slaves also.
- There is no suffering which may not be inflicted upon such slaves and no action which they may not be forced to do ([1625] 1901 VII, iii).

Grotius was one of many authors who proposed rules for war on their own authority and little by little, the principles they proposed began to be embodied in the regulations that European states issued for the conduct of their armed forces and their diplomatic missions, and in their treaties with other states. In the course of the eighteenth century, these became increasingly humane. A notable treaty concluded in 1785 between the kingdom of Prussia and the brand-new United States of America provided that in case of war between the parties,

> . . . all women and children, scholars of every faculty, cultivators of the earth, artisans, manufacturers and fishermen unarmed and inhabiting unfortified towns . . . shall not be molested in their persons, nor shall their houses or goods be otherwise destroyed, nor their fields wasted by the armed force of the enemy . . . but if anything is necessary to be taken for the use of such armed force, the same shall be paid for at a reasonable price . . . [Prisoners of war shall be] lodged in barracks as roomy and good as are provided by the party in whose power they are for their own troops (Friedman 1972).

With respect to the treatment of noncombatants, this is more humane than the practices of any modern government, including our own.

The international law experts of the nineteenth century rejected the authority of religion and natural law in these matters and identified the consent of sovereign states as the sole source of international law. This doctrine suggested that international law could be created by treaties and a long series of multilateral agreements intended to enact rules of war began with the Declaration of Paris in 1856, which prohibited privateering and expanded the naval rights of neutral states. It was followed by the Red Cross Convention of 1864, which provided for the immunity of hospitals, ambulances and medical personnel treating battle wounded and for the protection of wounded prisoners. The familiar Red Cross insignia was created by that treaty. Other rule-making treaties followed thick and fast until 1899, when an international congress—including non-European states like Persia and Japan—was convened at the Hague with the object of creating a comprehensive body of international law. The multiple Hague Conventions included provisions for the peaceful settlement of international disputes, limitations on the use of force to collect debts, elaborate rights for prisoners of war, and detailed rules about such matters as the treatment of noncombatants, the treatment of spies, the use of ruses and stratagems, declarations of war, surrenders and truces, and a host of other matters. Additional Hague Conventions drafted in 1907 attempted to prohibit the use of poisoned weapons, the bombardment of undefended places, aerial bombing, submarine mines, and any form of pillage.

The Blighted Hopes of 1907

The ten Hague Conventions that finished the series were signed by all the world's states having significant military forces. This extraordinary consensus was possible because the leaders of opinion in all the major countries were confident that war would soon disappear from the annals of civilized nations along with other barbaric customs inherited from the past. Their belief in moral progress rested on substantial evidence. During the nineteenth century, slavery and the slave trade, human sacrifice, judicial torture, female infanticide, blood feuds, burning at the stake and breaking on the wheel, flogging and keel hauling, piracy, serfdom, child labor, imprisonment for debt, the castration of boy sopranos, and a host of other traditional atrocities had been abolished almost everywhere.

By the same token, war had lost much of its former cruelty. The new rules of war devised at the Hague and ratified by every country with appreciable military power, prohibited the killing of enemy wounded, the mistreatment of prisoners, the pillage of captured towns, the seizure of private property, the impressment of recruits, and other indignities that had been visited on the less powerful players in the game of war since time immemorial. War itself seemed to be going out of style. The wars and military excursions of the European powers between 1815 and 1900 were brief and decisive.

It was generally understood after the second Hague conference of 1907 that war would be gradually legislated out of existence. In the interim, it would be closely controlled to prevent excesses. There was nothing absurd about this program. It assumed the continuation of an international system operated by half a dozen European great powers (France, Britain, Germany, Austria-Hungary, Russia, Turkey) and a score of peripheral powers including the weaker European states, the United States, and Japan—all Christian and Caucasian except Japan and Turkey, all relatively modernized, all committed to some form of parliamentary government, private property, and a highly stratified class system, all having more or less interchangeable military and diplomatic institutions. Turkey and Japan belonged to the system by virtue of having partially adopted western military and diplomatic institutions during the nineteenth century. Weak states like China and the Latin American republics were incapable of resisting the armed forces of any great power. Acting in concert, the great powers appeared fully capable of restraining and eventually abolishing war.

The Concert of Europe had continued to perform the double task for which it was formed in 1814: to prevent the domination of Europe by any single power and to prevent social revolutions modeled after 1789. The revolutions of 1830 and 1848, although exciting, did not change the foundations of the European order. The Paris Commune of 1871 was quickly suppressed. The partition of Asia and Africa by the colonial powers was accomplished with remarkably little friction. Writing around 1907, Max Weber ([1921] 1978) predicted that capitalist imperialism would persist for the foreseeable future.

The moral progress registered in the Hague treaties and in the actual conduct of war was regarded around 1907 as part of an irresistible trend towards the improvement of the human condition. Even in backward and despotic states, the nineteenth century witnessed the extension of political rights to formerly excluded groups, the disappearance of traditional forms of cruelty, the softening of penalties for crime, the extension of state welfare programs, and the proliferation of education, health and social services. The great powers claimed to have a civilizing mission in their foreign colonies and they did export many social improvements. Radicals believed as strongly in moral progress as conservatives. Secure in the belief that capitalism was the sole cause of modern war, they were confident that the replacement of capitalism by socialism would put a permanent stop to war (Kautsky [1892] 1973).

No one seems to have foreseen the future that happened. Even with hindsight, it is difficult to argue that World War I was inevitable. It began with accidents, garbled messages and mislaid orders. The fighting was supposed to be brief and decisive (Tuchman 1962, 19).

It turned out that the technical conditions of war had changed. The largest armies in history were able to keep the field throughout the year, and they discovered before the end of 1914 that the machine gun, the field telephone, barbed wire, and explosive shells gave the defense an overwhelming advantage. The casualties soon exceeded those of all previous wars. The only reason to continue was the investment already made.

The economic costs were high but were soon recouped. The moral costs were incalculable and are being paid to this day; they include the strengthening of the war system and the rise of violent political movements throughout the world.

As we suggested before, it is not unreasonable to visualize the two World Wars as a single thirty year conflict, with two active phases separated by two decades of uneasy peace. The victors of the first phase were unable to reestablish the Concert of Europe or to create effective peacekeeping organizations. The losing empires, German and Russian, replaced the tyrants who had failed them with bloodier and more bizarre tyrants and began to prepare for the second phase while the victors were still congratulating themselves on having achieved perpetual peace.

The first phase had been marked by serious violations of the newly enlarged body of international law: the invasion of neutral Belgium, the shelling of cathedrals, the use of poison gas, and unrestricted submarine warfare, but these were recognized as infractions even by the perpetrators, who pleaded military necessity. The second phase witnessed the complete abandonment of restraint by both sides: passenger ships sunk without warning, mass bombing of residential districts, the pillage of both enemies and allies, the wholesale demolition of cultural monuments, and the attempted extermination of entire peoples. The civilian populations of enemy territories occupied by either the Germans or the Russians were maltreated in every possible way and even in friendly territory the armies of both sides were careless about civilian rights and lives.

There was a precipitous decline in conformity to the rules of war from the bombing of Rotterdam and Coventry in 1940, which aroused universal outrage in Britain and America, to the more severe bombings that flattened Dresden and Tokyo in 1945 without arousing any outrage at all. The massacre of children and the destruction of temples had become normal acts of war and no longer called for excuse or explanation. It came to the point eventually that moral scruples were not even invoked to protect people on one's own side, as at Nagasaki, where the information that American prisoners of war were held in that city did not prevent its selection as a target for the second atomic bomb (Clark 1985).

Enforcement of International Law

That part of international law that regulates the conduct of war includes rules of four different kinds:

1.   Rules about the interaction of belligerents and neutrals.
2.   Rules for the interaction of hostile forces.
3.   Rules for the protection of noncombatants.
4.   Rules for the protection of property.

There are wide differences in the degree of obedience that warring governments and armed forces give to the four kinds of war rules. With a few important exceptions, notably the German invasion of Belgium in 1914, most of the rules about interaction with neutrals have been scrupulously respected in the major wars of the twentieth century, presumably because a violation of neutral rights carries the risk of turning the offended neutral government into an active enemy.

The rules concerning the interaction of armed forces have also been generally respected, although with more exceptions than in the previous category. The mutual advantage to belligerents of treating prisoners well is self-evident; today's captor may be tomorrow's prisoner. In World War II, while the German government was killing millions of innocent civilians in its death camps, its prisoner of war camps were operated in general accordance with international law. There were atrocities and a number of technical violations, especially regarding food near the end of the war when much of Germany was starving, but the overall picture was compliance. Interestingly, American and British prisoners were generally better treated than French or Russian POWs (Foy 1984, 139–156).

The rules about the protection of non-combatants are the least enforced; there were wholesale violations by every active belligerent in World War II. For example, although the relevant treaties provide that merchant ships may not be sunk unless the safety of the ship's crew is assured, that rule was not respected either by the German U-boats operating against Allied convoys in the Atlantic or by the American submarines operating against Japanese shipping in the Pacific. The rules about the immunity of civilian property, cultural and historical monuments and undefended places have also become dead letters.

A special gap in the rules of war is that their applicability to civil wars is uncertain. The refusal of quarter, the massacre of prisoners, the murder of hostages, rape and pillage and the wanton destruction of personal and public property have been routine practices in the civil wars of our era.

The Growth of International Law

International law continues to grow in scope and complexity. Trade relations between nations are now the subject of treaties covering a vast array of products and producers. Violations of the provisions of such instruments have so far led only to reciprocal violations and further negotiations. This process is facilitated by the mutual interlocking of the banking systems of the industrialized world—the principal assets backing national currencies and bonds are no longer metallic, but rather each others' currencies and bonds. The only international violence provoked by commercial disputes has verged on farce, as in the "fishing war" between Iceland and Britain.

A number of alarming externalities of global industrialization are reinforcing this tendency toward negotiated solutions to international problems. These externalities range from the fallout from nuclear accidents to the potential dangers associated with atmospheric pollution.

To sum up, it might be said that those parts of international law that are analogous to domestic civil law are, for the most part, effectively self-enforcing, but those parts that are analogous to criminal law are not.

For Further Reading

Daniel P. Moynihan, *On the Law of Nations*, Cambridge: Harvard University Press, 1990.

Adam Roberts and Richard Guelff, eds., *Documents on the Laws of War*, 3rd ed., New York: Oxford University Press, 2000.

5

The Contemporary War System

In Chapter 2 we noted that since 1944, a tendency towards political fragmentation (fission) has greatly outweighed any tendency towards political consolidation (fusion). More than a hundred new states have appeared since then. Each of them as it joins the system acquires its own flag, currency, constitution, passports, customs, diplomats and—with negligible exceptions—its own armed forces. Each is presumed to be absolutely sovereign, juridically equal to the most powerful nations, subject to no higher authority, free to maltreat its own people without outside interference, and free to make war on any enemy it chooses. The opportunity is not scanted. Of the 72 nations which became independent between 1945 and 1982, 59 had engaged in war by the latter date (Kidron and Smith 1983).

War in the Late Twentieth Century

The end of World War II left the world divided between two camps, each more or less committed to the destruction of the other. The military power of the western European powers had become negligible compared either to the vast armies of the Soviet Union, or to the enormous air and naval forces, and atomic weapons of the U.S. The most striking consequence was that the former colonial powers: Britain, France, Italy, the Netherlands, Japan, Belgium, and Portugal were unable to resist the dismantling of their empires promoted by the U.S. and the Soviet Union in tacit

cooperation. This released scores of new nations, bristling with
hostility, into the world arena, and the competition between the
superpowers for their support gave all of them ample access to
weapons and military technology from one side or the other,
or in many cases from both sides. The examples include India,
Pakistan, Iran, Iraq, Israel, Syria, Egypt, Libya, Morocco, Angola,
Ethiopia, Zaire, Nigeria, Uganda, Chad, Morocco, Guatemala, El
Salvador, Nicaragua, Cuba, Vietnam, Korea, Malaysia, Cambodia
and all the other killing fields of the late twentieth century.

The Cold War between the superpowers directly fueled a number
of proxy conflicts around the world and abetted a number of
others by obstructing efforts to achieve a resolution. As many
as 30 million people may have perished in about 80 wars that
were peripheral to the Cold War but still a part of it (Brogan
1990, vii). The end of the Cold War in 1989 saw several of these
wars end almost simultaneously (Ethiopia, Iran-Iraq, Afghanistan, Cambodia, El Salvador). Others sputtered on, but ceased to
be supplied by the superpowers (Somalia, Angola). At the same
time, however, a host of new conflicts related to the collapse of the
Soviet Union broke out into open warfare (Yugoslavia, Armenia,
Azerbaijan, Georgia). Other conflicts suddenly became more
ominous (North Korea/South Korea, Montenegro, Indonesia).

High-intensity and Low-intensity War

There are two distinct types of war in the world today: high-
intensity war, fought by governments that make their own
modern weapons and field large, professional armed forces, and
low-intensity war, fought by governments, would-be governments,
paramilitary forces, guerrilla armies, terrorists and bandits pursuing
diverse goals by violent means. Low-intensity war is characterized
by sporadic fighting, unpredictable casualty levels, the brutal
treatment of noncombatants and large refugee flows. According
to Van Creveld, we are witnessing the end of conventional
high-intensity war and the emergence of a new model of warfare
in which tribal, ethnic, commercial and religious factions do battle
with each other and with state-supported forces that lack formal

military organization. Van Creveld challenges the conventional Clausewitzian view of war as a continuation of politics by other means, "In the future," he writes, "there will undoubtedly be many cases in which the whole idea of fighting a war 'for' something will be largely inapplicable" (1991, 217). The theory also holds that regular military forces will seldom prevail over irregular forces in low-intensity wars.

The Distribution of Military Power

As of 1999, there were 20 governments in the world whose annual military expenditure exceeded $5 billion. They were supplied with such equipment as fighter planes, helicopters, tanks, howitzers, and radar by a small number of arms-exporting nations, principally the United States, France, Germany, and China. The largest armed forces, all over one million people on active duty, were maintained by China, the United States, India, North Korea, and Russia, in that order (International Institute for Strategic Studies 2000, 297–302).

Most of the world's nuclear weapons—about 20,000—were owned by the United States and Russia. France, Britain, and China had more modest nuclear arsenals of several hundred weapons each, efficiently deployed and capable of inflicting grave damage on targets anywhere in the world. India and Pakistan had smaller nuclear arsenals; their exact size was not publicly known. Israel is believed to have a nuclear arsenal. In 1993, South Africa became the first country to announce that it had indeed developed nuclear weapons but then had dismantled all of them. This was the first and so far the only instance of a nuclear-capable state reverting to non-nuclear status. Germany, Sweden, Japan, Brazil, Argentina, and perhaps Taiwan, have long had the capacity to go nuclear on short notice. Iraq and Libya have made frantic efforts to join the club; Iraq may have succeeded after the abandonment of international inspection in 1998. North Korea has agreed to give up the quest in return for various concessions from the United States.

The present distribution of military power in the world involves: (1) a distinction between nuclear-weapons states and non-nuclear states; and, (2) a more gradual distribution of modern, conventional power (the ability to make "high-intensity" war). Scoring high on both categories are a handful of states (e.g., China, Russia, France, Britain, India, Israel) which field deliverable nuclear bombs and have indigenous high-intensity conventional capability. Then there are states that field a high-intensity conventional force, but lack nuclear weapons (e.g., Germany, Sweden, Vietnam, Switzerland, Japan). A large group consists of states that do not possess either high-intensity conventional capability or nuclear weapons but do maintain fairly large military forces (e.g., Brazil, Indonesia, Sudan, Myanmar).

Looming over this distribution is the one remaining military superpower, the United States, which possesses both a large nuclear arsenal and the ability to project conventional military force anywhere on earth. Compared to the U.S., all other conventional forces are regional, not global in scope. As of 2000, the U.S. defense budget exceeded the combined defense budgets of all the other nations with substantial forces (International Institute for Strategic Studies 2000).

In addition to armed states, there are a number of small, clandestine military forces that engage in dramatic attacks on targets chosen for symbolic impact. This is the relatively new phenomenon of international terrorism. Some of these groups have been parties to a low-level civil war (as in El Salvador, Mexico, Colombia, Afghanistan), others have been nationalist movements seeking to accomplish the fission of an existing state (e.g., Hamas, Hezbollah, Tamils in Sri Lanka, the Irish Republican Army, Catalan nationalists, Basque separatists, Chechen rebels) and finally, one group, Osama bin Laden's Al Qaeda, has declared war on the United States of America.

The International Arms Trade

The worldwide trade in military hardware, and the training of local personnel to use the imported items, is a vast industry that accounts for a substantial portion of all worldwide merchandise trade flows. More importantly, at least since World War II, the existence of an unregulated arms bazaar has made many international wars and internal civil struggles far more costly in lives and property than they would have been if the participants had been limited to indigenous weapons. Long-standing tribal conflicts in countries without an internal ability to make a reliable pistol are enacted with advanced hand-me-down weapons from the industrial world. This can upset the calculations of local decision-makers, who lack experience in estimating the destruction that can be wrought by high-tech weapons.

There are numerous reasons for the amazing growth and size of the arms business:

1. Efforts to prevent sales must overcome the free-rider problem. Domestic pressure groups point out with some justification that "the other countries will sell if we don't."

2. Modern armed forces find third party conflicts to be excellent testing grounds for new weapons. Commercial advertisements for weapons frequently refer to their demonstrated effectiveness in recent battles. The French Exocet missile enjoyed greatly increased sales after its successful use by the Argentine Air Force in the Falklands War.

3. Arms sales are used diplomatically to reward friends and punish enemies. The relative political popularity of different countries and insurgencies in Washington, D.C. and other Western capitals is tangibly signaled by access to modern weapons.

4. Arms producers reduce the unit cost of weapons sold to their own governments by stretching out production runs with export sales. So much of the cost of a modern weapon system is in research, development, and the tooling of production lines that overseas sales can make the difference between profit and loss.

5. Military establishments seek to maintain their own defense industry base between procurement cycles by producing for export.

6. In some places, especially in the former Soviet bloc countries of Eastern Europe, over-production of arms resulted from misguided investment into heavy industries such as steel when civilian demand for their products was declining.

7. There is no real regulation of the arms business—that is, no effective transnational authority. Many arms merchants are shadowy private individuals with unusually good political connections and access to capital from dubious sources.

8. What little regulation has existed, in the form of arms embargoes imposed by individual countries or blocs, may in fact have accelerated the arms trade by forcing the targeted states to create indigenous arms industries which then compete in the world market.

Political Functions of Modern Armed Forces

Beyond their role in the international war system, many armed forces play a critical role in the internal politics of their countries. Indeed, in much of the world, suppression of dissent against the ruling regime has been the primary mission of the military (e.g., Nepal, Chile, Myanmar, Honduras, Nigeria, and Guatemala). In some of these countries, the military is a major political player in its own right, taking over the civilian government intermittently or permanently.

Janowitz (1964) identified three traditional patterns of military involvement in the history of Western nation-states: aristocratic, democratic, and totalitarian. In the aristocratic model, the political and military elites are tightly connected: "birth, family connections, and common ideology insure that the military will embody the ideology of dominant groups in society (3–4)." In the democratic model, civilian and military elites are sharply separated. Explicit understandings that command broad popular support carefully delineate the terms and conditions under which the military operates. These terms and conditions do not envisage military involvement in domestic politics, which is conceived as wholly civilian. Instead of a direct, e.g., family, stake in successful war-making, the officer in the democratic model is motivated by adherence to a professional code of ethics. In the totalitarian model, a "centralized and authoritarian one-party system" provides the military with resources but maintains tight control through the placement of party members into military units, the arming of special paramilitary party units, the existence of secret party security organizations, and party control over officer promotions. The military officer is confined to military affairs and shut out of domestic politics.

None of the foregoing models precisely describes the political functions of the military in most of the states that have gained independence since 1945. The wider involvement of armed forces in social and economic change in these societies is a new phenomenon that does not fit the aristocratic, democratic, or totalitarian models. Janowitz (1964, 6–7) described five new types of civil-military relations:

1. *authoritarian-personal control*, where the regime was based on a traditional right to command, as in Haile Selassie's Ethiopia, or where the regime was based on the personal autocracy of a military commander, as in Idi Amin's Uganda;

2. *authoritarian-mass party*, where the "civilian police and paramilitary institutions operate as counterweights to the military," as in Castro's Cuba;

3. *democratic competitive and semi-competitive systems*, where there are "competing civilian institutions and power groups," as in India;

4. *civil-military coalition*, where the civilian group is in power so long as it retains the support of the military, as in Indonesia; and

5. *military oligarchy*, where "political initiative" has passed to the military, as in South Korea, Turkey, and Pakistan at various times in recent years.

Despite many local peculiarities, the new nations can be roughly sorted into these types at any particular time. In some of these situations, the military is not directly involved in domestic politics but plays a critical role in legitimizing civilian regimes. In others, the military is more directly involved in domestic politics, either ruling directly or supporting a civilian clique. In either case, the participation of the military in politics offsets some of the "liability of newness" that suddenly independent states face.

From a slightly different standpoint, Finer (1988) identified three types of military regime. The first is indirect government, where a nominally civilian government seems to exercise its constitutional responsibilities but is controlled by the military, either by the exercise of pressure or by the control of civilian appointments. Such an arrangement can be intermittent, with the army intervening from time to time for limited objectives, or it can be continuous. In the second type of military regime, the army is in direct control, even if it appoints civilian ministers to carry out its policies. Finally, there is a dual type, in which the political system rests on two pillars, the army and a political party, both subject to a dictator or an oligarchy. Most military dictatorships have taken this form. The individual who seizes power as a military commander tends to become more and more involved in the task of governing and less and less identified with the armed forces. In some cases, this leads to his overthrow by another military coup; in other cases, to the reinstatement of a civilian regime.

Public Opinion and War

The argument that a transition from monarchical to republican constitutions would inhibit warmaking was articulated by Immanuel Kant in his famous essay on perpetual peace ([1795] 1917). Kant thought it self-evident that public opinion would be unfavorable to war and constitute an effective restraint on republican governments. After two centuries of practical experience, we know that it does not. Governments do not merely respond to public opinion; they create and manipulate it. An overwhelming body of evidence suggests that the populations of modern nations are very easily persuaded to support any war that a government elects to wage. The classic example is the sudden shift of opinion in favor of war that occurred in Britain, France, Germany, Austria and Russia in August 1914. The strong, pacifist commitment of the French and German socialists vanished overnight, as did the internationalist views of leading intellectuals. Among the unlikely supporters of the war were Mahatma Gandhi, Igor Stravinsky, Henry James, Sigmund Freud, and Max Weber (Stromberg 1982, Weber [1926] 1975). Bertrand Russell (1956, 31) wrote of 1914 that:

> I discovered to my amazement that average men and women were delighted by the prospect of war. I had fondly imagined, what most pacifists contended, that wars were forced upon a reluctant population by despotic and Machiavellian governments.

Sample survey data that provide reliable estimates of mass opinion are available for the U.S., Britain, and France for all conflicts since 1939. Each war these countries have entered during that interval has gained overwhelming public support at the outset; every military action by the U.S. since the invention of public opinion polling has caused an immediate large rise in the popularity of the President and his government. In a *Washington Post* poll taken two weeks after the outbreak of the Gulf War (27 January 1991), the proportion of survey respondents who agreed that "things in this country are generally going in the right direction" had risen from 19 percent to 49 percent. A similar change occurred in the aftermath of the destruction of the World Trade Center. Apparently, no nearby war in the past two centuries has failed to evoke massive public support in its initial stage in all the countries involved. But this support erodes during a protracted war so that there is ultimately a decline in national unity and growing criticism (Stein 1980; Mueller 1973).

For Further Reading

Martin L. Van Creveld, *The Transformation of War*, New York: The Free Press, 1991.

Robert K. Schaeffer, *Warpaths: The Politics of Partition*, New York: Hill and Wang, 1990.

§

Part Two

Military Systems

6

The Origins of Modern
Military Organization

Every armed group in human history has confronted choices
about such things as weapons, tables of organization, and tactics.
These choices have always been constrained by the characteristics, especially the status pattern and technological level, of the
surrounding society. A common source of inspiration for past
military organizations has been older military organizations. The
victories of ancient armed forces were attributed to various organizational features, which were then copied, with varying degrees of
accuracy and with various battlefield outcomes. Modern military
organization has evolved in this fashion from several archaic
military systems. In this chapter we will consider these systems in
their societal contexts. All of them are from the Western military
tradition because after the European armed conquest of the globe
between 1500 and 1900, few other sources of military inspiration
have been drawn upon.

The Roman Legion and the *Pax Romana*

The Roman legion provided the original model for modern
military units. Such features as uniforms, rank insignia, tables of
organization and equipment, division into subsidiary units, close
order drill, individual-level training in combat skills, an elaborate
division of labor on the battlefield and tactical manuals—all
regarded today as defining characteristics of military organizations, were first introduced and systematized by the Romans.[1]

The final defeat of Anthony and Cleopatra in 30 B.C. and the installation of Octavian as emperor consolidated two centuries of republican conquests: Spain was fully occupied and divided into three provinces; Gaul into four; Germany west of the Rhine, along with Switzerland, Bavaria, Austria, most of the Balkans, Macedonia, Greece, Croatia, Bulgaria, Anatolia, Asia, Galatia, Armenia, Syria, Egypt, and Libya were under Roman authority. Parthia, Dacia and the German barbarians were the important hostile powers (Luttwak 1976). The Roman empire lasted some four centuries after the conquest of Spain and Gaul around 20 B.C. Long periods of peace within the empire permitted considerable prosperity and an advanced civilization.

The military unit that maintained the empire was the *legion*—a multi-purpose infantry formation under a single commander, which directly anticipated the modern infantry *division*. Originally, the legion consisted of a mix of cavalry, artillery, and infantry. After the reforms of Marius, the legion became almost entirely a heavy infantry formation, with very limited cavalry and artillery (Luttwak 1976, 40). The infantry units were also trained as combat engineers.

The basic plan of the Roman legion consisted of a headquarters, a small cavalry unit, a small artillery unit, and ten large heavy infantry formations called *cohorts*. The legion headquarters contained a command element and staff personnel for technical, medical, and supply functions. Each cohort contained six *centuries* of eighty soldiers each and a small staff element, except for the first cohort, which had six double-strength centuries of 160 men each and a small staff element. About 5,300 soldiers were assigned to the cohorts. An additional 700 men in the headquarters, artillery, and cavalry units brought the legion up to about 6,000 men (Luttwak 1976, 14).

The legion employed a mix of carefully chosen weapons. For offense, infantrymen carried the *pilum* (resembling a javelin) and the *gladius* (a short, double-edged sword). For defense, infantrymen wore helmets and body armor. Each infantryman carried a light, oval shield. A combination pickax-shovel was also standard individual equipment.[2] The artillery unit used catapults to hurl stones and *ballistae* to throw large spears. Finally, the legion could build siege engines to overcome enemy fortifications (Luttwak 1976, 44–45).

The legion typically fought with the assistance of *auxiliaries* who were organized into cavalry, infantry, and mixed units. These less formal organizations were variously armed: bows, spears, lances, long swords, slings, javelins. Auxiliaries wore no body armor (making them ultimately vulnerable to the legion, should they be tempted to switch sides). The number of auxiliaries operating with a legion was about equal to the number of legionnaires (Luttwak 1976, 45).

The legion fought as little as possible; its primary purpose was deterrence. Its most characteristic device was the marching camp. At the conclusion of the day's march, legionnaires spent three hours or more to dig a perimeter ditch, to erect a prefabricated palisade and to pitch their tents, grouped by units, around a broad T-shaped roadway leading to headquarters. A gap of 60 feet was left between fence and tents. The marching camp was as much a psychological as a tactical device.

The legion was not suited to guerrilla warfare, cavalry engagements, or skirmishing, but it was almost irresistible in pitched battles with less disciplined forces. Its javelins had an accurate range of about 100 feet; it was trained to fight as a solid mass. This limited the legion's effectiveness to battles with a fixed objective, such as a city, a fortress or a bridge. The legion moved too slowly to engage cavalry formations such as existed toward the East in what is now Ukraine and Iran. It could not divide itself into small detachments to pursue guerrillas such as those deployed by the Germanic tribes north of the Rhine. These tactical limits of the legion ultimately defined the geographic limits of Roman power.[3]

The Roman empire fielded between 25 and 28 legions with a maximum strength of about 300,000 men, including auxiliaries. The empire's frontier was not defended in depth. The empire was organized in 3 zones for: (1) direct control; (2) indirect control; (3) influence. Only the zone of direct control had a perimeter defense.

Roads were an essential element of the Roman defensive system. Legionary fortresses developed later, along with local recruitment, baths in the desert, hospitals, and separate lavatories for each pair of rooms. In the second century, there were long intervals of peace, and consequently, a heavy emphasis on recruitment, training, and drill.

The legion fit nicely into the political formula of the *Pax Romana* ("Roman peace"): respect for local institutions and dignitaries, adherence to imperial cults by imperial officials, temporary tenure of officials, limited tax authority, a uniform coinage for imperial taxes, privileges of Roman citizenship given to local notables, subjection of provincial military forces to civilian command, ruthlessness in suppressing opposition, rapid communication and transportation, the strict accountability of commanders, the construction of sewers, aqueducts and markets on standard plans, and a refreshing absence of racism.

War in the Dark Ages

Between the fall of the western Roman empire and the establishment of feudalism, warfare in Europe reverted to a more primitive, disorganized style. Various tribes throughout Europe that had been enlisted into the service of the Roman empire found themselves in possession of pieces of the fallen power. With the important exception of Charlemagne's temporary centralization of military authority, warfare in Europe from A.D. 400 to A.D. 1000 was crude and undisciplined. The largest coherent group, the Franks, succeeded in stopping the westward advance of Islam, but had no ability to expand their domain. Light cavalry dominated the battlefield, but was undisciplined and not coordinated with other branches.

In the armies of the eastern Roman empire, Byzantium, the Roman legion was transformed into a unit of armored, mounted, horse archers. The longevity of Byzantium (about a thousand years separated the fall of Constantinople from the fall of Rome) testifies to the continuing power of the legion idea. Byzantine leaders had learned from the fall of Rome not to rely too much on their tribal allies, and continued to insist on some citizen service in the army. At the same time, soldiers from many different places served as mercenaries (Diehl 1957, 41).

Charlemagne's temporary reestablishment of central military authority did not survive the partition of his domain at his death. Viking raids encouraged local landowners to take responsibility for their own defense, beginning the development of feudalism.

Feudal Chivalry

The next phase in the development of Western warfare came as Europe emerged from the "Dark Ages." *Chivalry* (from the French word for horse) was based on the tactical advantage that the mounted, armored horseman enjoyed over other warriors in the long period between the introduction of the stirrup in the eighth century and of gunpowder in the fourteenth. In an age almost devoid of effective authority, chivalry subjected the military forces of the time to a measure of social control by imposing rules on their conduct (although these were much more effective within than outside the knightly class), making them responsive to ecclesiastical mandates limiting the application of force in various ways, and making feudal obedience a religious obligation and a sign of honor. Much of that code survives today in the idea of military (especially officer) honor.

Induction into knighthood was a religious ceremony. Loyalty to comrades was equated with loyalty to God. The knightly obligation to protect the weak was associated with the biblical virtues of compassion and charity. The element of fun and games was equally important. The great medieval tourneys were a mixture of Superbowl and film festival. Celebrities gathered from far and wide to enjoy gossip and amorous byplay and the great spectacle of mock battle.

Chivalry was more than a military code; it was the way of life of a powerful ruling class closely linked to religion on the one hand and to eroticism on the other. Thus, the contrasting phenomena of the military orders of knights who took monastic vows, and the courts of love in which knights and ladies raised flirting to an art form. Chivalry converted war into a game and linked it directly with eroticism: the lady's favor was the quid pro quo for the knight's prowess, he ran unnecessary risks and took dangerous vows as a sign of either love or religious fervor. Some similar linkages occurred in other places, notably among the *Mahabharata* warriors of India and the Japanese samurai, but the details were different.

Gilbert sums up the knightly culture:

> Spiritually as well as economically the knight was a characteristic product of the Middle Ages. In a society in which God was envisaged as the head of a hierarchy, all secular activity had been given a religious meaning. The particular task of chivalry was to protect and defend the people of the country; in waging war the knight served God. He placed his military services at the disposal of his overlord, to whom the supervision of secular services was entrusted by the church. Apart from the spiritual-religious side, however, the military bond between vassal and overlord also had its legal and economic aspects. The knight's land, the fief, was given to him by the overlord, and in accepting it, the knight assumed the obligation of military service to the overlord in wartime . . . A religious concept of war as an act of rendering service, restriction of participation to the class of landholding knights and their retainers, and a moral-legal code which operated as the main bond holding the army together—these are the factors that determined the forms of military organization as well as the methods of war in the Middle Ages . . . The purely temporary character of military service as well as the equality of standing of the noble fighters made strict discipline difficult if not impossible (1986, 12–13).

The modern understanding of the honor of military personnel, especially of commissioned officers (who go through a kind of knighthood ceremony), is inspired by the codes of chivalry. Honor is still defined today in elite military organizations as loyalty to Unit, Corps, Country, and God. The entire complex of ideas is justified by the responsibility to protect those who cannot protect themselves, but that theme tends to get submerged in practice. The cultural influence extends beyond purely military organizations to include, for example, some of the traits of the Boy Scout Oath (brave, loyal, courteous, reverent, etc.)[4]

In the more common, modern reading of the chivalrous tradition, honor is an attribute of officers but not of enlisted personnel. Thus officer prisoners are often released by their captors on parole, that is, on their promise not to return to the fighting, while enlisted prisoners are kept in strict confinement. The attribution of honor to officers alone is what supports the peculiarly large status gap between officers and enlisted personnel in some modern armed forces. It is clearly not a functional requirement either of the host society or of modern warfare (the Israeli Defense Force does well without it) and is hard to understand until the social distinction between knight and retainers (who cared for the horses and carried modest infantry weapons) is recalled. The knight was owner and ruler of a sizable estate, while the retainers were social ciphers. In modern Western forces, officers may barely keep pace with the professional middle classes, but still attempt to maintain a large status gap between themselves and the lower ranks.

The *Condottiere* System in Renaissance Italy

With the invention of gunpowder and the reintroduction of a money economy, the code of chivalry lost its power and war was transformed from a religious duty to a semi-commercial activity that enjoyed little esteem. In the most civilized parts of Europe soldiering came to be viewed with contempt.

As the citizens of the city-states of Italy became richer and more cultivated in the early Renaissance, they became increasingly reluctant to be personally involved in the degrading business of war. But they still needed to deal with hostile neighbors and invading armies and so they resorted to hiring mercenaries, who were paid at negotiated rates for their military services. The *condottiere* recruited a band of soldiers and offered them for hire at a set price to any prince or city needing a military force. Since the wars of the time were small-scale enterprises conducted for profit or territorial gain, there were few political issues at stake. The presence of the *condottieri*[5] tended to reduce the hardships of war, since troops hired for short engagements were not particularly eager to die for the benefit of their employers. Battles were likely to be brief and relatively harmless; they might be avoided altogether by negotiation or flight when there was an obvious disparity of forces.

The danger in the *condottiere* system was that a hired army might turn on its employers, and this happened from time to time as when Francesco Sforza made himself duke of Milan in 1450. But most city-states were more skillful in managing their contractors. Contracts were kept short, multiple contractors were hired with the object of keeping each other in check, and contractors were not immune to state authority. In 1429, the Venetians employed Francesco Carmagnola as their commander-in-chief at a salary of 1,000 ducats a month, payable even in peacetime, but in 1432, when he was suspected of collusion with the enemy, he was lured back to Venice, tried for treason, and executed (McNeill 1974, 70).

It is interesting that although the Venetians of the fifteenth century hired their soldiers, the state produced all the weapons of war; they had no military contractors in the modern sense. Indeed, Venice invented the assembly line by lining a canal with stations for the outfitting of warships (McNeill 1974, 6).

The system weakened when Italy was invaded by foreign armies and war became more desperate and more serious, but it never entirely disappeared. Centuries later, wars regarded as unimportant were still being fought by mercenaries; the most familiar example is the extensive use of Hessian mercenaries by the British in the American Revolutionary War. And mercenaries are still in considerable demand today: the U.S. recruited a mercenary army to fight in Nicaragua; Colombian drug warlords hire Israeli ex-servicemen; and the post-colonial civil wars in Africa involved substantial numbers of mercenaries. Some spent entire careers fighting in one small war after another throughout the 1950s, 1960s, and 1970s.

Maurice of Nassau and the Choreography of Drill

Machiavelli's *Art of War*, originally published in 1521, was the precursor work with its emphasis on a hierarchical chain of command, functional specialization, and military competence based on constant drill and training. A disciple of Machiavelli, Justus Lipsius, published a book on the art of war in 1589 and presented a copy to his student, the young prince Maurice of Nassau. War, according to Lipsius, was not a condition of uncontrolled violence but the orderly application of force in the interest of the state. His ideal officer was a thoroughgoing professional dedicated to public service.

Discipline, drill, and training were the keynotes. The Roman legion was the model. Maurice's military career started in 1588 when, at 21, he was appointed Admiral-General of the United Netherlands and Captain-General of Brabant and Flanders. But he was always under civilian control, operated through a web of boards and committees. The Dutch had revolted against Spain in 1566; they were in the course of being subjugated when the defeat of the Spanish Armada gave them a breathing space. The troops were all mercenaries; the Dutch themselves served in the Navy. Maurice began by reducing the size of his army to about 12,000 men. He introduced close-order drill, martial music, the manual of arms, and the performance of military tasks by the numbers and in unison. There were 56 invariable steps in the loading and firing of a musket. Instant obedience and unit cohesion were the objectives of drill. Units were of standard size: companies of 150 men and battalions of 550. Officers were recruited by ability and promoted by merit rather than nepotism. Another significant feature of Maurice's new system was the extensive use of the shovel for field entrenchment. His troops received adequate wages, punctually paid. Looting and pillage were not allowed.

This mode of discipline, an explicit reinvention of Roman practice, was overwhelming on the battlefield, and spread rapidly throughout Europe. A few years later, Gustavus Adolphus of Sweden adopted the same system but added conscription. Other European military leaders were quick to follow. However, with rare exceptions, close-order drill did not spread beyond Europe for many years, although the Ottoman empire tried in fits and starts to adopt the new style. Japan, in the late nineteenth century, was the first non-European state to adopt European military discipline along with European technology. But Maurice's program is standard in nearly all national armed forces today. Officers in underground command posts launch intercontinental ballistic missiles by the numbers; all competent armies pay standard wages and pay them promptly.

The American and French Revolutionary Armies

During the past two centuries the differences in military organization that may now be observed in the world began to appear. Some of these differences can be traced to different national experiences of war. The first important differentiation of modern military organizations into national types began with the revolutions that established the American and the French republics.

Political revolutions in America and in France were ignited and sustained by ideologically motivated civilian participation in a new kind of mass army. In America, the ability of the Massachusetts irregulars to stand off British troops at Lexington and Concord and then at Bunker Hill enabled the Continental Congress to declare independence in 1776. Winsor (1972, 133–134) estimates the number of American forces who made themselves available for the Battle of Bunker's Hill in June 1775 at 16,000. They were all volunteers or militia; the Continental Army had not yet been organized (see Galvin 1996). In France, the passive resistance of the Royal Army to police duties in 1789 undermined the monarchy in its struggle with the rebellious Parisians (Scott 1978, 46, 80; Bertaud 1979, 41–46).

From the military standpoint, there were many similarities between the two revolutions:

- Both involved the successful defense of a home territory against invading forces, although the French made some temporary conquests in the Netherlands, Germany and Savoy, and the Americans attempted the invasion of Canada.

- Both revolutionary armies were administered by an improvised legislative body, which lacked almost everything required for the task but nevertheless achieved ultimate success. But both armies suffered acutely from deficiencies of provisions, weapons, and pay because of the weakness of the administrative machinery. In 1779, for instance, when much of the American army was in rags, 10,000 uniforms lay in storehouses in France and another large quantity in the West Indies when the various agents of Congress could not decide whose business it was to ship them (Higginbotham 1978, 57).

- Both revolutions developed a tripartite military structure composed of a national army, local units of volunteers (the National Guard in France, the armies of the several colonies in America) and a pre-existing militia. In both cases, the first two were eventually amalgamated into the regular forces. In both revolutionary armies, the aims of the leadership were fully shared by the rank and file, in contrast to their adversaries. Both armies contained a large core of volunteers but were brought up to their maximum strength by conscription.

- The scale of military effort was unprecedented in each case. The best numerical estimate (Peckham 1974, 131–134) is that 200,000 men saw military service on the American side of the Revolution—about 40 percent of the adult male population. (The maximum number under arms at any one moment probably did not exceed 50,000.[6]) The French figures are more elusive but Bertaud (1979, 240) suggests a maximum strength at the end of 1793 of 700,000 men under arms out of a population of 24 million—a similarly large proportion.

- Both revolutionary armies had severe disciplinary problems, reflected in high rates of desertion and numerous mutinies and riots.

- Both armies practiced the appointment and expulsion of officers by the rank and file, the election of soldier's councils, and other democratic innovations.

- Both armies were commanded by general officers of traditional type, nobles in France, landowning gentry in America, but the lower levels of the officer corps were largely filled by promotion from the ranks.

- Both armies suffered heavy casualties in battle and equally heavy losses from sickness. The 25,234 who were killed in the American service amounted to 0.9 percent of the general population. The equivalent French losses in 1794–1795 are estimated at 200,000 (Bertaud 1979, 248), which was proportionately comparable.

The American revolutionary army was created *de novo*. The French revolutionary army was created by the gradual transformation of a Royal Army organized on quite different principles, officered almost exclusively by nobles, and intended for the defense of the *ancien régime*. That transformation involved much more internal conflict than was ever experienced by the American forces.

The American forces had a single commander in chief from the outset. The French forces at the height of the war were divided into eleven armies, each under separate command.

The French forces were much more politicized than the American forces and their political actions, beginning with the participation of soldiers on active duty in the attack on the Bastille, had much more impact on civilian politics. The French Revolution was fought within and around the armed forces, while the American army, despite many grievances and intrigues, retained its ideological solidarity from beginning to end.

The loyalty of the armed forces to the central government was never called into question in the American Revolution. It was a point of acute concern throughout the revolutionary period in France, which explains the almost continuous reorganization of the Army between 1789 and 1795 as new factions came to power in Paris.

In each case, the revolutionary experience imprinted itself on the national consciousness with profound consequences for the future.

Cincinnatus rather than Caesar remained the American ideal. "The fear of a standing army, was by 1775 an old and accepted political tradition, bound up inextricably in the Revolution itself" (Kohn, quoted by Higginbotham 1978, 104). The anti-military biases of the colonists were strengthened by their success in raising a large army overnight and finding able commanders for it. Thereafter, the American way of war was to recruit a mass army when needed, and to disband it as soon as the need passed. Washington, as president, calculated that a permanent force of 2,500 men, plus some naval vessels, would satisfy the peacetime requirements of the United States. Not until the 1950s and under the pressure of the Cold War did the U.S. abandon the practice of disbanding its forces after each war.

In the whole course of the American Revolution there was only one challenge to Congressional authority by the generals, and that one, the so-called Newburg conspiracy, quickly evaporated. These two features of the American polity—subordination of the military to civil authority and the abstention of the armed force from party politics—have survived all the twists and turns of American history. On the few occasions when popular generals were tempted to challenge their civilian superiors— notably McClellan in 1862 and MacArthur in 1952—they found it impossible to do so. Lesser-known American generals find themselves suddenly retired when they question civilian leadership (as did General Singlaub under President Carter), when they make rash statements to the media (the Air Force chief of staff under President George Bush), and even when they orally denigrate the Commander-in-Chief (an Air Force general in Europe under President Clinton).

In addition to the authority of the Executive Branch, Congress' fiscal watchdog, the General Accounting Office (GAO), provides the informational support for Congressional committees to exercise considerable oversight in military matters.

In France, by contrast, the whole revolutionary experience reinforced the old idea of the army as the bulwark of national power, and joined it with the newer idea of the "nation in arms" (Brubaker 1990). Napoleon took the patriotic, mass army that the Revolution had created and made it an instrument of conquest and political proselytization that was irresistible until his ill-fated invasion of Russia. Under every subsequent French regime, from the Restoration to the Fifth Republic, the army has played a critical role in support or in opposition. The peacetime military establishment has been as much taken for granted as the post office, but it has been only intermittently attached to the principle of civilian supremacy. At nearly every major turn of French history, the attitude of the armed forces, and particularly of the officer corps, has weighed heavily in the political balance.

The American Civil War

The war between the United States of America and the newly formed Confederate States of America (1861–1865) had a peculiarly modern character and foreshadowed the wars of the twentieth century both in technology and in organization. It was, for example, the first war in which the movement of troops by railroad, permanent trenches, aerial observation, field telegraphs, repeating rifles, explosive shells and armored warships were important. It was also the first modern war to mobilize most of the available manpower on both sides, to convert civilian industry to large-scale war production, to have full and contemporary press coverage, to be photographed and to develop anti-war movements on the home front.

The foreshadowing was not coincidental. No war in history harbored so many foreign military observers and they were quick to learn the technical and tactical lessons of the innovations they observed and to carry them back to Europe.

The idea of war as a spectacle for the civilian population might be said to originate in the first major engagement of the Civil War, at Bull Run, when crowds of well-dressed spectators came from Washington in carriages and on horseback to view the battle. Throughout the war, journalistic accounts of every major action were illustrated by battlefield artists and appeared almost immediately on the nation's breakfast tables. Overnight, public opinion came to exert a powerful influence on day-to-day military management, and success or failure in the field began to be weighed in terms of its effect on the next election. The foreign press coverage was almost equally extensive and eventually persuaded the British to abandon their initial support of the Confederacy.

Another peculiarly modern feature was the evolution of the scale and purpose of the war as it progressed. When the first shots were fired at Fort Sumter, no one on either side anticipated a long and destructive war, and no issues were involved beyond a difference of opinion between the government in Washington and the governments of the southern states about whether the Constitution permitted secession. It was not even certain that secession would be contested. But as events developed and each side threw more and more of its resources into the cauldron, the war changed into a crusade against slavery on one side and against foreign tyranny on the other—causes worth dying for.

Finally, there was a modern cast to the political consequences of the war, which were largely unforeseen and unintended—the failure of Reconstruction, the substitution of collective for individual slavery, and the installation of a one-party system in the South.

The Great War

As we suggest in Chapter 1, it is convenient for some purposes to combine World War I (1914–1918) and World War II (1939–1945) into a single war between Britain, France, the U.S., Russia, and their allies on one side, and Germany, Austria and their allies on the other, with two phases of intense activity separated by an uneasy twenty-year truce.

What makes this combination plausible is that the two world wars greatly exceeded all previous wars in military and civilian casualties, in the destruction of cities and cultural monuments, in geographic scale, and in political and social consequences. The principal adversaries were the same, although Turkey, Japan and Italy changed sides between the first and the second phase. The major European fronts—western, eastern and Atlantic—were the same, although theaters outside Europe played a larger part in the second phase. But the most important consideration is that the second phase resulted directly from the first.

The Great War was the first, and perhaps the last, fully industrialized war. It involved the total dedication of the world's most advanced industrial economies to war production, and the almost total dependence of combat forces on sophisticated machinery, including tanks, fighter and bomber aircraft, long-range artillery, land mines, submarines, battleships, cruisers, aircraft carriers, radio, radar, rockets, and ultimately the atomic bomb. These enabled the protagonists to kill about 100 million people and to permanently injure as many more.

Tactically, each phase of the war involved a major, initial surprise. In the first few months of fighting on the western front in 1914, the German, French and British armies discovered that infantry defense—based on entrenchment, machine guns and barbed wire—was conclusively superior to infantry attack, when the opposing forces operated at the same technological level. Despite major efforts to overcome that superiority by means of tanks, poison gas and tunneling, it persisted through 1918. Victory was eventually achieved by the exhaustion of the attacker, not by any significant breakthrough.

In the first few weeks of fighting on the same front in 1940, the German, French and British armies discovered that infantry attack—in highly mobile armored vehicles supported by dive bombers—was now conclusively superior to old-style infantry defense. That discovery nearly ended the war immediately but in the remaining years of the war, as both sides acquired armor, mobility and air cover, the odds evened out, and victory was eventually achieved by the side with the larger industrial capability.

Colonization and Decolonization

The development in the fifteenth century of ships that could carry batteries of cannon, sail to windward, and navigate distant seas, allowed the western European nations to begin a long sequence of discoveries, conquests and annexations that continued until 1914, by which time nearly all the world was dominated politically and culturally by Europeans or their descendants. The cultural domination has persisted but the political domination dissolved very rapidly in Asia and Africa after 1945. Numerous features of modern military organization can be traced either to the successful experience of Western military forces in conquering and administering the world or to the successful experience of national liberation movements after 1945.

During the 400 years from Cortez to the Mau-Mau there were continual indigenous revolts against Western imperial domination. Most of these were ruthlessly suppressed. The common elements of European imperial success were:

- superiority in maneuver, firepower, and seapower;
- incessant diplomacy, on the principle of *divide and rule*;
- religious indoctrination;
- reliance on mestizo administrators (of mixed European and native descent);
- recruitment of indigenous troops and allies;
- implantation of a colonizing elite;
- withdrawal from untenable positions; and
- ruthless cruelty in the suppression of uprisings.[7]

The European colonial empires, with more than four centuries of development behind them, were still largely intact in 1945. Britain, France, Belgium and Spain controlled most of Africa and the Middle East; India, Canada, Australia, New Zealand, and most of the Caribbean islands were still attached to Britain; the Dutch ruled most of the East Indies. Smaller British, French, Dutch, Belgian, Portuguese and Danish colonies were scattered around the globe. This entire structure collapsed within 25 years after the end of World War II.

The loss of every significant Western colonial possession after 1945 was accelerated by several factors. As the sole surviving military powers, the United States and the Soviet Union enthusiastically championed the dismantling of the British, French, Dutch, Spanish, Belgian and Portuguese empires. The major imperial powers' home countries had been battered, their armed forces exhausted or destroyed, and their overseas bases obliterated during the war. Western moral authority—the belief in the White Man's

Burden and the manifest destiny of Europeans to civilize the world—had been totally undermined by mass slaughter, death camps and bombed-out cities. The idea of empire had become morally offensive.

Independence was granted voluntarily to many colonies such as the islands of the British West Indies. But wherever decolonization was resisted by the imperial power—in Indonesia, Vietnam, Algeria, the Congo, Kenya—it happened anyway, and with great speed. The military balance had shifted so far in favor of national liberation movements that none of those movements failed. Aside from the open or covert support of the superpowers, these movements benefited from effective radio communication, the availability of cheap, portable explosives and automatic weapons, the invention of new guerrilla tactics and a coherent theory of guerrilla warfare, and the evaporation of the moral authority of colonial regimes.

For Further Reading

Edward Luttwak, *The Grand Strategy of the Roman Empire from the First Century A.D. to the Third,* Baltimore: Johns Hopkins University Press, 1976.

Brian Lapping, *End of Empire,* New York: St. Martin's Press, 1985.

Notes

[1] McNeill (1982) makes a strong case for granting priority to the Assyrians who created an army that had standard ranks, equipment, units, and promotion ladders based on merit. However, our knowledge of this comes from archeological investigations undertaken in recent decades. There is little evidence that later innovators, such as Maurice of Nassau, knew much about Assyria, but certainly Rome was well known to them.

[2] The pickax-shovel is so valuable that it reappears in the modern U.S. Army as the "entrenching tool."

[3] To the south was the Sahara desert; to the West, the Atlantic Ocean.

[4] The other Boy Scout virtues derive from a different cultural source: the Protestant Ethic, especially as propounded by Benjamin Franklin (Weber [1905] 1958). A Scout is prepared, dependable, prompt, and thrifty. The Boy Scout virtues thus uneasily combine chivalric honor and the work ethic of the Industrial Revolution.

[5] A *condotta* is a contract, the *condottiere* (plural *condottieri*) was a military contractor but not in the modern sense of building weapons for the armed services. The *condottiere* provided troops and led them into combat on behalf of his employers.

[6] An inference from the tabular information presented by Lesser 1976, xxxi; the maximum strength of the rank and file was 40,962 in October 1776.

[7] "Relational distance between the third party and the adversaries has the same effect as social superiority: The greater it is, the more violent the settlement is likely to be . . . Repressive pacification in colonial settings again defines the extreme: The administrators are usually not only socially superior but also entirely unacquainted with the people they handle (Black 1998, 87)."

7

Modern Military Organization

The principal features of modern military organizations are:

- a standard hierarchy of ranks with standard pay and privileges for each rank;
- an elaborate etiquette of rank;
- promotion by seniority qualified by merit;
- pyramidal tables of organization;
- vertical replication of functions, including command, administration, intelligence, operations, supply;
- horizontal replication of structures to make units interchangeable;
- standardization of specialties to make personnel interchangeable;
- procedures for rapid expansion and contraction of rosters; and
- a portable bureaucracy centered on the muster roll, the pay book, the field manual, written reports, and written orders.

Horizontal, Vertical and Zonal Differentiation

The modern development of armed forces has been marked by increasing differentiation in three dimensions: the vertical dimension of rank and command, the horizontal dimension of functional specialization, and the spatial dimension of zone. *Vertical differentiation* involves very stable ladders of rank and units of command; *horizontal differentiation* involves specialization by branch of service, battle function and military occupation; *spatial differentiation* involves the distinction between domestic bases and operational theaters and within theaters among front, intermediate, and rear areas.

Vertical differentiation in the armed forces of modern states has been very stable. The general arrangement of rank and units of command for land forces has scarcely changed in the past two centuries. The classic arrangement looks like this:

Rank	Unit of Command
Marshal	army group
General	army
Lieutenant General	corps
Major General	division
Brigadier General	brigade
Colonel	regiment
Lieutenant Colonel	battalion
Captain	company
Lieutenant	platoon
Sergeant	squad
Corporal	fire team

In the contemporary U.S. Army, there are eleven grades of commissioned officer, four grades of warrant officer, and nine grades of enlisted personnel, from recruit to sergeant major. The ranks are grouped as follows: general officers, field-grade officers, company-grade officers, warrant officers, and enlisted personnel (Table 3).

Naval ranks are differently titled but exactly equivalent to army ranks (Table 4). The Air Force and the Marine Corps use the same names for the commissioned ranks as the Army (Tables 5 and 6). Each of the services, however, uses its own names for the enlisted ranks. In addition to these ranks, there is another

Table 3. Number and Basic Pay of U.S. Army Personnel, July 2001

Rank	Number on Active Duty	Basic Monthly Pay Range ($)
General officers		
General of the Army*	0	
General (O-10)	10	8,519 – 12,951
Lieutenant General (O-9)	44	7,550 – 10,356
Major General (O-8)	95	6,838 – 9,383
Brigadier General (O-7)	147	5,682 – 8,323
Field-grade officers		
Colonel (O-6)	3,538	4,211 – 7,310
Lieutenant-Colonel (O-5)	8,693	3,369 – 5,965
Major (O-4)	14,229	2,839 – 4,987
Company-grade officers		
Captain (O-3)	21,500	2,638 – 4,580
First Lieutenant (O-2)	8,764	2,301 – 3,688
Second Lieutenant (O-1)	8,179	1,998 – 3,120
Warrant officers		
Chief Warrant Officer (W-5)	386	4,641 – 5,120
Chief Warrant Officer (W-4)	1,307	2,688 – 4,591
Chief Warrant Officer (W-3)	3,057	2,443 – 4,045
Chief Warrant Officer (W-2)	4,695	2,140 – 3,503
Warrant Officer (W-1)	1,915	1,783 – 3,019
Noncommissioned officers		
Sergeant Major (E-9)	3,069	3,127 – 4,061
Master Sergeant (E-8)	10,857	2,622 – 3,613
Sergeant First Class (E-7)	37,024	1,831 – 3,251
Staff Sergeant (E-6)	56,444	1,575 – 2,421
Sergeant (E-5)	71,723	1,382 – 2,040
Corporal/Specialist (E-4)	96,367	1,289 – 1,653
The rank-and-file		
Private First Class (E-3)	63,439	1,215 – 1,385
Private (E-2)	36,988	1,169
Recruit (E-1)	24,503	965 – 1,043

* Only appointed during major wars.
Sources: http://web1.whs.osd.mil/mmid/military/ms11.pdf, and
http://www.dfas.mil/money/milpay/pay/07-2001.pdf

Table 4. Number and Basic Pay of U.S. Naval Personnel, July 2001

Rank	Number on Active Duty	Basic Monthly Pay Range ($)
General officers		
Fleet Admiral*	0	
Admiral (O-10)	8	8,519 – 12,951
Vice Admiral (O-9)	29	7,550 – 10,356
Rear Admiral (UH) (O-8)**	72	6,838 – 9,383
Rear Admiral (LH) (O-7)	108	5,682 – 8,323
Field-grade officers		
Captain (O-6)	3354	4,211 – 7,310
Commander (O-5)	6,979	3,369 – 5,965
Lieutenant Commander (O-4)	10,471	2,839 – 4,987
Company-grade officers		
Lieutenant (O-3)	17,338	2,638 – 4,580
Lieutenant (j.g.) (O-2)***	6,589	2,301 – 3,688
Ensign (O-1)	7,560	1,998 – 3,120
Warrant officers		
Chief Warrant Officer (W-4)	350	2,688 – 4,591
Chief Warrant Officer (W-3)	376	2,443 – 4,045
Chief Warrant Officer (W-2)	959	2,140 – 3,503
Noncommissioned officers		
Master Chief Petty Officer (E-9)	3,079	3,127 – 4,061
Senior Chief Petty Officer (E-8)	6,261	2,622 – 3,613
Chief Petty Officer (E-7)	21,797	1,831 – 3,251
Petty Officer First Class (E-6)	55,323	1,575 – 2,421
Petty Officer Second Class (E-5)	71,262	1,382 – 2,040
Petty Officer Third Class (E-4)	66,172	1,289 – 1,653
The rank-and-file		
Seaman (E-3)	48,732	1,215 – 1,385
Seaman Apprentice (E-2)	25,926	1,169
Seaman Recruit (E-1)	18,192	965 – 1,043

* Only appointed during major wars.
** Rear admirals are divided into an "upper half" and a "lower half."
*** "j.g." means "junior-grade."
Sources: http://web1.whs.osd.mil/mmid/military/ms11.pdf, and
      http://www.dfas.mil/money/milpay/pay/07-2001.pdf

Table 5. Number and Basic Pay of U.S. Air Force Personnel, July 2001

Rank	Number on Active Duty	Basic Monthly Pay Range ($)
General officers		
General of the Air Force*	0	
General (O-10)	11	8,519 – 12,951
Lieutenant General (O-9)	38	7,550 – 10,356
Major General (O-8)	80	6,838 – 9,383
Brigadier General (O-7)	137	5,682 – 8,323
Field-grade officers		
Colonel (O-6)	3,832	4,211 – 7,310
Lieutenant-Colonel (O-5)	10,081	3,369 – 5,965
Major (O-4)	15,405	2,839 – 4,987
Company-grade officers		
Captain (O-3)	23,220	2,638 – 4,580
First Lieutenant (O-2)	5,964	2,301 – 3,688
Second Lieutenant (O-1)	9,921	1,998 – 3,120
Noncommissioned officers		
Chief Master Sergeant (E-9)	2,820	3,127 – 4,061
Senior Master Sergeant (E-8)	5,731	2,622 – 3,613
Master Sergeant (E-7)	29,463	1,831 – 3,251
Technical Sergeant (E-6)	42,139	1,575 – 2,421
Staff Sergeant (E-5)	69,634	1,382 – 2,040
Senior Airman (E-4)	52,705	1,289 – 1,653
The rank-and-file		
Airman First Class (E-3)	54,041	1,215 – 1,385
Airman (E-2)	11,704	1,169
Airman Basic (E-1)	11,770	965 – 1,043

* Only appointed during major wars.
Sources: http://web1.whs.osd.mil/mmid/military/ms11.pdf, and
   http://www.dfas.mil/money/milpay/pay/07-2001.pdf

Table 6. Number and Basic Pay of U.S. Marine Corps Personnel,
          July 2001

Rank	Number on Active Duty	Basic Monthly Pay Range ($)
General officers		
General (O-10)	4	8,519 – 12,951
Lieutenant General (O-9)	13	7,550 – 10,356
Major General (O-8)	23	6,838 – 9,383
Brigadier General (O-7)	40	5,682 – 8,323
Field-grade officers		
Colonel (O-6)	632	4,211 – 7,310
Lieutenant-Colonel (O-5)	1,787	3,369 – 5,965
Major (O-4)	3,447	2,839 – 4,987
Company-grade officers		
Captain (O-3)	5,070	2,638 – 4,580
First Lieutenant (O-2)	2,686	2,301 – 3,688
Second Lieutenant (O-1)	2,456	1,998 – 3,120
Warrant officers		
Chief Warrant Officer (W-5)	86	4,641 – 5,120
Chief Warrant Officer (W-4)	225	2,688 – 4,591
Chief Warrant Officer (W-3)	441	2,443 – 4,045
Chief Warrant Officer (W-2)	719	2,140 – 3,503
Warrant Officer (W-1)	479	1,783 – 3,019
Noncommissioned officers		
Sergeant Major (E-9)	1,381	3,127 – 4,061
Master Sergeant (E-8)	3,290	2,622 – 3,613
Gunnery Sergeant (E-7)	8,949	1,831 – 3,251
Staff Sergeant (E-6)	14,176	1,575 – 2,421
Sergeant (E-5)	23,469	1,382 – 2,040
Corporal (E-4)	29,231	1,289 – 1,653
The rank-and-file		
Lance Corporal (E-3)	42,534	1,215 – 1,385
Private First Class (E-2)	20,696	1,169
Private (E-1)	10,818	965 – 1,043

Sources: http://web1.whs.osd.mil/mmid/military/ms11.pdf, and
         http://www.dfas.mil/money/milpay/pay/07-2001.pdf

category of officers ranking below the commissioned officers. These are warrant officers, who typically serve in some technical role after rising from the enlisted ranks as experts in their field. Warrant officers are found in the Army, Navy and Marine Corps, but not the Air Force.

A large *status gap* between officers and enlisted people is part of the standard military hierarchy. It originated in the eighteenth-century distinction between gentlemen and the common people, viewed almost as separate species.[1] Officers have personal honor, enlisted people do not. Hence officers are presumed to be trustworthy and to perform their duties without severe coercion. Enlisted people are presumed to be irresponsible and to be motivated to perform their duties by the fear of punishment. Officers are held to deserve better clothing, equipment, pay, food, and quarters, and to require only minimal supervision. Fraternization and marriage between the two groups are discouraged, as in other caste systems.

For obscure reasons, these archaic arrangements have been preserved to a greater extent in the U.S. military than in most other modern armed forces. Janowitz (1971, 216–217) comments on their curious origin:

> The military forces of the United States had their origins in a revolutionary political movement—in an anti-colonial struggle. Yet their code of honor derives from the aristocratic forms against which they struggled. Forms of officership and honor were transferred, if only because key officers in the Revolutionary forces had direct contact with British military institutions and there were no other directly available models. At least four basic elements operated in the code derived from British aristocratic institutions . . . Military honor meant, first that officers were gentlemen; second, fealty to the military commander was personal; third, officers were members of a cohesive brotherhood which claimed the right to extensive self-regulation; and fourth, officers fought for the preservation and enhancement of traditional glory.

Horizontal differentiation involves specialization by branch of service and occupational specialty.

As far back as the Roman legion, there were at least five discernible branches: infantry, cavalry, artillery (catapults), engineers (siege machines), quartermaster, and headquarters. Modern land formations include specialized units for wire and radio communication, transportation, intelligence, ordnance, medical treatment, legal proceedings, construction and demolition, graves registration, public relations and numerous other specialized functions. The division between infantry and cavalry—now infantry and armor—is still primary, however.

Another form of horizontal differentiation is by the distribution of personnel into what the U.S. Army calls "military occupational specialties." The trends in the military division of labor in this century have been roughly parallel to those in the civilian labor force—a great increase in the number and complexity of occupations and a sharp decline in the proportion of workers engaged in direct production. In modern armed forces, there are far more mechanics, truck drivers, radiomen, clerks, cooks, medical attendants and computer operators than "trigger pullers." This numerical comparison is sometimes called the "tooth-to-tail" ratio.

Zonal differentiation by battle position is fundamental in wartime and more or less disappears in peacetime. In its simplest form, it looks like this:

- enemy territory
- no man's land
- front
- support positions
- rear area
- supply lines
- safe territory

In addition to these flat zones, there is an important vertical differentiation between high ground that commands terrain and low places dug into the earth for cover and concealment. The greatest fortresses, such as Gibraltar and Iwo Jima, combine both of these virtues. Any piece of land that provides clear observation and fire over adjacent territory has obvious tactical value. In World War I, the famous "Hill 60," which offered these advantages on the battlefield of Ypres was the object of frantic struggle between British and German forces from 1915 to 1918. Tunnels were dug and filled with explosives. Chlorine gas was used to clear trenches. Mining and bombardment eventually reduced the height of the hill from the 60 meters for which it was named to 42 meters. In one operation alone, the British lost 100 officers and 3,000 men seizing and trying to hold a patch of ground about the size of the "center part of Trafalgar Square (Cowley 1992a, 342)."

Vertical and Horizontal Replication

The ubiquity of both vertical and horizontal replication is the most distinctive feature of military organizations compared to other large-scale organizations. The principal administrative functions —command, personnel, intelligence, operations, supply—are configured in the same way in every unit from the smallest to the largest, although the number of positions allotted to each function increases with each step up the ladder from company to battalion to brigade to division to corps to army.

Horizontal replication is achieved by imposing the same table of organization, the same tables of equipment, and the same operating procedures on all the units of a given type at the same level, all infantry companies or all armored divisions, for example.

Vertical replication in naval forces works a little differently than in land forces. The permanent units of operation are ships, and all ships are organized on the same template. The size and importance of the ship determines the rank of the officers and the elaboration of each function. But command is an indivisible function and the command of ships is rigorously separated from the command of fleets. The admiral does not command his flagship. The petty officer in command of a Coast Guard patrol boat has the same prerogatives as the captain of an aircraft carrier.

Horizontal and Vertical Mobility

Horizontal mobility within modern armed forces involves both geographic movements to new duty stations and transfers to different functional areas of the organization. A typical modern military career involves numerous geographical moves from one duty station to another at intervals of three or four years, but there is some variation in geographic mobility between ranks. Junior officers and junior enlisted persons move more often than their seniors. Among the American services, the Marines move the most and the Air Force the least.

High rates of geographic mobility reduce the institutional memory of particular units and entail considerable expense. However, rapid exchanges of personnel between the schools where doctrine is promulgated and units where it is practiced are a crucial method of insuring the interchangeability of units, even those of battalion size and larger. In other words, institutional memory is visualized as a potential problem rather than as an asset.

There are lower, but still significant, rates of individual mobility among the functional areas of a military organization. Infantrymen or parachutists can request retraining and reassignment as personnel clerks or helicopter pilots. If the request is refused, they may take the seemingly drastic step of leaving the service, waiting for a brief period, and then reenlisting in the desired specialty. Often the acquisition or abandonment of particular equipment systems creates personnel imbalances that are filled by encouraging reassignment to new specialties.

Officers are expected to be generalists at some stages of their careers, so that their mobility between organizational functions is greater than that of enlisted people. Officers are also expected to understand a much wider array of the organization's operations in preparation for eventual assignment to command or senior staff posts.

Modern armed forces maintain extensive career ladders that define an elaborate sequence of steps for a normal career in a particular specialty. "Career managers" at the central personnel office shepherd groups of specialists in and out of school and duty assignments.

The modern military promotion system, which emphasizes seniority, with some allowance for individual merit, is particularly susceptible to the Peter Principle, whereby individuals rise to the level of their incompetence and stay there, causing trouble and feeling miserable (Peter and Hull 1969). The solution is a curious policy called "up or out." Soldiers, especially officers, who fail to be promoted to certain levels after a fixed number of years are forced out or retired. This somewhat ruthless winnowing process keeps the average age of the force low, and maintains the shape of the pyramidal hierarchy. Its harshness is mitigated by a substantial cushion: military retirement benefits start immediately, not on the attainment of age 65. Thus, U.S. Army majors who are not promoted to lieutenant-colonel may have lost their career at the age of 42, but they begin at once to draw generous retirement checks and to enjoy other valuable benefits, such as free health care and air travel.

Social Control in the Armed Forces

There has been in recent years a notable transition in the modes of social control practiced by modern armed forces. For millennia, immediate painful death was the routine punishment for serious infractions of discipline. Minor infractions incurred punishment that seems fantastic today. The lash was standard military equipment. A British colonial officer, Richard Meinertzhagen, was forced to watch the punishment of one of his men for the offense of telling a sergeant that the sergeant's parents were a crocodile and a hyena:

> The culprit was lashed to a triangle, his breeches removed, and he was then flogged by a hefty Sudanese with a strip of hippopotamus hide; he was bleeding horribly when it was over and I was nearly sick (Jones 1992, 256).

Not long after this incident, however, Meinertzhagen shot some of his own troops during a battle for disobeying orders regarding the treatment of civilians.

Military history is replete with astonishingly harsh punishments of common soldiers and sailors. Sailors were put on bread-and-water or summarily hanged for offenses that today seem quite trivial. The primary goal of military social control was and still is to prevent desertion. An army or navy is a prison in motion. The closer it comes to combat, the more dangerous is the decision by a single soldier to avoid peril by fleeing. Panic is highly contagious. Closer to the battlefield, punishments for desertion become swifter and harsher. For the individual soldier in any battle, participation is, in many cases, not strictly voluntary. Until very recently in human history, the individual soldier in combat was usually caught between the enemy who was trying to kill him and his own leaders who would kill him if he attempted to escape his situation. Some "barbarian" tribes went into battle with the women following along behind to kill the men who left the field. At Gettysburg, thousands of military police were stationed behind the Union lines to prevent unauthorized retreat. The taboo against cowardice "in the face of the enemy" is a constant of military history.

Curiously, while the direct avoidance of combat by running from battle is severely punished, there are usually respectable ways of avoiding combat, for example, by choosing a rear echelon specialty. During the Vietnam War, American draftees, who were most often assigned to the infantry, suffered proportionately more casualties than Regular Army enlistees, who had the option of volunteering for service at large, well-guarded bases or in other countries (Gabriel and Savage 1978, 189). But even draftees could escape from combat duty by re-enlisting for a longer term, with the stipulation that they would be removed immediately from Vietnam (Baskir and Strauss 1978, 61).

Amitai Etzioni (1961, 10) classified organizations according to their prevailing "compliance relationship," which is determined by the intersection of three kinds of power (coercive, remunerative, and normative) and of three kinds of involvement (moral, calculative, and alienative).

Coercive power rests on the threat of the application of pain, mutilation, or death; or confinement; or the deprivation of physical satisfactions.

Remunerative power is based on control over material resources and rewards through allocation of salaries and wages, commissions and contributions, "fringe benefits," services, and commodities (Etzioni 1961, 5).[2]

Armies and navies have historically provided at least a minimum level of food, clothing and shelter for the troops. Current U.S. military personnel enjoy generous compensation packages, including relatively high salaries, free housing, free medical care, subsidized grocery and department stores, free air travel, and extremely lucrative retirement benefits. The potential increase in access to these rewards in return for good conduct and their potential loss for misconduct are powerful motivations.

But even minor rewards can be effective incentives. U.S. submarine commanders reward exemplary conduct with "Hollywood" showers: five minutes of continuously running hot water.[3]

Normative power rests on the allocation and manipulation of symbolic rewards and deprivations.

Military organizations recognize the crucial symbolic functions of leadership and devote extensive resources to the enhancement of leaders' images.[4] A plethora of decorations, ribbons, and insignia denote symbolic rewards within a prestige order that functions in tandem with the hierarchy of rank. Some of these symbols have currency far beyond the military. A Medal of Honor winner makes a strong political candidate.

Etzioni divided normative power into the manipulation of symbols (*pure normative power*), such as occurs in prestige systems, and the manipulation of acceptance (*social power*). The first is more characteristic of vertical social relationships, the second is more important to horizontal social relationships. In a military context, pure normative power is generally wielded by commanders, while social power is exercised by peer groups.

As often happens with ideal-typical analyses, all three types of power can be found in most live organizations. But Etzioni proposed that one type of power would usually predominate in a given type of organization because the three forms of power are partially exclusive: the use of coercive power leads to alienation which makes normative power less effective; and the use of remunerative power undercuts symbolic values.

No modern army can supply remuneration high enough to induce most lower participants to risk life and limb. Even an attempt to compensate for other deprivations, such as separation from family and home, interruption of a career pattern, lack of amenities, and so on, would call for more funds than any modern organization could recruit (Etzioni 1961, 56–57).

Consequently, combat organizations must rely on normative and coercive power. As examples of normative power, Etzioni listed resocialization in basic training, further military schooling, the influence of chaplains, prayer before battle, heroes' funerals, and medals. Coercive power in combat includes withdrawal of leave privileges, imprisonment, execution, and "firing at retreating troops."

While Etzioni's emphasis on coercive power in combat organizations is generally accurate, there are important exceptions, both in the past and currently. In recent years, the United States and other countries have experimented with high levels of compensation and low levels of coercion in their armed forces. It is now clear that it is possible to raise remuneration to levels consistent with precisely the deprivations and risks Etzioni outlines without spending "too much." American troops sent to Saudi Arabia for the Gulf War seem to have been powerfully motivated by the contract that they understood themselves to have with the military. Television reporters asked numerous enlisted people how they were bearing the hardship and the danger. Their responses often referred to their financial contract with the military.

Remunerative power is not confined to modern armed forces and small mercenary armies of earlier periods. Historically, the hope of booty has been one of the most important inducements to war. The long struggle between the cities and steppe peoples of

Eurasia was precisely so motivated. The plundering of captured places by individual soldiers was not prohibited by European armies until the nineteenth century.

Military Law

A body of law that applies to military personnel but not to civilians is what separates them juridically. Recruits become subject to military law the moment they are sworn in and remain so until they are formally discharged. Military law imposes numerous obligations on members of armed forces that do not apply to civilians: obedience to lawful commands, respectful behavior towards superiors, not running away from or communicating with the enemy, not deserting or going absent without leave, not sleeping on guard, protecting government property, and so forth. These laws are enforced by special tribunals composed of military personnel, called *courts-martial*. The military punishments administered by courts-martial were traditionally severe (Valle 1980). As late as World War I, U.S. soldiers who fell asleep on sentry duty were routinely sentenced to be shot by a firing squad, though such sentences were usually commuted to imprisonment.

The traditional justification for severe military punishments was that it deterred others from the same offenses. For that reason, punishments were customarily carried out in full view of the offender's comrades, assembled for "punishment parade." The Duke of Wellington is quoted by Babington (1983, vii):

I consider all punishment to be for the sake of example and the punishment of military men in particular is expedient only in cases where the prevalence of any crime, or the evils resulting from it, are likely to be injurious to the public interest.

However, a careful review of the executions in the British Army in World War I by Babington (1983) and by Putkowski and Sykes (1992) does not support the idea that harsh discipline supported the public interest in that particular war. The executed soldiers were a freakishly selected lot whose most important similarity was an inability to present an articulate defense at the court-martial. At other times and places, the purpose of military executions has not been to encourage other soldiers in their duty but rather to sway public opinion on the home front. Two Australian soldiers were shot during the Boer War in South Africa for the explicit purpose of deflecting criticism of army policies.[5]

In the United States and other advanced industrial societies, military law has recently lost most of its rigor and simplicity, and has converged with civilian law. The old *Articles of War* were read aloud by commanders to their assembled unit on ceremonial occasions and the reading took less than half an hour. They prescribed death as either a mandatory or an optional penalty for all serious offenses. These were replaced in 1952 by the much longer and more complex *Uniform Code of Military Justice* (UCMJ).

Prior to the revisions, American military law was not obsessed with due process. In 1890, Private Dell P. Wild was court-martialed for disobeying an officer's order to perform a personal service and for "conduct prejudicial to good order and discipline." The judge advocate (prosecutor) at the trial, Lieutenant Matthew F. Steele, was the very same officer Wild was alleged to have disobeyed. The judge was the company commander, both men's direct superior. Not surprisingly, Wild was found guilty and sentenced to dishonorable discharge, forfeiture of all pay and allowances, and imprisonment for one year. Public outcry led to a White House meeting between the Secretary of War and the President. The Secretary ordered Wild released.

Cases such as this generated pressure for incremental reforms of the military justice system (Foner 1970, 105–106), but major changes did not occur until after World War II, when the new Code introduced elaborate provisions for the appeal and review of court-martial sentences, for appeals to civilian courts and for lawsuits by military personnel against military authorities. The influence of commanders over courts-martial was drastically reduced by federal court decisions and by the increasing presence and autonomy of military lawyers.

The new principle that "command influence" in court-martial proceedings is improper was a long step away from the original purpose of military law—the maintenance of command authority. Other reforms included requiring access to legal counsel at the time of confinement by a commander, changing the law so that the testimony of officers and NCOs was not automatically true in the absence of witnesses, and requiring probable cause before searches of military personnel and their effects.

The sentences for military offenses were greatly reduced and, after the arrival of the All-Volunteer Force (AVF) in 1972, courts-martial practically disappeared from the U.S. Army—the rate of general courts-martial (the highest type) fell precipitously from 19 per thousand soldiers during and after World War I to 2 per thousand in the 1970s and 1980s (Lennon 1991, 52). There was a parallel decline in the lower types of court-martial; dismissal from the service became the standard punishment for military offenses.

These changes corresponded to a number of social and organizational trends: (1) the lessened isolation of military commanders; (2) the increasing resemblance of military service to civilian employment; (3) demographic changes in the military population, who are now older and better-educated than formerly, and more likely to be married and living with their families; (4) the increasing litigiousness of American society; (5) the creation of new rights for minorities,[6] women, and other categories of military personnel; and (6) perhaps most important, changes in the technology of war that make personal initiative and high morale more useful in combat than traditional discipline.

For a considerable time, the reduced juridical authority of U.S. commanders was blamed for a host of problems, including the loss of the war in Vietnam, the bored, sullen military of the 1970s, and operational fiascoes such as the invasion of Grenada. Officers lamented that:

> You people don't realize how important swift, sure punishment is in the control of an Army unit. I always felt that strapping on my .45 [pistol] and marching a troublemaker to the stockade had a powerful influence on the rest of the men (Ingraham 1984, 184).

But contrary to expert expectations, the abandonment of punishment eventually led to a force better disciplined than ever before.

Observability and Conformity

The relationship between observability and conformity in organizations was investigated by Coser (1961). Her finding that observability is structurally determined and in turn determines the type of conformity helps us to understand how recent changes in the technology of war have affected observability and conformity in armed forces. Thus, in the infantry, there has been a fairly steady and substantial decline in observability from the days of massed musket formations to the present. The initial decline, in the nineteenth century, followed the introduction of railroads, telegraphs and mobile artillery. Many battles of that period involved the defeat of technically backward, high-observability units by technically advanced, low-observability units.

Today, in the presence of chemical weapons, laser-guided missiles, cheap armor and three-dimensional mobility, military units "button up" and spread out. Entire divisions can deploy tactically and operate coherently without any commander being able to see more than a handful of his subordinates. Telecommunications equipment has created a novel type of "mediated observability," by technical means, whose effectiveness depends on the good will and good faith of the unseen units. Much of the most sophisticated military technology is now controlled from lonely offices such as the command posts of fields of missile silos. The military understanding of observability was traditionally subsumed under the aphorism "command and control" that then became "command, control, and communications," and more recently "command, control, communications, and intelligence."

Research on Military Organizations

Modern military sociology is descended in a fairly straight line from pioneering work done during and immediately after World War II, especially *The American Soldier*, a monumental compilation of research findings on the American Army in World War II by Samuel Stouffer (1949) and a staff of brilliant collaborators. That study centered on the causes and consequences of variations in morale. It was funded by the Pentagon because it promised immediate, practical returns. Other early work was similarly motivated. For example, early findings stressed the importance of informal organization and morale factors in raising combat effectiveness (Shils and Janowitz 1948).[7]

The field received extensive treatment in Morris Janowitz' *The Professional Soldier*, a work greatly influenced by Max Weber's typology of legitimate authority. The heroic leader, according to Janowitz, is traditionally oriented; he takes the relationship between means and ends for granted. The pragmatic military manager is oriented to discrete individual purpose. The absolute military manager is motivated by unquestioned collective values (Janowitz 1971, 278).

One of Weber's major themes was the tendency for technical rationality and industrial efficiency to weaken traditional authority. Since honor is an essential component of traditional authority, the growth of rationalism in the military establishment means the growth of a critical attitude, not only in technical and administrative matters, but toward the purposes and ends of one's profession. Each service, each weapons system, must consciously develop a "philosophy" because traditional assumptions about the efficacy of violence in the control of international relations no longer seem applicable (Janowitz 1971, 235).

Janowitz has synthesized two ideas from earlier sociologists: the Marxist theory that ideology emerges from relations of production (in this case the production of violence) and the Weberian theory that rationalization undermines the traditional basis of authority which must then be legitimated on some rational basis.

The complex technology used by modern armed forces is crucial to understanding their structure and behavior. The "technological paradigm" in the field of organizational studies holds that variation in the technologies used by organizations accounts for much of the variation in their structures and practices. Janowitz employed the technological paradigm extensively (1971, 21–54). More recent research has followed this lead. Martin's (1981) work on the French military since 1945 used technology as an important independent variable. Demchak (1991) traced the organizational effects of the U.S. Army's shift from the M60 tank to the M1 tank.

The American military itself is sensitive to the relationship between technology and organization. This is expressed as a concern about a possible lack of fit between the technological sophistication of current weapons systems and the personnel that can be recruited to operate them (Binkin 1986; Zurcher, Boykin, and Merritt 1986). Another expression of this sensitivity is the continuing debates within the services about the "warrior" ethos versus the "managerial" ethos, or "leadership" versus "management" (see, for example, Gabriel and Savage 1978).

There are some other value conflicts inherent in the soldier's occupation (see Moskos 1970, 1988). The military institution imposes special conditions on those who work within it—such as "subjection to military discipline and the incapacity to resign, strike, or negotiate over working conditions" (Moskos 1970, 42). But military occupations are increasingly managed like civilian occupations and increasingly motivated by pay and benefits rather than by coercion.

Military Sociology

Military sociology is now an established specialty.[8] It has its own professional association (the Inter-University Seminar on Armed Forces and Society) and its own journal *(Armed Forces and Society)*. The field has branched-out in many directions but its central theme has been the application of contemporary sociological concerns to the military environment. Military organizations have been studied as formal organizations, subject to the same principles as other formal organizations. They have been examined in relationship to the state they defend and the society from which they are drawn. They have been studied as the active agents of war and peace. The incentives they offer have been analyzed from various perspectives. They have been described as an arena of gender struggle. Indeed, issues of race, gender, and class are the focus of much recent sociological research about the military.

A considerable portion of military sociology focuses on the practical concerns of modern military organizations. For example, sociologists (e.g., Teachman, Call, and Segal 1993) study the "propensity to enlist" because this is a crucial issue for armed forces that depend on volunteers.

Sociologists who specialize in other areas often include the military as a special setting for the phenomena that command their attention. There are extensive writings on women in the military, homosexuals in the military, minorities in the military, conservatives in the military, violent "dysfunctional" men in the military, alcoholics in the military, child abusers in the military and so forth. For example, one group of investigators studying family violence has claimed that child abuse in U.S. Air Force families is more common if the parent in the service has a combat role; they speculate that "war legitimates violence as a means of correcting wrongs, and this principle spills over to include violence to correct 'wrongs' by children" (Straus 1992, 226).[9]

For Further Reading

Morris Janowitz, *The Professional Soldier: A Social and Political Portrait*, New York: The Free Press, 1971.

Douglas Porch, *The French Foreign Legion: A Complete History of the Legendary Fighting Force*, New York: Harper Collins, 1991.

Anna Simons, *The Company They Keep: Life Inside the U.S. Army Special Forces*, New York: Free Press, 1997.

Notes

[1] This in turn was a faint echo of the distinction under feudalism between knights and serfs.

[2] The word "salary" in fact derives from *salarium:* "money allowed to Roman soldiers for the purchase of salt." *Oxford Dictionary of English Etymology,* s.v. "salary."

[3] A scarce resource on older submarines.

[4] Even to the extent of blaming the U.S. defeat in Vietnam on the military's lack of control over American news organizations, a deficiency rectified in time for the Gulf War.

[5] The subject of a successful film, *Breaker Morant.*

[6] Burchett examined "the administration of military justice in the United States Army during the last three years of the Vietnam War" using empirical data collected while he was a legal clerk in the Army (1984, i). Contrary to his expectations, he found that the defendant's race had almost no effect on the verdict or the sentence.

[7] Recent work has indicated that similar factors can also degrade combat performance (Bearman 1991).

[8] For a tour de force overview of a century of American military sociology see Boëne's 100-page précis of his habilitation thesis (2000).

[9] This conclusion seems to ignore the conventional view that much child abuse has nothing to do with correcting children's offenses.

8

Military Culture

The armed forces of any society develop separate cultural patterns that arise from their peculiar function of wielding deadly force for approved collective purposes. These patterns differentiate armed forces so sharply from the surrounding civil society that the passage from civilian to soldier involves abrupt changes in the way the individual views himself and others, as well as profound shifts in his or her attitudes and values. The military world has its own distinctive rituals, etiquette and language and a unique status order. It generates relationships and experiences that have no exact counterparts in civilian life.

Rituals

The principal military rituals are drills, parades, inspections and military etiquette. *Close-order drill*, originally designed to permit the maneuvering of troops in battle, has now been largely reduced to ancillary functions—to teach mechanical obedience, to instill the sentiments of unit solidarity that come from moving in unison, and to provide the sense of security that comes from immersion in a cohesive and apparently invulnerable group.

> For when a group of men move their arm and leg muscles in unison for prolonged periods of time, a primitive and very powerful social bond wells up among them . . . Perhaps even before our prehuman ancestors could talk, they danced around camp fires, rehearsing what they had done in the hunt and what they would do next time.

> Such rhythmic movements created an intense fellow feeling . . .
> Military drill . . . tapped this primitive reservoir of sociality directly
> (McNeill 1982, 131).[1]

Long before McNeill, Émile Durkheim ([1915] 1965, 414) had seen such rituals as the basis for social phenomena in general. Beyond its psychological and tactical functions, drill constitutes preparation for the public spectacle of the parade.

A *parade* is a public spectacle of military units marching according to the commands learned in close-order drill. Parades have both internal and external functions. Internally, parades enhance the psychological impact of drill on the participants. The individual and his preferences disappear in the collectivity. Externally, the rhythmic music, precise choreography, bright colors and sparkling metal of the parade produce strong feelings of excitement and identification in spectators.

As recently as fifty years ago, most military units, both land and naval, could put on a respectable parade on relatively short notice. Ceremonial events were routine occurrences at peacetime army bases and on board naval ships. In modern times, some of the functions of parade have been changed by making parade duty (and other related ceremonies) the sole mission of particular units, thereby relieving other units. When called upon to be in a parade, a non-ceremonial unit often withdraws from its primary mission for a considerable time to prepare for the event. A large parade at a military base in the United States today will exhibit a wide variation of unit competence at ceremonial tasks. Some units, such as the military police, which perform ceremonies regularly, will approach eighteenth-century standards of precision. Others, such as the medical unit, which works full-time at the base hospital, will be embarrassing to watch, even after several nights and weekends of panicked practice under the alternately amused and disgusted guidance of an experienced drillmaster. Despite the straightforward explanation for this distinction, a certain stigma attaches to units that cannot march in a straight line. The internal stratification of armed forces reflects this difference: the top echelon of elite combat units can parade almost as well as ceremonial units, middle-range groups such as chemical warfare units do less well;

and units at the bottom of the stratification system, such as intelligence and personnel administration, can hardly march at all.

Various symbolic artifacts, from the units' banners to the
national flag, are essential elements of parades.

Inspections have multiple purposes: the achievement of an
extreme degree of obedience, precision and uniformity; the
detection of dangers, impurities, and unlawful acts; and the
assessment of readiness to perform missions. Although we usually
think of inspections as taking place in a barracks, anything
and anyone in the military can be inspected: immunization
records, weapons, personal equipment, vehicles, supply stocks,
food quality, knowledge of correct radio procedure, execution
of tactical maneuvers, motor pool maintenance bays, mobile
kitchens, hospital dispensaries, aircraft engines, office equipment
and files, and so on *ad infinitum*. Inspectors use a variety of means
to these ends: the white glove to detect dust on locker tops, or the
cotton swab inserted into the deep recesses of a gun.

Especially in formal training situations, such as Officer
Candidate School (OCS), there is an emphasis on precise performance of trivial tasks: the underwear folded in exactly the
prescribed manner, the boots brought to a mirror polish, the rifle
with the smoothest possible coating of oil, the perfect shaves
and haircuts. Inspections attempt to suppress individual differences and that function is reinforced by the customary practice
of punishing the whole unit for individual faults discovered in
an inspection. At the same time, records are kept of individual
performance in inspections and those records affect class standing,
promotion opportunities and the like.

Beyond this, inspections are used to assess the readiness, clean-
liness, healthfulness and morale of military units. Inspections are
also performed as an inventory control device whenever a unit
changes commanders. In the U. S. armed services, virtually every
piece of equipment, however trivial and inexpensive, is listed
on the unit's property book. Its presence and condition must be
certified by the incoming commanding officer before the departing
commander can leave. Periodically, examples are made of officers
who fail to account carefully for equipment by holding them

financially responsible for the missing items. In the case of very expensive equipment, certain limits and waivers come into effect, but the principle is taken seriously—the commander does not own the unit's equipment, but is very definitely responsible for its loss.

That responsibility is often in conflict with the demands of unit readiness. Given the vast number of items in the military's inventory and the difficulties of maintaining proper stocks of parts and so forth at every location, military units quickly develop informal arrangements involving the hoarding, borrowing, and trading of useful supplies. When units prepare to deploy for exercises in the field or at sea, they "top-off" their supplies by calling in chits with other units who are not scheduled to deploy soon. Complicated cross-borrowings develop over time. These are sustained by personal relationships between personnel working in the supply areas of different units. When a unit in this network undergoes a change of command, and hence, a "property book inspection," unusual behavior occurs in the supply function. There is an urgent need to have items actually on hand (as opposed to the ability to recover or borrow them from a neighboring unit) and an equally urgent need to dispose of equipment and supplies that the unit is not authorized to possess. In extreme cases, the first problem can result in units stealing from each other, whereas the second problem can result in valuable equipment thrown into trash containers or dumped into the sea. This complex of behaviors is not intentional malfeasance, much less sabotage. Rather, units respond more or less rationally to an environment with incompatible demands for combat readiness and administrative accountability.

Analogous situations occur in the unauthorized modification of equipment. Many items of military equipment are more or less easily modified to accomplish their intended purposes more efficiently or to accomplish some other purpose. Military equipment is necessarily designed to fit a particular function. Because units' actual requirements often deviate from this function, a plethora of adaptive alterations to military equipment are usually visible to the trained eye. These may be very small, as when an

American infantryman uses a belt to make a sling for his M16 rifle because the authorized sling is designed to hold the rifle upright behind the user—the parade position that is less useful in practical situations than that achieved with the ersatz sling. On a larger scale, units may accumulate small unofficial funds to pay either civilians or off-duty personnel to modify equipment.

Military Etiquette

Military etiquette has the primary purpose of maintaining awareness of rank at all times and the secondary purpose —analogous to civilian etiquette—of specifying the appropriate behavior for a given situation. Rank awareness is maintained by saluting, standing to attention, oral and written forms of respectful address to superiors, peremptory forms of address to subordinates, rules for entering and leaving in order of rank, the prohibition of uninvited physical contact with superiors, and the use of differentiating language for relations and appurtenances, e.g., "officer's ladies and enlisted men's wives." American enlisted personnel on gate guard duty are even required to salute officers' civilian automobiles even if the car's sole occupant is the officer's teenage son or daughter.

Appropriate behavior is much more elaborately specified in the military environment than in civilian life. Military etiquette applies to sociable occasions—parties, excursions, weddings—as well as to working situations, and to leisure activities, politics, and family life, for all of which there are some norms of etiquette that apply to all military personnel and others that apply particularly to officers or enlisted people.

Military Language

The distinctive character of military culture appears very clearly in its distinctive vocabulary and syntax, which makes most military communications unreadable to outsiders.

Only the military could call a tent a "frame-supported tension structure"; a parachute, an "aerodynamic personnel decelerator"; a life jacket, a "personal preservation flotation device"; and a zipper, an "interlocking slide fastener." It's not a toothpick, but a "wood interdental stimulator" not a pencil but a "portable, hand-held communications inscriber" (Lutz 1989, 163).

Some of these excesses represent the efforts of a highly bureaucratized purchasing system to justify its refusal to buy ordinary civilian goods at ordinary prices. The object of these strange designations is to convert everyday objects into military commodities that must be procured through the same channels as weapons and combat equipment, instead of being bought at the corner store.

A more basic function of military language is, of course, to promote group solidarity. The recruit who learns to divide the day into periods named after bugle calls from reveille to taps has placed himself closer to other soldiers and further from civilians than he was before.

For purposes of clarity in communications, the military created standards such as "Alpha" for the letter "a," "Bravo" for the letter "b," "Charlie" for the letter "c," etc. Codewords and passwords are often used to protect armed forces during wartime.

Another important function of the military vocabulary is euphemism. Many unpleasant and grisly events occur in combat. By using euphemistic labels, military personnel are able to shield themselves from confronting these events psychologically. And, needless to say, the same euphemisms can be used to conceal certain aspects of combat from the civilian audience. Lutz provides numerous examples: "friendly casualties" caused by the "accidental delivery of ordnance equipment" are American troops killed by American bombs or shells; "own goal" stands for shooting down friendly planes;[2] "servicing the target" means killing the enemy; "collateral damage" stands for killed or wounded civilians and the destruction of civilian property.

The Stratification of Armed Forces

Armed forces are stratified in numerous dimensions. The most important dimension is also the most explicit: military rank. Each member of the military is assigned a rank that is both a role and a status. Beyond specifying to whom one owes deference and obedience and to whom one may issue commands, rank entails a complex set of rights, duties, and expectations. Unlike assigned status in many civilian organizations, the military rank system possesses certain almost mathematical properties: at the level of individuals, it is ordered and transitive. A ranking of a set is *ordered* if it is always possible to determine which of two members of the set ranks higher. This is not true of, for example, of all the employees of a large bank. Nor would it be meaningful to invent a way to order all the bank's employees. In the American military, however, any two persons in a particular branch of service can be ordered by rank. For examples, two Army captains would each have a "date of rank" (which bears a complicated relationship to when they were actually promoted from first lieutenant). The officer with the earlier date of rank is senior to the officer with less "time-in-grade." If their dates of rank are identical, then recourse is had to the date they entered military service. The officer with more time in the military is then the senior in rank. If these two criteria fail to solve the problem, the older officer is the senior. Military rank is also perfectly *transitive*: if A is senior to B and B is senior to C, then A is necessarily senior to C.

The relationship between officers and enlisted personnel in most western armies represents the class structure of the eighteenth-century more faithfully than that of the twenty-first. It has preserved more of its archaic character in the American armed forces than in most others. Different moral personalities are ascribed to each group: officers as gentlepersons are presumed to be trustworthy, chivalrous, conservative and conscientious; enlisted people are presumed to be irresponsible, unreliable and potentially dangerous. Traces of the eighteenth-century doctrine that the object of military training was to make the soldier fear his officers more than he feared the enemy can still be seen in some U.S. training facilities, such as Marine boot camp. Open conflict between officers and men is not uncommon either. In Vietnam, unpopular American officers were commonly "fragged," i.e., murdered, by their own troops; the practice was not new. The recruitment of officers predominantly among college graduates and of enlisted people among high school graduates tends to sustain the perception that the officer-enlisted relationship reflects a difference of social class.

But there is some evidence that the status gap has recently been narrowing. The gap in wealth and income between the highest-and lowest-ranking members of modern military organizations is smaller than in most other work organizations. Beyond this, the provisions for education, health care, disability and retirement systems in the military are much more egalitarian than in large civilian organizations. The scandals that are raised from time to time when officers' children are accused of receiving favored educational treatment in schools operated by the army suggest how much the privileges of rank have recently diminished. American base commanders have on occasion perceived a need to order their subordinate officers not to suggest to the base school principal which teacher would be appropriate for their child.

A significant exception to the pattern of diminishing privilege is the quality of housing on military bases, which is elaborately graded by rank. Enlisted personnel with families tend to be assigned apartments off a common stairwell. Enlisted rank differences are not normally reflected in apartment size or quality—only the number of family members is considered relevant. Officers, on the other hand, are assigned duplexes or single-family detached houses according to their rank. Thus, the base commander will occupy a large mansion, suitable for entertaining. Other senior officers will occupy large houses with at least some possibility of hosting a respectable dinner party. Junior officers are assigned more modest middle-class houses such as three-bedroom ramblers. When residing off-post in civilian housing, American military personnel are provided a cash allowance that varies considerably from the top of the officer hierarchy to the bottom of the enlisted ranks.

Beyond the formal rank system, many unofficial status distinctions can be observed in the military, and they tend to qualify and complicate the official ranks. Some of these distinctions are intentionally generated inside the organization and involve special decorations like the Meritorious Service Medal or special training such as that offered by the U.S. Army's Ranger and Special Forces schools. "SF'ers" in the base bar sometimes simply will not talk to non-Green Berets and have little difficulty ignoring enlisted persons who may nevertheless outrank them. Condescension may even be heaped upon officers, especially lowly lieutenants, though more subtly. Airborne soldiers, graduates of the Army's three-week jump school, refer to all other soldiers as "legs." Similar distinctions according to military training and duties exist in other services. Naval fliers, and military pilots in general, are notorious for their disregard of the rank privileges of "ground-bound" personnel.

An important qualification of officer rank is source and type of commission. "Regular Army" (RA) officers have higher status than officers called to active duty from the reserves. Officers who received their commissions by graduating from one of the military's own service academies (West Point, Annapolis, and Colorado Springs) have a subtle status advantage over officers commissioned through the Reserve Officer Training Corps (ROTC) and a somewhat larger status advantage over officers commissioned through Officer Candidate School (OCS).[3] Officers commissioned under emergency battle conditions have such a lowly position that they are in danger of reverting to enlisted status when hostilities end. This curious pattern of veteran officers being cashiered to free up promotions for new graduates of the service academies indicates how powerfully the core of the organization protects itself from non-elite invasions. This practice is not an innovation of the U.S. military; long ago, Frederick the Great swelled his officer corps with competent commoners when needed in war, then promptly purged them after hostilities ended.

The prestige of branches of the armed services varies according to their proximity to danger and their faithfulness to traditional military values. At the top in the U.S. Army for example, are elite combat units such as the Ranger battalions, Special Forces groups, cavalry regiments, and airborne divisions such as the 82nd and 101st. Immediately below are combat infantry, armor, and artillery units (Moskos 1970, 116). Then come direct combat supporters such as the amphibian engineers. All the units that normally operate outside the zone of danger—communications, supply, medical, judicial, and financial units among others, are scorned by combat soldiers (Spector 1992, 532). Core military values are the key to internal stratification by unit type. The offense of support troops is distance from danger, in which they are seen to resemble civilians. Modern warfare, of course, has extended the zone of danger almost indefinitely and this may begin to have effects on prestige stratification based on risk. However, there are other core military values that sustain this status order, such as masculinity, strength, and propensity to violence.

Another type of informal status derives from combat experience. Combat veterans of whatever rank look down on those who have only practiced for combat. The importance of this distinction fluctuates with its scarcity, which in turn depends on the time elapsed since the last major war. Scions of military families have another important special status. Military personnel who are the sons and daughters of senior officers may not automatically convert their heritage into faster promotion, but their advantage is real.

Other informal distinctions in the military are imported from the larger society. Especially under conscription, the military sometimes takes account of civilian status. Yale University students who dropped out to join the Navy in World War II were routinely commissioned (one of them was the elder George Bush); orthopedic surgeons enter the service as lieutenant colonels. But the accommodation only reaches so far. The induction of wealthy and famous draftees like Elvis Presley has on occasion turned into a disruptive circus, and the military would probably find a convenient pretext to discharge a private who had just won a $20 million lottery.

Other Military Relationships

Besides the officer-enlisted relationship discussed above, there are
two other distinctive military relationships: the military-civilian
relationship, and the friendly-hostile relationship. As we have seen,
the officer-enlisted relationship ascribes different moral personalities to each group—officers as gentlepersons are expected
to be trustworthy, chivalrous, conservative, and conscientious;
enlisted personnel to be irresponsible, unreliable and potentially
dangerous. In the relationship with civilians, both officers and
enlisted men hold themselves superior because they *serve* and
put their lives at risk by doing so, while civilians are thought to
be pursuing only private and selfish purposes. In Shakespeare's
King Henry V, the outnumbered English are trapped in France, far
from help. One of the king's lieutenants wishes that they could
have "one ten thousand of those men in England that do no work
today!" The King responds by rousing his soldiers for the battle
of Agincourt:

> He that shall live this day, and see old age,
> Will yearly on the vigil feast his neighbors
> And say, "Tomorrow is Saint Crispian."
> Then he will strip his sleeve and show his scars
> And say "These wounds I had on Crispin's day."
> Old men forget; yet all shall be forgot,
> But he'll remember, with advantages,
> What feats he did that day. Then shall our names,
> Familiar in his mouth as household words—
> Harry the King, Bedford and Exeter,
> Warwick and Talbot, Salisbury and Gloucester—
> Be in their flowing cups freshly rememb'red.
> This story shall the good man teach his son;
> And Crispin Crispian shall ne'er go by,
> From this day to the ending of the world,
> But we in it shall be remembered—
> We few, we happy few, we band of brothers;
> For he today that sheds his blood with me
> Shall be my brother. Be he ne'er so vile,
> This day shall gentle his condition;

And gentlemen in England now abed
Shall think themselves accursed they were not here,
And hold their manhoods cheap whiles any speaks
That fought with us upon Saint Crispin's day.
(*King Henry V* Act IV Scene III)

The soldier thinks of himself as protecting the civilian's life and property and freedom and getting little thanks for it. But of course this situation varies from country to country and from peace to war. The U.S. is fortunate in having an apolitical military establishment, a condition that dates back to the American Revolution and contrasts dramatically with the historic role of the military in most other countries, including France, Germany, and Russia, where the military has often exercised political influence, and the nations of Eastern Europe, Latin America, Asia, and Africa, most of which have been ruled by military dictators at one time or another and are always in some danger of falling under military rule if the regime is unable to keep the armed forces happy.

Another aspect of the relationship to civilians is the transfer of status claims from the military to the civilian sphere. How military status translates into civilian status is affected by many factors, but especially by the prestige of the military services in the larger society, which fluctuates with the fortunes of war and of politics. Veterans of the unpopular Vietnam War were more despised than respected when they returned home. Argentine officers hid in shame after the Falklands War.

Victory is much more popular. After the brief Gulf War, employers pledged to hire veterans of that operation, vendors offered them a smorgasbord of free and discounted products, and political parties begged the senior commanders to run for public office—a pattern not seen in the U.S. since the end of World War II. Aside from these fluctuations in the general prestige of the military services, retired officers, especially senior officers, are commonly equated with civilian executives and recruited for major managerial positions. At a lower level, the specific job training in military specialties like air traffic control, is easily carried over into civilian employment.

Civilians often have only a dim understanding of military ranks. A Navy captain is exactly equivalent to an Army, Air Force, or Marine colonel, but the public may not know it, as Adam Smith ([1776] 1937, 109) remarked more than two centuries ago:

> The great admiral is less the object of public admiration than that great general, and the highest success in the sea service promises a less brilliant fortune and reputation than equal success in the land. The same difference runs through all the degrees of preferment in both. By the rules of precedency a captain in the navy ranks with a colonel in the army: but he does not rank with him in the common estimation.

The British Royal Navy long suffered from a less favorable image than the land services. Upon being warned against upsetting Navy traditions, Winston Churchill, newly appointed as First Sea Lord, is said to have asked "What traditions? Rum, sodomy, and the lash?" In America today, the Air Force seems to enjoy greater prestige than the other services, whether because of its association with high technology or its perceived distance from manual labor.

The relationship of soldiers to their adversaries is complex and often ambivalent. The enemy is commonly dehumanized and treated with great cruelty—the refusal of quarter and the killing of prisoners is commonplace in modern warfare—but there can also be admiration and sympathy, and when circumstances permit, fraternization. Ashworth (1980, 19) records the unofficial truces and the harmless firing that Allied and German troops arranged in defiance of their higher commands on the Western front in World War I, which he calls the "Live and Let Live System." It involved a process whereby each side did its best to minimize the infliction of death, discomfort or injury on the other side in exchange for reciprocal consideration. Another example comes from the North African front in World War II, where in the midst of a bitter struggle that would eventually destroy the *Afrika Korps*, German and British reconnaissance battalions arranged a daily cease-fire called "tea time," during which they exchanged news, prisoners, cigarettes and medicine (von Luck 1992, 433).

One author summarizes the perceptions of the enemy by various fighting forces in a few illuminating phrases: The Egyptians of the New Kingdom, the enemy as non-people; the early Israelites, the enemy as ritual outlaws; the Spartans, the enemy as political obstacles; the Athenians, the enemy as opponents of democracy; the Carthaginians, the enemy as economic rivals; the Romans, the enemy as uncouth barbarians; the Crusader knights, the enemy as unbelievers; the Mongols, the enemy as effete degenerates; the Aztecs, the enemy as ritual fodder; the Zulu, the enemy as colonial intruders; the Nazis, the enemy as racial inferiors; the Maoists, the enemy as class antagonists (Carlton 1990).

Battle Experience

Beginning with World War II, a considerable body of empirical research on the experience of battle began to accumulate (Stouffer 1949–1950; Shils and Janowitz 1948) and there were serious attempts to extract data on the subject from historical documents (Keegan 1977, Ashworth 1980, Pope 1981, Bertaud 1985). Five important points emerge from these investigations:

1. Men approach battle with a mixture of fear and excitement; the ratio between them is a measure of morale.

2. The average participant's view of battle is disjointed and fragmentary; he often has no idea of how the battle is progressing.

3. The motivation to fight is more often induced by attachment to a peer group than by attachment to larger formations.

4. Combat soldiers are typically cynical about the declared aims of their war, but this varies greatly among armies and among wars.

5. The motivation to fight weakens steadily under the stress of combat; battle fatigue is experienced by individual soldiers at different rates, but almost all soldiers and all units eventually become ineffective in protracted engagements. According to Gabriel (1987, 4), "Given enough

time in combat, every soldier will eventually suffer a mental collapse."

The Demography of Armed Forces

As far back as it can be traced, armed combat has been almost exclusively an activity of young men. The age range for soldiers has been historically stable: the rank and file consisting of men aged 17 to 25, junior officers slightly older, noncommissioned officers between 25 and 40, and senior and general officers aged 25 to 60, or older in a few cases.

There are several reasons that armed forces are predominantly composed of young men. We quote Adam Smith again, who wrote in 1776 that:

> The contempt of risk and the presumptuous hope of success, are in no period of life more active than at the age at which young people chuse their professions . . . Without regarding the danger . . . young volunteers never enlist so readily as at the beginning of a new war; and though they have scarce any chance of preferment, they figure to themselves, in their youthful fancies, a thousand occasions of acquiring honour and distinction which never occur. These romantic hopes make the whole price of their blood. Their pay is actually less than that of common labourers, and in actual service their fatigues are much greater ([1776] 1937, 109).

Compared to most historic armed forces, or earlier American armed forces, today's U.S. military population is relatively mature and the age distribution is compressed by early retirement. The median age of active duty personnel in 1999 was just over 27 years. About 7 percent were under 20 and the same proportion were over 40.[4] But the outstanding difference between them and earlier uniformed forces is the very high proportion who are married and living with their spouses and children. In traditional armies and navies, enlisted men were either single or treated as such and officers were inclined to avoid marriage until they reached senior rank. Their pay was not intended to support a family. By contrast, in today's U.S. forces more than half of the people in uniform are currently married, with the highest proportion in the Air Force and the lowest in the Marine Corps. Moreover, these married couples average 1.5 minor children, so that the military dependents for whom the Department of Defense is responsible considerably outnumber active duty personnel.[5]

Female soldiers have not played an important direct role in warfare. Indeed, the distinction between a boy and a man in many societies is that a man must have proved himself as a warrior. All large armies probably contain a few women disguised as men or boys and there have been numerous instances of women as guerrilla fighters. Queens, empresses and other female heads of governments have often had a voice in strategy, but Joan of Arc seems to have been the only woman in western history who led a large body of troops into battle. On the other hand, armies throughout history have been accompanied by large groups of women as wives, cooks, laundresses, nurses, merchants, and prostitutes.

Current practice regarding women in the military is highly uneven. Some very liberal states like the Netherlands allow women full equality in combat roles. Others, like Israel, enlist large numbers of women but keep them out of combat. The role of women in the U.S. armed forces steadily expanded until the mid-1980s when a partial retreat began. Some jobs formerly open to women, such as those in the U.S. Army's units that defend against nuclear, biological, and chemical contamination, were closed by administrative order. Basic training, which had been combined for men and women in the early 1980s, was resegregated. Today, women constitute about 14 percent of the U.S. armed forces and hold jobs sufficiently close to combat to insure that there will be some female casualties in any large operation like the Gulf War. In the 1990s, rules about the military assignments of women were changed again, allowing women to fly fighter planes and to serve on warships specially fitted with separate quarters. The four services differ somewhat in their receptivity to women (from 18 percent in the Air Force to under 6 percent in the Marine Corps) but in all four services, women make up the same proportion of the enlisted ranks as of the officers' ranks (Caplow, Hicks, and Wattenberg 2001, 205).

Another way in which U.S. forces today differ from all their predecessors is the allocation of rank by formal education. Historically, rank was most often a function of social class, but commissions were often awarded by nepotism (as in all medieval armies), election (as in some units in the American Revolution), purchase (as in the British Royal Navy for two centuries), or battlefield valor (as in both Union and Confederate forces). In today's U.S. services, education is the principal criterion that separates officers from enlisted personnel. As of 1998, nearly all active duty officers had graduated from college and about 40 percent had gone on to advanced degrees, while only 3 percent of enlisted personnel were college graduates.[6]

Sexuality and the Military

The primordial masculine character of military organizations is directly related to human sexuality. It is not too great an exaggeration to say that for at least five thousand years, armies have been fighting to keep or acquire women, as well as food, territory and other scarce goods. Helen of Troy had "the face that launched a thousand ships" in Homer's *Iliad*. U.S. recruiting posters in World War I showed sub-human males—"Huns"—drooling over helpless American women.

Sexuality is important to the military not only in war but also in peacetime. Soldiers often regard deployment as a holiday from marital fidelity—the longer the deployment, the larger the proportion of military personnel who adopt this view. U.S. commanders of week-long military exercises in Germany were enjoined not to bring their units in from the field early, because so many married soldiers would arrive home to find non-deployed soldiers in their bedrooms.

Besides conquest and infidelity, sex for pay has accompanied militaries for millennia. Large military bases usually have large prostitution districts nearby. Overseas bases have even larger numbers of sex workers in the vicinity. The U.S. Navy's huge base at Subic Bay in the Philippines supported thousands of prostitutes, despite official efforts to prevent sexually-transmitted diseases (Enloe 1989).

Sex is also an important source of military symbols:

- The Supreme Allied Commander, General Eisenhower (1948, 225) was ordered to "enter the continent of Europe" and "undertake operations aimed at the heart of Germany and the destruction of her Armed Forces."
- Naval vessels are also invariably "she."
- A Soviet battlefield rocket was nicknamed "Stalin's organ."
- Bomber crews paint pictures of scantily-clad women on the side of their airplanes.
- Nuclear war planners describe the spasmodic release of missiles and bombs as a "wargasm."

For women to have "voluntary" sex with the enemy is one of the most violently punishable offenses. As the Allied forces liberated Europe in 1944 and 1945, women in France, Belgium, the Netherlands, etc., who had hosted Nazi soldiers were stripped, shaved, driven through the streets, and beaten. Some were killed along with their infants of improper paternity. At the other end of the spectrum are stories from the French Resistance of women who slept with Germans until the invasion alert, when they killed their mates as they slept.

Rape has been associated with war throughout history. The sack of a city by nomads routinely included the violation of every female inhabitant. Japanese soldiers in World War II raped Chinese, Korean, and Filipino women by the thousands (see, e.g., Chang 1997). When the Red Army took Berlin, the surviving women of the city were treated quite brutally.

But sex in war is not all about conquest, prostitution, and rape. Quite the opposite can be the case: in 1944 and 1945, some western European women thanked their liberators with their bodies. The return of GIs to the U.S. in 1945 triggered a huge baby boom nine months later.

Sex powerfully disturbs the status order of military organizations. To prevent breakdown of discipline, modern militaries typically forbid sex between members, or forbid sex between members of different ranks, or at least between officers and enlisted persons.

These prohibitions have not prevented a raft of scandals in the American military. Drill sergeants at Aberdeen Proving Ground turned groups of trainees into harems. General officers have coerced the wives of their subordinate majors and colonels into affairs with threats to damage their husbands' careers. And it is not only men who are charged with sexual offenses. A female B-52 pilot was discharged for sex with the civilian husband of an enlisted woman.

Less dramatically, the introduction of women into the military has turned the institution into an unofficial marriage market, not unlike high schools and colleges. Many military members now find a spouse in the service. This creates an administrative problem when the couple seeks to be stationed together.

Homosexuality is also a powerful disturbance of the military status order and is even less tolerated than heterosexual activity. Except for a handful of "postmodern" militaries,[7] all military organizations forbid homosexuality. But homosexuality has probably been present in most military organizations. Current U.S. policy is a bizarre convention: "Don't ask; don't tell." Gays are not supposed to disclose themselves and commanders are not supposed to inquire (Moskos, Williams, and Segal 2000, 271; Burk 1998).

Ethnicity in the Military

Almost all large armies and many small ones in history have been composed of two or more ethnic groups. The armies of large empires tended to be quite colorful. For example, the Byzantine army employed:

> in the sixth century . . . Huns and Vandals, Goths and Lombards, Heruls and Gepids, Antae and Slavs, Persians, Armenians, Arabs from Syria, and Moors from Africa. In the tenth and eleventh centuries there were Khazars and Pechenegs, Phargans and Russians, Slavs, Iberians, Georgians, Mardaites of Lebanese descent, hillmen

from the Caucasus, Arabs, Turks, Norsemen from Scandinavia, and Normans from Italy (Diehl 1957, 41).

In the past, multi-ethnic armies commonly arose from the more or less forced induction of defeated armies into the victorious body. This was easier when military skills were relatively primitive. In the modern age, military forces are rarely composed of defeated personnel, though the practice recurred occasionally during World War II. The other common source of multi-ethnic forces, recruitment from a diverse population, remains important today. Modern multi-ethnic military forces are often drawn from such large and diverse societies that the military leadership faces the headache of training and leading soldiers who speak many different languages, as in the forces of the former Soviet Union.

Typically, the leadership of a fighting force is more ethnically coherent than the rank-and-file. Legion commanders tended to be Romans; the French Foreign Legion has French officers. The dominance of one ethnic group can be expressed in other dimensions of military stratification. For example, the Soviet Union strongly preferred to assign ethnic Russians to the Strategic Rocket Forces and other elite units.

Another recurrent pattern of ethnicity in armed forces is the specialization of small minorities in fierce roles within large armies where they are employed as shock troops or as guards for the senior commanders (Dreisziger with Preston 1990). The British Empire employed Gurkhas in this fashion, and used them in combat as recently as the Falklands War in 1982.

The ethnic experience of American armed forces involves several curious twists. A disproportionate number of military bases today are located in the states of the Confederacy. American military culture is more heavily influenced by the South than by other regions of the country and Southerners are more likely to have seen active service.

The other large ethnic pattern in the American military experience is the changing military situation of African-Americans. Originally brought as slaves to the New World, free blacks fought in the American Revolutionary War, the War of 1812, and other smaller actions. Serving in frontier units, they were known as "buffalo soldiers," supposedly because Native Americans thought their hair resembled that of the bison.[8] In the American Civil War, African-Americans were employed by the North in support positions until late in the war when combat units were formed. These were segregated and led by white officers.

Segregation remained in effect throughout World Wars I and II, but was ended quite rapidly in the late 1940s, largely on the initiative of Secretary of Defense James Forrestal. Various discriminatory barriers to desirable duty, promotions, and so forth, were slowly removed in the decades that followed. Today, more than a third of the American armed forces is made up of minorities. In 2000, African-Americans constituted 29 percent of enlisted personnel in the U.S. Army and were disproportionately represented in the other three services (Caplow, Hicks, and Wattenberg 2001, 203). This is generally attributed to continuing discrimination in the civilian world that leads minorities to seek opportunity in the military.[9] Unlike women, however, minorities were not as well represented in the commissioned as in the enlisted ranks. This appears to reflect the relative educational deficits of African-Americans and Hispanics rather than discriminatory barriers.[10] Unlike many civilian institutions, however, members of minority groups have served at the very pinnacle of the U.S. armed forces: General Colin Powell as Chairman of the Joint Chiefs of Staff and General Eric K. Shinseki as Chief of Staff of the U.S. Army.

Conscription

Until quite recently, all of the western European nations (with the exception of Britain and Ireland) required all healthy young men reaching a certain age to serve for a fixed period of time in the armed forces and thereafter to remain in the reserves until reaching a prescribed age. Universal military service was regarded as the most convenient way of filling the ranks of a mass army and also as a way of strengthening national integration.

The United States never had a peacetime system of universal military service but in all of its major wars from the Revolution to Vietnam, a draft was introduced to make up a shortfall of volunteers. The Civil War draft allowed draftees to escape service if they could afford to pay for a substitute. It provoked extensive urban riots. The Vietnam-era draft exempted college and university students; it too was widely resented and seriously resisted. By contrast, the World War II draft was generally regarded as fair and no sharp distinction was drawn between volunteers and draftees in that conflict. The creation of the All-Volunteer Force in the early 1970s ended the draft that had been in place for most of the Cold War. Although the machinery of conscription is still retained in skeletal form, it is unlikely to be used again.

Meanwhile, conscription is being rapidly abandoned in Europe, and with it the concept of the mass army that originated in France in 1792. Conscription will end in France in 2002. It has already been abolished in Belgium and the Netherlands and abolition seems imminent in Germany, Italy, Spain, Norway and Denmark (Boëne and Dandeker 1998). The future armed forces of the NATO allies, like those of the United States, are expected to consist of people who have chosen the military as a profession like any other.

For Further Reading

Robert Cowley, ed., *Experience of War: An Anthology of Articles from MHQ, the Quarterly Journal of Military History*, New York: Norton, 1992.

John McPhee, *La Place de la Concorde Suisse*, New York: Farrar, Straus & Giroux, 1984.

Thomas E. Ricks, *Making the Corps*, New York: Scribner, 1998.

Endnotes

[1] See also McNeill's *Keeping Together in Time: Dance and Drill in Human History*, Cambridge: Harvard University Press, 1995.

² The problem of military accidents has attracted sociological attention. Hicks (1993) described "friendly fire" as a species of "normal accidents."

³ In the U.S. Army, the graduates of West Point are sometimes referred to as "ring-knockers" after the elaborate graduation rings acquired at the Academy. The special influence of West Pointers is expressed by the metaphor of knocking on a conference table to express authority.

⁴ www.defenselink.mil/pubs/almanac/almanac/people/how_old.html, 9/2001

⁵ www.defenselink.mil/pubs/almanac/almanac/people/families.html, 9/2001

⁶ www.defenselink.mil/pubs/almanac/almanac/people/military_ education_ stats.html, 9/2001

⁷ Booth, Kestnbaum, and Segal (2001) suggest that the language of postmodernism is at least partially useful in describing changes that have happened since the end of the Cold War.

⁸ Nothing but respect was meant by this; Native Americans revered the bison (Nalty 1986, 54).

⁹ This is a fact that the contemporary American military is proud to emphasize.

¹⁰ www.defenselink.mil/pubs/almanac/almanac/people/minorities.html, 9/2001

9

Military Technology

Most wars are won by a combination of material and social technology. The material technology provides the weapons, the vehicles, the equipment, and the construction methods. The social technology provides the battle order, the command and control network, the capacity to maneuver, the motivation of troops, and the cohesiveness of units. Most of the great conquests of history were achieved by new forms of military organization that swept everything before them. From the Macedonian phalanx to the mass armies of the French Revolution, these new forms had certain common features—enhanced discipline, concentration of striking power, maneuverability, and interchangeable units.

Material and Social Technology

Superiority in material technology is expressed both by the quality of weapons and equipment and the quantity available, both immediately and as a stream of supplies for future operations. Japanese weapons in World War II were generally equal or superior to their American equivalents, but Japan had fewer of them and a much smaller capacity to produce replacements. Even before the massive bombing of the Japanese mainland, the U.S. was out-producing Japan by enormous margins, often tenfold or more. U.S. shipping was being built faster than it could be sunk by enemy submarines. The Japanese lost a large proportion of their total aircraft carrier strength in a single day at the Battle of

Midway, while the U.S. launched twenty-one new fleet carriers between 1941 and 1944 (Keegan 1993, 377).[1] American planes might attack a Japanese base shortly after dawn. Japanese planes would rise to meet them. There would be approximately equal losses on both sides. Before noon the American planes would be back in greater numbers. Fewer Japanese planes than before would rise to defend the area. In the afternoon, the American planes would return and have the air to themselves. But a quantitative advantage is not always sufficient. U.S. forces in Vietnam were so well supplied that they could replace 5,000 helicopters during the war, but that war was still lost.

A quantitative advantage can often be sustained by a third party: the Soviet Army held out against the Nazi onslaught partly because American and British ammunition, fuel, trucks, aircraft, and weapons were being unloaded in Russian ports as fast as possible. Similarly, Israel was reinforced during the 1973 war by U.S. tanks taken directly from the NATO front in Germany.

When one side has an unmistakable advantage in both social and material technology, the relative size of forces is almost irrelevant, as in the Spanish conquests of Mexico and Peru. Cortez faced some 80,000 Aztec warriors with fewer than a hundred men. But numbers usually determine the outcome when the adversaries are roughly equal in both material and social technology, as in the American Civil War. When one side has an advantage in material technology and the other in social technology, as in Vietnam, the odds seem to favor the superior social technology.

Technological Evolution

Cave remains and other archeological evidence indicate that men have been fashioning stone weapons for tens of thousands of years. River beds in Africa contain what appear to be stone weapons that are 100,000 years old. One of the earliest vestiges of human settlement in the western hemisphere is the collection of flaked-stone spear points known by the name of the town in New Mexico where they were found: Clovis. These early weapons were undoubtedly used to hunt game and defend against predators but quantities of human bones that show unmistakable signs of injury from stone weapons have been unearthed all over the world.

At the dawn of civilization, warfare was already well established. The earliest pictorial records include images of weapons and of the artisans who made them. Concurrently with the rise of the earliest empires in Mesopotamia and Egypt about 3500 B.C. stone spear points and arrowheads were replaced by much more lethal weapons made of bronze. The technological arms race was on.

The next major inventions appeared together around 1800 B.C.—the two-man chariot and the compound bow. Both of them demanded a relatively high level of industrial competence, since the chariot rolled on spoked wheels that had to be accurately round and dynamically balanced, while the compound bow was skillfully crafted of wood, sinew and bone. This pair of devices, operated for the most part by horsemen from the steppes of Eurasia, enabled them to conquer the settled agricultural societies of the Near East, India and China. But in Greece, where the terrain was too rugged for the effective use of chariots, these innovations were successfully resisted. The Greeks used chariots for show, not for combat. High-ranking warriors drove themselves to the battlefield in one-man chariots but dismounted to fight (McNeill, 1982, 11). And without the mobility provided by the chariot, the operator of the compound bow was too vulnerable to survive.

Around 1200 B.C., the art of making iron weapons spread throughout the ancient world. They were stronger than bronze weapons and very much cheaper, so that ordinary people could own and wield them. Military predominance abruptly shifted from noble warriors like the Homeric heroes to disciplined bodies of troops recruited from subject populations. The ancient Assyrian army had standard tables of organization and equipment, regular ranks, promotion by merit, and written rules of engagement. They were the earliest group of combatants to resemble a modern army.

The next and most enduring innovation was cavalry—massed bowmen on horseback. Mounted raiders from central Asia destroyed the Assyrian empire in the seventh century B.C. and harassed the Greeks. A little later, horsemen from the same areas began to raid China. The pattern of raids and conquest by cavalry hordes from the steppes continued for many centuries. Often the raiders settled in the countries they conquered and were raided in turn by their successors. A few great captains like Attila and Genghis Khan acquired huge domains that their successors were unable to hold.

They were eventually checked by another and very different form of cavalry—armored knights on much larger horses, wielding iron lances, maces and swords, and immune to arrows. A charge of knights against foot soldiers or light cavalry was irresistible. Two innovations—the breeding of heavy horses and the adoption of the stirrup—made this new type of warfare possible. Introduced into Europe in the eighth century, it enabled Charlemagne to revive a semblance of the Roman empire and created the complex social pattern called feudalism.

The knight was neither a lone warrior, like the Homeric hero, nor a member of a disciplined band. Each knight required a sizable entourage—squires, grooms, farriers, messengers—to take care of his equipment and his horses, help him to mount and dismount, and assist him with the rituals of knightly combat. Feudal armies were voluntary assemblages of such small units. They could be extremely effective when they kept together, as they did in the First Crusade and the capture of Jerusalem, and much less effective when they quarreled with each other, drifted away or attacked friendly populations, as they did in the later Crusades.

Nevertheless, the military superiority of the knights endured in Europe for half a millennium until it was countered by the construction of fortified castles and the introduction of the crossbow. The crossbow had been known in China for centuries and had been used to defend merchant ships from pirates for some time before its introduction in land warfare. Instead of an arrow, it shot an iron bolt that was capable of penetrating armor at 100 yards and it required no particular strength or skill to operate. When rulers began to recruit companies of crossbowmen, the mounted knights became obsolete. The disruption of feudal warfare was completed by the introduction of gunpowder—another Chinese invention—in the same century.

Cannon were at first used mostly for psychological effect, being inaccurate and dangerous to their users. But they spread fast and were soon so much improved that by the middle of the fifteenth century, existing castles and fortresses were virtually useless. They could be knocked to pieces by artillery in a few hours.

For the first hundred years or so, cannon were made of bronze and were extremely expensive. That fact helped to start the long development of the modern state, since only the most important feudal rulers could afford cannon, and those cannon greatly increased their relative power. As the evolution of gunpowder weapons continued, cannon became lighter and more mobile, iron was substituted for bronze and iron balls replaced stone.

The Age of Discovery

The European conquest of the world that began around 1492 and was completed around 1912, was the direct consequence of a cluster of inventions—compass, square sails, seaborne artillery—that produced a floating fortress invulnerable to the military forces of other societies, capable of going anywhere in the world and returning under its own power, and of controlling any port that it entered.

The Chinese had built and used powerful long-distance warships two centuries earlier but abandoned them in the early fifteenth century, for internal political reasons. Likewise, although the Chinese put gunpowder to use in cannon a little sooner than the Europeans, they were not very interested in improving them. By the time that European ships came to the coasts of China and India, European artillery was so much more advanced that the locally made cannon were useless:

> The Chinese, like the Turks and the Indians, lagged hopelessly behind the times in understanding the true potentialities of naval artillery . . . When they eventually realized that times had changed, it was too late . . . Western guns were always much superior to any

non-European product and their superiority was universally recognized (Cipolla 1965,126–128).

Attack and Defense

The alternation of advantage between attack and defense is a striking feature of military history. At the beginning of the medieval era, the stirrup and the war horse enabled armored knights to overwhelm foot soldiers armed with pikes and swords (White 1962). The advantage was sufficient to allow feudalism to develop; the knights took control of Europe and temporarily of the Near East, including the occupation of Jerusalem for 120 years. Attack had the advantage on the battlefields of the early middle ages, but the moated castles built in the eleventh and twelfth centuries were almost impregnable to siege by feudal armies and the new crossbows and long bows of archers on foot were able to penetrate armor and halt mounted charges. Defense retained an advantage until the introduction of artillery around 1400 made it easy to knock down castle walls and the invention of chain mail gave the advantage again to cavalry. But shortly thereafter, Italian fortress-builders learned to construct walls of loose dirt that were invulnerable to artillery and to reinforce them with ditches and outworks. The advantage shifted back to defense. The raising of mass armies and the introduction of field artillery in the eighteenth century restored the advantage to the attack.

The attack retained its advantage throughout the nineteenth century, as armies used railroads to become more mobile, and increased their firepower by means of automatic weapons. But in World War I, the machine gun, explosive shells, barbed wire, poison gas, and entrenchment gave overwhelming superiority to the defense. That was overcome in World War II by the blitzkrieg,[2] which involved fast-moving breakthroughs by motorized armored columns under heavy air cover, and by airborne and amphibious operations. In conventional warfare, the advantage still lies with the attack. Even relatively weak forces can inflict surprising damage on modern defenders, as the North Vietnamese showed during the Tet offensive. Powerful armed forces on the attack, like the U.S. armored corps in Desert Storm, are almost impossible to stop with conventional weapons. Recognition of this fact made the Soviet threat to Western Europe at least tactically plausible for decades.

Nuclear weapons reinforced the advantage of the attack, perhaps permanently. But efforts to strengthen the defense continue. President Reagan called for development of an anti-missile defense system that would render incoming nuclear missiles harmless. There was never any serious likelihood that such a defense could be successful[3] but the prospect was so tantalizing that tens of billions of dollars were spent in the attempt, and the project was renewed in 2001 by the incoming Bush administration.

Nuclear Weapons

The development of the atomic bomb by U.S. scientists late in World War II, and the subsequent improvement and mass production of nuclear weapons by the United States and the Soviet Union raised the technical means of inflicting death and destruction to an unprecedented level of efficiency. The bomb dropped at Hiroshima leveled the center of that city and killed about 100,000 of its inhabitants. It had the explosive power of 12,000 tons of TNT. But the power of many nuclear weapons in current stockpiles is measured in megatons. A megaton is the equivalent of a million tons of TNT. To get some perspective on these numbers it is helpful to note that the energy released by the Hiroshima bomb was equivalent to simultaneous head-on collisions at 60 miles an hour of all the motor vehicles in the U.S.; that the existing nuclear arsenals are equivalent to at least a ton of TNT for each of the 6 billion people on earth; and that a modern bomber, armed for a nuclear mission, carries more explosive power than the total used thus far in all the wars since the invention of gunpowder.

A one-megaton nuclear bomb exploded 6,000 feet above the center of a city on a clear day would create a blast overpressure of 5 pounds per square inch and deliver about 110 calories per square centimeter at a radius of 4 miles from the center (Warf 1989, 213–214). Divided into five 200-kiloton bombs, the same charge would level any city in the world and kill nearly all of its inhabitants.

But the blast is only the beginning. There are other effects:

- Thermal energy is 25 percent of the total energy released in a nuclear explosion. A one-megaton bomb can burn the retinas of viewers 50 miles away and blind them. Closer in, it can ignite a paved road.

- Direct radiation in the form of gamma rays and neutrons is lethal over a wider area than the blast.

- The radioactive fallout from nuclear explosions can spread over an entire continent or even further and harm people and animals thousands of miles away. The explosion of a hydrogen weapon emits about three hundred radioactive products. Their half-lives range from fractions of a second to thousands of centuries. Aside from their radioactive effects, some of these products are extraordinarily poisonous.

- The electromagnetic pulse was the last effect of nuclear explosions to be discovered and it is still not very well understood. It is known to be capable of disrupting all electrical systems over a wide area but it is uncertain whether and to what extent these systems could be restored to operation.

There are also two speculative effects that are still being debated among experts: nuclear winter and ozone depletion.

According to one computer model, now somewhat discredited, a full-scale nuclear exchange would release so much dust and smoke into the atmosphere that sunshine would be totally shut off; a year later, there would be no place on earth, even in the tropics, that had a summer temperature above freezing, and the result would be universal famine. A less extreme "nuclear autumn" would still have grim implications for the food supply.

Among the products released by nuclear explosions are nitrous oxides that could destroy the ozone layer that shields the surface of the earth from harmful ultraviolet radiation. The effect might be temporary or permanent. Nobody knows.

The travel time of nuclear warheads from launch site to target started out as 10 to 12 hours in the 1950s and huge quantities of warheads and aircraft were manufactured because the aircraft that carried the warheads were considered highly vulnerable to air defenses.[4] The habit of redundancy through over-building persisted after the reason for it disappeared. Present flight times are 25 to 30 minutes for intercontinental missiles, 10 to 12 minutes for "theater" weapons, and as little as 3 minutes for "depressed trajectory" submarine-launched missiles.

A full-scale nuclear attack on the U.S. by the USSR would have killed around 100 million people immediately and tens of millions more within days or weeks. Whole states, such as Nebraska, would have received lethal doses of radiation. Similar destruction would have been visited upon the Soviet Union. Eventually, additional hundreds of millions of people, mostly in the Northern Hemisphere, would have died as the effects spread through the air and water. Even more devastation could be wrought by targeting nuclear power plants with hydrogen bombs—such a strategy could render huge areas uninhabitable for decades (Warf, 219).

There is no way of telling how extensive an actual nuclear exchange would be. But the means of something close to universal extinction are in place.

Conventional Weapons

The bombing of Hamburg, Dresden, Tokyo, and Osaka in the closing days of World War II demonstrated that conventional bombs in sufficient numbers could achieve nearly the same level of urban destruction as an atomic bomb. Since then, the size, force, precision, and accuracy of explosive projectiles have been greatly increased. Explosives can now be delivered over intercontinental distances by ballistic missiles and cruise missiles as well as by manned bombers. Air-mist and cluster-bombs have achieved new levels of "anti-personnel efficacy." Battle between evenly matched conventional forces has become almost as impracticable as nuclear battle. Overwhelming technical superiority makes war a reasonable enterprise for the stronger side, but casualties on the weaker side are necessarily very high.

Chemical and Biological Weapons

Most of the chemical weapons stockpiled by the United States, the successor states of the Soviet Union, and about twenty other states are variants of the corrosive agents introduced in World War I, or nerve agents—more sophisticated compounds that kill by disrupting the human nervous system. Nerve gas is more lethal than the other gases—a single drop on the skin is sufficient to cause death—but since a simple and reasonably effective antidote is available, it has no great military usefulness, except against civilians, or as a psychological weapon that subjects enemy troops to fear and to the inconvenience and discomfort of protective clothing. Nerve gas is dangerous to its users; it is difficult to store and handle safely. The principal technical development of recent years is a binary form of nerve gas, whose two components are relatively harmless until combined inside a bomb or artillery shell on the way to the target. More than twenty other chemical agents, including non-lethal gases and herbicides, are currently stocked by the United States, the Soviet Union, Burma, China, Ethiopia, Iran, Israel, North Korea, Syria, Libya, and Vietnam.

The ban on poison gas enacted after World War I by the Geneva Convention of 1925 was generally respected (except by the Italians in Ethiopia and the Japanese in China) until the Iran-Iraq War in which poison gas was freely used by Iraq against Iranian troops and against unarmed Kurdish civilians. But Iraq did not use gas in the Gulf War, despite repeated threats to do so. In 1990, the United States and the Soviet Union signed a new convention calling for the gradual reduction of the chemical arsenals of each government to 5,000 tons by the year 2002. The 1993 Chemical Weapons Convention calls for a global ban on the production and stockpiling of chemical weapons.

Biological weapons have so far mostly remained in the laboratories and in developmental experimentation. But the laboratory work was extensive, especially in the U.S. in the 1950s and 1960s and in the USSR in the 1970s and 1980s (Miller, Engelberg, and Broad 2001). The Biological and Toxin Weapons Convention of 1972, which went into effect in 1975 and has been ratified by 110 nations, now forbids the production or stockpiling of biological weapons. But it would not restrain terrorist groups or rogue governments. Some alarming scenarios have been presented: a study by the Congressional Office of Technology Assessment warned that 100 kilograms of anthrax spores dropped on the Washington, D.C. area on a clear night might kill as many as three million people (U.S. Congress, 1993).

For Further Reading

James F. Dunnigan, *How to Make War: A Comprehensive Guide to Modern Warfare for the Post-Cold War Era*, 3rd ed., New York: William Morrow, 1993.

Manuel de Landa, *War in the Age of Intelligent Machines*, New York: Zone, 1991.

Judith Miller, Stephen Engelberg, and William Broad, *Germs: Biological Weapons and America's Secret War,* New York: Simon and Schuster, 2001.

Notes

[1] The Japanese managed to build five in that time.

[2] German for "lightning war."

[3] The two problems that made the "Star Wars" project implausible were: (1) that to be useful, any system of defense against nuclear missiles, would need to be close to 100 percent efficient; and (2) that any system of defense against ballistic missiles could easily be countered by substituting cruise missiles or other methods of delivery.

[4] One of the Soviet Union's major service branches, on the same organizational level as the Ground Forces or the Navy, was the *PVO*, or Air Defense Force.

10

Military Success and Failure

Like other large-scale organizations, military organizations are continuously preoccupied with achieving success and avoiding failure. But while the successes and failures of most other organizations are defined rather flexibly, i.e., making a reasonable profit or showing a steady growth in membership, military organizations have only the polar alternatives of victory or defeat, and even during long periods of peacetime activity, all of their planning and training is focused on the achievement of victory and the avoidance of defeat in hypothetical future battles.

The VISA Model

All organizations must satisfy the same constant set of requirements. They must hold the allegiance of their participants; maintain a high level of communication among their working parts; get people to conform to their assigned roles and procedures; and achieve at least some of their stated goals. VISA is an acronym for this set of requirements, in which V stands for Voluntarism, I for Integration, S for Stability, and A for Achievement.[1]

When we measure the voluntarism, integration, stability and achievement of an organization, we quickly discover that they are connected in intricate ways and that a change in any one of the four measures is *always* followed by changes in one or more of the other measures, and that the direction and magnitude of these changes are roughly predictable.

We can get a clearer view of how the VISA model works by looking at any two persons—we will call them A and B—who cooperate on common tasks in an organization. To do so, they must develop a relationship characterized by slightly different forms of the same variables. To keep the VISA acronym, the variables of a pair relationship may be designated as Valence, Interaction, Status, and Activity. The reason for using similar terms is that when these measures of individual relationships are combined, they account for the group measures mentioned above.

Valence is the average attraction of A for B and B for A. (The term is borrowed from chemistry where it signifies the attraction of one atom for another.) It might be described as friendliness, or liking, or positive affect; the basic element is that the parties want to continue their interaction. *Interaction* as a variable is a measure of how much A and B communicate—a measure that ideally includes both frequency and intensity. *Status* is a measure of differential power in an organizational context. To say that A has higher status than B is to say that the organization expects A to influences B's behavior more than B influences A's behavior. *Activity* is a measure of the joint contribution of A and B to the organization's program.

With status at zero, i.e., when A and B are peers, an increase of interaction is followed by an increase of valence and an increase of activity. Likewise, an increase of activity is necessarily followed by an increase of interaction. This is the social mechanism on which all armies depend when they throw recruits together for 24 hours a day and engage them in varied and strenuous activities. The presence of other peers keeps the values of interaction, valence and activity for the A/B pair from spiraling up indefinitely, but military organizations do count on the development of close "buddy" relationships within the solidarity of the small military unit.

The mechanism also works in reverse. A decline of activity leads to a decline of interaction and of valence. Confined to barracks in bad weather, some As and Bs are likely to fight.

When there is a difference of status between A and B, the increase of activity stimulated by an increase of interaction is much greater. The larger the status difference, the less interaction is needed to sustain a given amount of activity. In general, the interaction between an unequal pair is proportional to the amount of their joint activity and inversely proportional to the status difference between them. That is what authority is all about; the initiation of activity by a superior is less dependent on the willingness of the subordinate and requires less discussion.

In unequal relationships, an increase of interaction or activity may lead either to an increase or a decrease of valence, depending on the circumstances. In peer relationships, the valences of the parties are generally equal or close to equal, the valence of a superior toward a subordinate is likely to be higher than the valence of the subordinate towards the superior.

Turning back to the organization as a whole, we can see that *Voluntarism* is the willingness of the organization's members to participate in its program, *Integration* is the result of effective internal communication, *Stability* is the maintenance of the organization's prescribed statuses, and *Achievement* refers to the accomplishment of the organization's goals (Caplow 1964).

As every manager knows, voluntarism and integration tend to vary together and to contribute directly to achievement. But the more stable the organization, i.e., the more authoritative, the less its achievement will depend on the maintenance of voluntarism and integration.

Military organizations are unusual in having two distinct modes of operation—peacetime and wartime—with very different types of achievement. In peacetime, their goal is to maintain their own structure with a minimum of internal friction and external disturbance. The necessary levels of voluntarism, stability and integration in peacetime are not very high.

But because combat imposes imminent risks of life and limb, wartime military units must develop a high level of voluntarism in order to fight effectively. Since success in combat also depends on the coordination of diverse activities in a rapidly changing environment, high levels of stability and integration are required at the same time.

But as our model suggests, a simultaneous increase of all three variables is difficult to accomplish because an increase of stability normally leads to a decrease of voluntarism, and a decrease of voluntarism has an adverse effect on integration. Every serious military organization must find some response to this dilemma.

The classic solution is to emphasize voluntarism in the smallest units of the organization—squads and platoons—and stability at the higher levels. That the formula works is shown by studies of rank-and-file soldiers that find attachment to comrades to be a more important incentive in combat than attachment to any larger cause.[2]

Modern military organizations, including guerrilla forces specializing in "low-intensity combat" and high-technology forces like U.S. armored divisions, seem to be evolving a different formula, in which small units and even individual combatants are allowed unprecedented autonomy and formal orders are reduced to a minimum. In this mode, stability is minimized in favor of voluntarism and integration, except at the top of the status order, where general objectives are set.

But even under the most favorable conditions, there is always some friction between the organization's efforts to maintain its own structure, particularly the prerogatives of military rank, and its need to maintain the allegiance of rank-and-file participants. Only extraordinary and repeated success in battle can reduce this friction but that solution is not routinely available.

Success in Battle

Success in battle depends on seven factors: (1) numbers; (2) personnel factors; (3) organizational factors; (4) technology; (5) strategy and tactics; (6) accident and luck; and (7) hunger, disease, fatigue.

Numbers: Numerical superiority in personnel, weapons, or supplies is a powerful advantage on the battlefield. Larger numbers of troops can achieve otherwise impossible maneuvers such as surrounding an enemy force. By the same token, a larger army is harder to surprise and harder to surround than a small one. For forces evenly matched in personnel, the quantities of weapons and ammunition determine the density and rate of fire—a crucial variable. Modern forces equip themselves with an amazing number of weapons per soldier. Finally, a large quantity of supplies allows more flexibility and implies less fear of enemy operations against logistical targets. Superiority in manpower, weapons, or supplies makes it possible to embark on a strategy of attrition, trading losses with the enemy until his smaller force is reduced to ineffectiveness, as Grant did to Lee.

Prussian, and later, German military planners knew that a prolonged war on two fronts would involve such disadvantageous numerical odds that all of their other advantages (internal lines, superior training and tactics, and the element of surprise) might be nullified. German attempts in World War II to compensate for numerical inferiority by using auxiliary troops, such as Romanians and Italians, were largely unsuccessful. Even Admiral Yamamoto recognized that the great damage inflicted in the attack on Pearl Harbor would only be effective if the war was very short, since in the longer run, the American superiority in manpower and productive capacity would surely prevail. Other things being equal, a numerical advantage is usually conclusive.

But other things are often unequal. History is filled with the victories of small forces over large ones. Superior strategy and tactics enabled Lee and Jackson to defeat larger Union forces on several occasions. When contending forces are drawn from societies with entirely different military cultures, astonishing numerical imbalances can sometimes be overcome, as in Cortez' conquest of Mexico with a handful of Spanish soldiers.

Personnel factors include training, experience, discipline, and morale. The better-disciplined force has a marked advantage. A high degree of discipline cannot be achieved without intensive training. Battle-experienced troops also have a powerful advantage over the inexperienced. Many great battles, like Waterloo, were decided by small differences in discipline. High morale by itself does not guarantee success, but conspicuously low morale insures failure. Historically, victory has probably been won as often by the better-disciplined force as by the larger or better-armed one.

The idea that social order originated in war is very ancient. Weber mentions that Homer knew of the danger of fighting "out of the line." The Greek phalanx owed its effectiveness in part to superior armor and in part to superior discipline, achieved by long years of practice. The Roman legion offered great rewards for service, with lifetime security for the legionnaire and his family and land ownership for his descendants. Machiavelli ([1521] 1965) perceived the advantages of modern citizen armies before any of them existed.

According to Michael Mann (1986) social power comes in four forms: ideological, or normative power; economic power; military power; and political power. Mann's "IEMP" model clearly has room for military discipline as an important variable. Indeed, the earliest, barely visible forms of discipline combined all four power sources into one: the early military leaders became permanent political leaders who attained semi-divine status and presided over the collection and distribution of economic surpluses. In the beginning, discipline was unitary. As far back as the Sumerians (163), "Cohesion and morale, faith in the man next to you, was essential for infantry." The city-states of Sumer were either democracies or relatively benign oligarchies, and this provided the social basis for their military success.

Mann explains the victories of the Greeks over the Persians as due in part to the superior discipline and obedience of free men (244), and the rapid and the sustained success of the first Islamic armies by the superior discipline fostered by their religious doctrine. For the Islamic cavalry,

> a disciplined life entailed military drill . . . In many cases the Islamic forces defeated better-equipped armies by means of superior coordination and mobility, rather than undisciplined fanatical charges . . . It [Islam] conquered those areas whose rulers' armies were not sustained by a comparable morale (346).

Islamic expansion was eventually checked by warriors with equivalent religious motivation rather than technological superiority: Frankish knights and Byzantine soldiers.

In *The Modern World System*, Wallerstein includes military discipline as a variable in his analysis of European expansion in the sixteenth century. In his overview of the "medieval prelude," he contends that technological innovations procured an enhancement of military discipline:

> a technological shift [occurred] in the art of war, from the long bow to the cannon and the handgun, from the cavalry war to the one in which infantry charged and hence in which more training and discipline was required (1974, 28).[3]

Organizational factors: Decisive victories are often secured by social inventions (i.e., new organizational forms). The line between organization and tactics is not easily drawn because any given type of organization suggests particular tactics. Social inventions that achieved spectacular military success include: the Viking raid, the three-line formation of musketeers, the infantry hollow square, the *levée en masse,* the blitzkrieg, and modern guerrilla tactics.

Technology: This includes not only weapons and personal equipment but the technology of transport, communication, intelligence, and supply. The range and power of weapons and the quality of defensive equipment are always crucial. The most successful innovations in military technology are those that can damage or destroy the adversary before he can bring his own weapons in range, or that enable one's own forces to maneuver more rapidly or that provide more information about the enemy's capabilities and movements than the enemy can obtain about one's own. Inventions like the chariot, the bridle, the catapult, the crossbow, the long bow, chain mail, shipborne artillery, ironclads, the machine gun, the tank, the submarine, the airplane, radar, and the atomic bomb, have each in turn revolutionized warfare.

Strategy, tactics: Many battles have been fought between forces that were sufficiently equal to make the outcome quite unpredictable. The greater the equality, the more decisive the strategic and tactical skill of the commanders. Military genius enables some commanders repeatedly to win battles with smaller forces or under less favorable conditions than their adversaries. The great commanders of history—Alexander, Caesar, Napoleon, Lee,

Halsey—repeatedly won against the odds and at ridiculously low cost. The minor military geniuses that appear in every war—the consistently successful platoon sergeants and battalion commanders—do the same things on a smaller scale. What they seem to have in common is the ability to predict the actions of the enemy, to understand and adapt to a given terrain, to move their own forces with uncommon speed, and to accomplish unconventional maneuvers.

For thousands of years, writers have sought to discover timeless general principles of war. War has been as much an enduring puzzle for successful generals as for armchair theorists who never saw a battle. Attempts to systematize these insights go as far back as the Chinese strategist Sun Tzu (ca. 500 B.C.), whose strategic and tactical maxims are still considered useful. By far the most important author in this tradition was Carl von Clausewitz whose principal work, entitled *On War* (1832–1834), can be viewed as a systematic sociology of military interaction. Most of the other important strategic theorists, from Machiavelli to the academic designers of nuclear deterrence, have preached more restricted strategic principles based on the conditions of a particular era.[4]

For all of this intellectual effort, there has been little progress toward a unified "science of war." There are innumerable strategical theories, many elegant analyses of battles and campaigns, and many formulas for victory, but all of them turn out on close analysis to refer to particular styles of war in particular circumstances.

Luck: Military luck, good and bad, comes in many forms and has accounted for the outcome of innumerable battles: the stray arrow or bullet that kills the enemy commander (as in the Norman invasion of England in 1066), the order accidentally intercepted, the fog that rolls in to conceal a target, the sudden storm that destroys a fleet (as a "divine wind" saved Japan from a Chinese invasion), the misunderstood message that launches a surprise attack. The effects of luck can be cumulative—the lucky unit believes itself to be invulnerable and good omens shower upon it.

Disease, hunger, fatigue: As many battles are decided by the physical condition of the troops engaged as by their fighting ability. Prior to the twentieth century, disease accounted for more casualties than enemy fire in nearly every protracted war. Under primitive sanitary conditions, any large body of troops would eventually be swept by epidemics. And soldiers have sometimes unintentionally infected the enemy with unfamiliar diseases, causing astonishing devastation, as the Europeans did to the Meso-American empires (Crosby 1972, Diamond 1999). In pre-industrial eras, agricultural surpluses were limited, provisioning was generally uncertain, and it was seldom possible to keep a large force intact through the winter months. In the modern era, these limitations are more easily surmounted and battles and campaigns have become more protracted than ever before. The Battle of Stalingrad in World War II raged for more than a year without interruption. But a mass of empirical evidence has accumulated to show that the combat effectiveness of units declines steeply and virtually all soldiers break down mentally or emotionally if exposed too long to the stress of battle.

Success in War

Success in war is quite distinct from success in battle. Many wars have been won by the side that lost most of the battles but resisted exhaustion longer and states have often been unable to derive any lasting benefit from military victories. In both World Wars, the most brilliant and conspicuous victories were won by the alliance that was eventually defeated. After both World Wars, the economic growth of the loser nations considerably exceeded that of the winners.

For Further Reading

Mark Bowden, *Black Hawk Down: A Story of Modern War*, Thorndike, Me.: G.K. Hall, 2000.

John Keegan, *The Mask of Command*, New York: Viking, 1987.

William Odom, *The Collapse of the Soviet Military,* New Haven: Yale University Press, 1998.

Notes

[1] Talcott Parsons' AGIL problems (Adaptive, Gratificatory, Integrative, Pattern-Maintenance) are alternative descriptions of the same requirements (Parsons 1956).

[2] The study most often cited is Shils and Janowitz (1948). Its findings about Wehrmacht soldiers in World War II have often been over-stretched to support the conclusion that all soldiers are indifferent to official war aims—very doubtful in the cases of the Union or Confederate armies or the Israeli Defense Force. Their finding may be an artifact of the data collection process. The authors were, after all, interrogating prisoners who had every reason to deny allegiance to Nazi war aims.

[3] This explanation differs somewhat from those of Weber and McNeill, both of whom observed that gunpowder and other lethal innovations lay unused until a form of discipline was devised that could take advantage of the new technology.

[4] For an excellent survey of strategic theory, see Paret 1986.

11

The Social Effects of War

War seems to accelerate social change in every possible way, from technological development to shifts in moral standards. No aspect of a country's life is unaffected by participation in a major war. Literature, music and art take new directions. Political parties are restructured. Religion, family life, education and leisure are modified in innumerable ways. The composition of the population is permanently altered. Defeated nations are likely to show more drastic changes—especially political changes—in the short run, but in the long run, it becomes difficult to say which side was more affected by a particular war.

War and Social Structure

Despite his insistence on deriving social structure from relations of production, Karl Marx understood clearly that the technical means of warfare conditioned the whole universe of social relations. His running commentary on the American Civil War, written for a London newspaper, was a model of strategical analysis. But for the most part, he left the systematic study of military effects to his partner, Friedrich Engels (nicknamed "The General" for his continuing interest in military affairs). Nonetheless, because the bulk of their writings focused on relations of production it has appeared to generations of Marxists that the effects of violent coercion on social structure were relatively marginal, and Marxist theories of war do not amount to much more than the dubious proposition that war would disappear if capitalism were replaced by socialism.

Max Weber was the first sociologist to deal with the effects of war on social structure in a comprehensive way. The organization of violent coercion was central to his understanding of history. In this respect, Weber agreed with orthodox thinkers as far back as the ancient Greeks.[1] But with his characteristic originality and unmatched erudition, Weber studied the social, political, economic and ideological aspects of organized violent coercion in a bewildering array of historical contexts. Most historians had written about battles, campaigns, strategies, and commanders. Weber was intrigued by the *patterns* of organized violent coercion more than by the details of particular conflicts. This important theme in Weber's work has been carried further by his successors.

Weber regarded violent social action as primordial. The "political community," he wrote, rests on the "readiness to resort to physical force, including normally force of arms." With few exceptions, a "readiness to apply violence normally accompanies domination over a territory" ([1921] 1978, 901–902).

Charisma, the possession of unique personal qualities that form the basis for leadership, can depend on military fortunes. Weber noted the charismatic ruler's vulnerability to defeat in war and how ruling elites fear the charisma accruing to victorious generals. He described kingship as "normally charismatic war leadership that has become permanent and has developed a repressive apparatus for the domestication of the unarmed subjects" (1135).[2]

Weber showed how the "sociologically basic change of the army from the combat of heroes to disciplined formations," (158) matched the "stages of political association," (905–908) and he challenged Marxist materialism by stressing the role of weapons technology (rather than means of production) in determining the details of military organization and the broader development of social structure.[3] This assertion was supported with examples ranging from Greek hoplites to the military revolution in seventeenth- and eighteenth-century Europe. Elsewhere, Weber took account of relationships in the opposite direction, for example the effect of innovative military technology in changing the infantry-cavalry balance of power and the military consequences of the introduction of iron and horses.

Weber discussed at great length the role of warfare in creating social discipline and showed how discipline, originating in war, became the basis for other types of rational collective activity and furnished the common element in ancient projects like pyramid building and modern capitalist projects, like railroad building. This thread of discipline is almost independent of its political context, whether patrimonial, charismatic or bureaucratic. Innovations in European military discipline eventually contributed to bureaucratic rationality and the rise of capitalist industry.

If this view is pushed a little further, a seemingly peaceful business enterprise that pays its employees in money can be seen as employing "coercion once removed." The reasoning runs as follows:

> Any organization involves authority, the power of certain people to give and enforce orders which others carry out. The basis of authority is a chain of communications. The ultimate sanction of a lower-level manager over a worker is to communicate to others in the management hierarchy to withhold the worker's pay; the sanction in a military organization is to communicate orders to apply coercion against any disobedient soldier. *The civilian case is founded on the military one*; control chains based on pay or other access to property are ultimately backed up by the coercive power of the state (Collins 1981, 270–271, emphasis added).

The Rise of the State

Weber noted that gunpowder was a curiosity until Maurice of Nassau created a disciplined force trained to use the new weapons in a controlled, massed fashion. The effect was a transformation of war and a vast increase in the power of sovereign princes at the expense of the city-states and feudal lords with whom they contended. Wallerstein comments further on this point:

> the cost of war increased, the number of men required rose, and the desirability of a standing army over ad hoc formations became ever

more clear . . . neither feudal lords individually nor the city-states could really foot the bill or recruit the manpower. . . (1974, 29)

He later reiterates this view:

> We have also mentioned the evolution of military technology which made obsolete the medieval knight and thereby strengthened the hand of central authorities who could control large numbers of infantrymen (134).

Other authors discuss the rapidly rising military expenses of the nascent state bureaucracies: "the growth in the financial size of the state . . . was a product of the growing costs of war" (Mann 1986, 430), and:

> Preparation for war has been the great state-building activity. The process has been going on more or less continuously for at least five hundred years (Tilly, quoted in Mann 1986, 433).

The appearance of large standing armies—the *sine qua non* of the new European states—raises the question of where the manpower was found. McNeill answers the question thus:

> Human flotsam and jetsam found an honorable refuge from a world in which buying and selling had become so pervasive as to handicap severely those who lacked the necessary pecuniary self-restraint, cunning, and foresight (1982, 13).

Another scholar who has examined the larger impact of war-and-peace on society is Theda Skocpol. In *States and Social Revolutions*, she discussed the factors contributing to social revolutions and noted the importance of military discipline in two situations: in coups d'état where the crucial question is, "Who will the troops obey?" and after foreign wars that have reduced the reliability of armed forces and thereby their usefulness for internal repression.

The relative discipline of the regime's military forces and of the revolutionary party's cadres goes far to explain the outcome of attempted revolutions. Skocpol considered three cases: the Russian, French, and Chinese revolutions. In Russia, the World War I defeat discredited and demoralized the Tsar's armed forces, and they ceased to be usable as instruments of internal repression. Party discipline was the crucial asset of the Cheka and other organs of the revolutionary party that filled the power vacuum.

The Bolsheviks' discipline allowed them to rule the peasants "by command and terror" (Skocpol 1979, 279). In France, the refusal of royal troops in Paris to open fire on rioters, and their participation in the attack on the Bastille, was the turning point of the revolution. Thereafter, France was invaded by an alliance of hostile states seeking to restore the monarchy. The revolutionary government mobilized the entire male population of military age to defend the country. Civilian resistance to this *levée en masse* as punished as a military crime thus extending military discipline to the entire population and blurring the civilian/soldier distinction. In China, the state was not finally organized until after World War II, by which time, the disciplinary mechanisms of the Communist Party, forged during a long period of guerrilla warfare, were overwhelmingly powerful and well adapted to serve a dictatorial regime.

The Costs and Benefits of War

Warfare has paradoxical effects on the national societies that engage in it. It is obvious, of course that the outcome of a war can be the devastation of one side and the aggrandizement of the other. But the overall consequences of war are much more difficult to specify. To some observers, war is merely a giant social cost, a useless waste of collective resources. The original sociological view of war, that of Herbert Spencer ([1892] 1914, 414) and other nineteenth-century evolutionists, envisaged it as a mechanism that selected the fittest for survival. Werner Sombart ([1937] 1969, 25) proposed an economic model for this evolutionary process. Pitirim Sorokin (1928, 309–356) reframed the evolutionary position in more modern terms. Toynbee (1961) and Spengler ([1926–1928] 1961) described the mediation of historical cycles by war.

By the 1950s, this essentially positive evaluation of war had been largely reversed,[4] and most social scientists perceived war as inimical to social progress (e.g., Nef 1950). In a related development, some nuclear strategists began to refer to war as "unthinkable" (Kahn 1962).[5] This reversal of previous thinking probably went beyond the evidence. For example, Sorokin had pointed out that "the unusual stimulation of the inventive power of a nation for the sake of military victory has often facilitated the invention of a new method or the improvement of the old methods of wealth production" and that "warring periods are marked by an extraordinary progress of science, arts, and philosophies, and of all kinds of intellectual achievements" (1928, 339, 350).

Home Front Effects

Using empirical data on the home front effects of four U.S. wars (World War I, World War II, the Korean War, and the Vietnam War), Stein (1980) showed that after an initial surge of national cohesion (absent in the case of the Vietnam War) domestic disunity, as measured by crimes, strikes, and race riots, increased sharply during each war. The increase of violent crime was especially marked. Similar results are shown for Great Britain. These wars also brought about significant declines of social inequality. Other effects were large increases in governmental powers, non-defense government employment, and taxes, which in each case persisted after the war.

Among the effects not covered in that study are: demographic dislocation, the acceleration of institutional change, the rapid introduction of new habits and ideas, and the creation of a war-disabled population.

In general, the social effects of war are more extensive in defeated than in victorious states. But even in victorious states, major wars generally mark a kind of cultural watershed. Post-war politics, literature, popular culture, and social problems always show new departures.

Demographic Consequences

War has keenly interested demographers since their science began. Thomas Malthus theorized that the consequences of a geometrically increasing population trying to survive on an arithmetically growing food supply would lead to war as the price of survival of some at the expense of others. Modern demographers tend to discount Malthus's warnings but the logic of including population pressure among the factors leading to war remains persuasive. Certainly, some military leaders have explicitly identified the need for more land as the impetus for war. It is not always possible to draw a clear distinction between a ruler wanting more territory and a population requiring more room.

Apart from population pressure, the composition of population is profoundly affected by warfare. Because soldiers have historically killed or enslaved men on the opposing side, while taking their women as mates, human biological variation has been magnified by continual mixing and re-mixing. Without war, human subpopulations would probably be much more distinct than they are today.

Within populations, war has profound effects on the components of demographic change: mortality rates, fertility rates, and migration rates. War has the obvious effect of increasing mortality rates. Combat deaths are typically concentrated among young men, leading to changes in the age and sex structure of the population. Whole generations of young men sometimes vanish from populations, as in France during World War I. The shift in the sex-ratio of particular cohorts of marriage-age individuals may lead to temporary polygamy or a rise in out-of-wedlock births. Fertility rates are often affected in the short term by war: the absence of American men depressed birth rates in the early 1940s and their triumphant return ignited the "baby boom." The growth of defense industries during and after World War II led to massive migration of the American working age population, especially to the Sun Belt.

Fertility has recently fallen below replacement in most industrial nations and to low levels in some developing countries. It is too early to be sure if these trends will continue but if they do, war may be profoundly altered. If population pressures decline as a result of fertility declines then Malthusian theory would predict a reduction of, or even an end to war.

Effects of Defeat

After a lost war, the leaders of defeated governments are almost always repudiated and the political system transformed, sometimes under the surveillance of the victors. These effects appear even after defeat in distant, non-threatening wars: the American frustration in Vietnam discredited the administration of Lyndon Johnson and provoked a social upheaval that stopped only a little short of outright revolution. Military defeat was the proximate cause of the Bolshevik and German revolutions after World War I, the creation of democratic systems in West Germany and Japan after World War II, and the fall of the Argentine junta after the Falklands War.[6]

Despite the massive destruction of the infrastructure that generally accompanies defeat in modern war, the economic and political consequences of defeat are as likely as not to be favorable. The crushing defeat of France in 1815 was followed by a period of extraordinary prosperity and creativity. The defeat of France in 1871 was followed by an equally glorious era. The economic and military growth of Germany between the two world wars greatly exceeded that of Britain and France. The economic achievements of Germany and Japan after World War II surpassed those of the victorious allies.

Much thought has gone into explaining this "phoenix effect," whereby the losers in modern wars have gone on to win the peace by out-developing and out-competing the apparently exhausted victors. Some scholars point to "imperial overreach" to explain the exhaustion of victors (Kennedy 1987).

The Last War and the Next

Military planning for the next war is necessarily based on the experience of the last war; there is little else to go on. After being convinced by the experience of the Franco-Prussian War that the offensive was the only way to victory, both the French and the Germans persisted in deadly and fruitless assaults on enemy trenches in World War I. Understandably shocked by their losses and noting the eventual triumph of defense, the French reversed their strategy and built the Maginot Line while the Germans were developing the blitzkrieg. U.S. strategy in the Gulf War was explicitly intended to avoid the errors of Vietnam. The tendency of losers to innovate somewhat more than winners encourages alternation in the fortunes of war.

> New organizations, making use of newly created means of harnessing wealth, power, and moral commitment to organizational purposes . . . destroy the old forms of organization by competition . . . Armies that do not adapt are defeated in war . . . Natural monopolies like . . . armies under stable governments are in much different types of Darwinian processes than . . . armies in time of revolution (Stinchcombe 1971, 287).

War and Religion

The Enlightenment expectation that reason would displace religion has nowhere failed more conspicuously than in the realm of war-and-peace. The European wars of religion ended in the seventeenth century. Eighteenth-century philosophers believed that wars of that type were obsolete. In the long run, they were wrong. Wars of religion are still being fought at the beginning of the twenty-first century. Many of the world's most bitter conflicts have religious overtones: Sunnis and Shi'ites in Iran and Iraq; Catholics and Protestants in Ireland; Muslim Bosnians and Orthodox Serbs; Palestinian Muslims and Israeli Jews; Hindu Indians and Pakistani Muslims; and Islamic fundamentalists and the United States. Western nations are not immune from the entanglements of religion and foreign policy.

War and Education

War has significant interactions with the institution of education. Modern armed forces run the largest training programs ever seen. The American armed forces are a perpetual motion machine of classes, courses, reviews, tests, exams, exercises, credentials, degrees, diplomas, and certificates. Basic training consists more than anything else of sitting through one classroom lecture and one practical experience after another, covering everything from sexually transmitted diseases and the metabolism of alcohol to landmines and the Laws of War. Western, and especially American armed forces, invented a large part of modern educational technology, including simulators, multimedia, and computer-based training (Noble 1989; 1991). At sea and at remote frozen bases, education at all levels from high school to graduate school is continuously conducted in person, by videotape, by satellite and by computer.

Military organizations also pay for the civilian educations of many of their members, before, during, and after military service. The GI Bill after World War II is the famous American example but the policy continues today with similar impact.

War and the Family

For millennia, families and other civilians followed military forces in their campaigns. Sometimes this constituted their established life style, as among warring nomadic bands in Eurasia. The long train of camp followers did not begin to thin out until the mechanization of war increased mobility above walking speeds and made the areas around the battlefield increasingly dangerous for noncombatants. Tension between the military and the family is a common feature of modern armed forces. The Army and the family are both "greedy institutions" (Segal 1988). They both ask for large, open-ended commitments, especially from their lower-ranking members, whose marriages are newer and whose children are younger, so that the greatest demands for commitment are directed to those for whom the demands of military service are the least flexible. Naval service, with its long deployments at sea, is especially threatening to family life.

Recent U.S. policy has aimed at co-opting the spouses. Their status was upgraded: "dependents" became "family members." Base housing was dramatically improved—a large proportion of defense spending under the Reagan administration went to building apartments, bowling alleys, and shopping facilities on bases in the U.S. and abroad. But a dilemma results: as soldiers with spouses are treated with more understanding by the military, heavier burdens fall upon the shrinking number of single soldiers who live on the post.[7] "Off-post" personnel are often exempted from the endless inspections and petty chores that constitute barracks life.

The integration of women into Western armed forces has caused the two institutions to overlap to an even greater degree. A recent phenomenon in the American armed forces is a rapid increase in the population of families with both husband and wife in the service.

War and Science

Especially in recent times, the military is one of the few organizations with the resources to invest in basic scientific research. Only powerful institutions with stable resources can afford to take the long view: private foundations, government agencies devoted to science for itself (e.g., the National Science Foundation or the United States Geological Survey), and the armed forces. The Pentagon's National Security Agency is almost certainly the world's largest single employer of mathematicians. Vast resources are funneled into basic research laboratories at Los Alamos, MIT, Johns Hopkins, Livermore, and many other places (de Landa 1991).[8]

War and Technological Innovation

War has often been a profound spur to technological innovation. For example, metallurgy has focused around producing better edge weapons and better armor for at least 4,000 years. Medicine has been a primary military concern since ancient times. The Romans developed capable and effective battlefield surgery and public health measures. The U.S. military invented or pioneered all sorts of medical breakthroughs: triage, blood storage, helicopter evacuation, surgical techniques, vaccines, antibiotics, and so forth.

The overall effect on technology today is enormous. Modern America abounds with converted military technologies: radar, jet aircraft, the integrated circuit, plywood, cellphones, helicopter ambulances, Magnetic Resonance Imaging (MRI), night vision goggles, the Global Positioning System (GPS), the Internet—the list is practically endless.

War and the Economy

The military is a key player in the American economy. It is a major consumer of goods and services—taking about 3 percent of the nation's total production in 1999 (International Institute of Strategic Studies 2000, 297). For some major industries, such as aircraft, radio and TV communication equipment, and shipbuilding, military procurement accounts for more than 40 percent of the market (Reppy 1983, 31).

The logistic burden of equipping and supplying military units has been growing without apparent limit since the Industrial Revolution. According to Van Creveld:

> A division during the Franco-Prussian War consumed about 50 tons a day on average, consisting mainly of food and fodder. By 1916 the figure had risen to approximately 150 tons, most of the increase being accounted for by ammunition, fuel, spare parts, and engineering supplies. In 1940–42, the German General Staff worked on the assumption that an armored division in the Western Desert needed 300 tons daily to remain operational. Allied planners in 1944–45 postulated 650 tons a day per American division in Western Europe, a figure that has probably doubled or tripled during the decades since then (1991, 106).

The U.S. military practice of requiring adherence to detailed requirements, known as military specifications or "milspec" is blamed for the high cost of defense hardware and praised for providing materiel that does the job under extreme conditions.[9] It certainly spurs and channels (and sometimes directly pays for) much final product development. The innumerable scandals in military procurement have been responsible for the development of a special branch of contract law.

On the other hand, there is much that the military does *not* want sold—the secret designs of state-of-the-art weapons, of course, but much more besides: cryptographic software, intelligent machine tools, communication monitoring devices, special laser applications, and naval radar for example. An international consortium of non-sellers (COCOM), a logical inversion of a trading bloc, was formed to prevent commercialization in some fields.

In addition to purchasing equipment and supplies, the military services move hundreds of thousands of people around the country, and are major owners and operators of local real estate.

The military services play a major role in the labor market too, especially the market for workers in the demographically relevant group: young men. The military's demand since 1980 for an ever more qualified labor force has had profound effects on the economy. Downsizing after the end of the Cold War has had even more obvious and wrenching effects.

Modern management theories draw extensively on military sources and models. The American armed forces have been at the leading edge of technology since World War II and were among the first economic organizations to enter the "post-industrial age." One feature of this transition is the decline of mass production; many significant military products are now bought in lots of fewer than 100 items. More and more materiel is made by artisans. Cruise missiles are hand-crafted, as are nuclear warheads, stealth aircraft, and reconnaissance satellites.

War and Leisure

The vicarious experience of war is a conspicuous mode of leisure in modern societies. Nostalgia for the American Civil War has produced a vast complex of leisure activities: battle re-enactments; battlefield and campaign tours; conventions and campouts; a vast trade in uniforms, period costumes, and equipment, including not only virtually authentic weapons, uniforms, insignia, and accoutrements for reenactors who take the roles of Union and Confederate soldiers, but also hoopskirts for their wives and period toys for their children. Dozens of magazines and hundreds of books and films feed the same interests. Other wars have similar, if smaller, followings.

The subindustry of recreational war games interacts in an interesting way with the war gaming of military command schools and think tanks. Much of the activity of National Guard and reserve units, and of military schools, is almost indistinguishable from the forms of play that draw upon the inherent fascination of military activities and artifacts (Allen 1987).

War and Culture

The celebration of battle is a primary theme of the world's literature, second only to the celebration of sexual love, and often intertwined with it. In pre-industrial works like the *Iliad*, the Old Testament, the Norse sagas, the Chanson de Roland, the Morte d'Arthur, and the plays of Shakespeare and Racine, battle is heroic, glorious, tragic, divinely inspired. From the Napoleonic Wars onward, the tone changes. An abhorrence of war qualifies its continued, dramatic importance in thousands of fictional works from Tolstoy's *War and Peace* to Tolkien's *The Lord of the Rings*.[10]

When electric entertainments began to supplement novels and plays, war remained an important topic. Among the many war movies are some of the greatest films of all time: *Patton*, *Spartacus*, *Apocalypse Now*, *Saving Private Ryan*, *Gallipoli*, and *Kagemusha*. *Star Wars*—the most successful movie franchise ever—is, of course, about a long, long war.

War invades the TV screen as well. Cable television's History Channel is often called the "Hitler channel" for its concentration on World War II. Even TV sitcoms have focused on war: Gomer Pyle, Hogan's Heroes, M*A*S*H, and Major Dad.

The availability of movies and television has not diminished literary interest in war. War books like Stephen Ambrose's *Citizen Soldiers* and Tom Clancy's military novels sell millions of copies and remain on the best-seller lists for months.

For Further Reading

David Kaiser, *Politics and War: European Conflict from Philip II to Hitler*, enl. ed., Cambridge: Harvard University Press, 2000.

Stephen Vincent Benét, *John Brown's Body*, London: David Bruce & Watson Ltd., 1970. Originally published in 1922.

Notes

[1] For example, consider Heraclitus' pronouncement that "war is the father of all things," as translated by Pitirim Sorokin (1928, 309). Also translated as "strife is the basis of all things" by Collins (1981, 19) and as "strife is the origin of everything" by Van Creveld (1991, 218).

[2] "In China the charismatic quality of the monarch, which was transmitted unchanged by heredity, was upheld so rigidly that any misfortune whatever, not only defeats in war, but drought, floods, or astronomical phenomena which was considered unlucky, forced him to do public penance and might even force his abdication" (Weber [1921] 1978, 243).

[3] Collins (1981, 41) was careful to distinguish qualification from repudiation: "Weber is best known for a series of contributions that apparently break the Marxian mold . . . [but these contributions] remain within the conflict tradition, and supplement rather than negate the model of conflict over material goals and through material resources."

[4] It revives periodically, however. For a recent expression see Kennedy 1987.

[5] For an attempt to rebut the view that nuclear weapons change the rules of geopolitics see Collins 1986, 167–185.

[6] Which may also have contributed to the recent decline of military prestige throughout Latin America.

[7] Married servicemen as a proportion of all American servicemen rose from 38 percent in 1953 to 61 percent in 1980 (Segal 1988, 89).

[8] For overview of the relationships among war, science, and technology see Mendelsohn, et al., 1988; Smith 1985; and Parry and Yapp 1975.

[9] The specifications for fruit cake are 18 pages long and include a discussion of how to soak the raisins.

[10] Tolkien was inspired by the origins of northern European culture, especially the sagas of the Vikings.

§

Part Three

Peacekeeping Systems

12

Peace Projects

The idea of preventing war by political rearrangement is as old as the art of writing, and the main possibilities have all been recognized for a long time.

Millennial Movements

The rejection of violence was at the core of early Christianity and early Buddhism, although each adapted itself to warfare when it became a state religion. The recurrent hope that universal peace might be achieved by a millennial movement finds voices in every era: Francis of Assisi, George Fox, Leo Tolstoy, and Mahatma Gandhi. For over a decade, the Maharishi Yogi has taken out full-page newspaper ads to announce that war could be abolished by transcendental meditation.

The word *millennium* means a thousand years, just as the word century means a hundred. As this is written, we are just beginning the third millennium in our calendar, based on the assumed birth year of Jesus of Nazareth. But figuratively, the *millennium* is an indefinite future era in which society shall have been perfected and evil removed from the world.[1]

Millennial movements that looked forward to a total transformation of the secular world have marked the entire history of Christianity down to the present day. Islam too has had such movements since its founding. The French Revolution turned into a secular millennial movement after its initial success, began a new calendar and installed the Goddess of Reason along with the guillotine. In the ensuing two hundred years, there have been a great many political movements that promised to transform the world out of all recognition, to restore the natural goodness of man, and almost as an afterthought, to abolish war. Utopian socialism, Comtean positivism, scientific socialism, anarchism, fascism, Soviet technocracy, the counterculture of the 1960s, and dozens of obscure cults have held forth this promise. All the branches of Marxism, including Soviet and Chinese communism, have been millennial, promising eventually to bring about a world cleansed of all the troubles that stem from capitalism, including crime and war.

Given the extreme threat presented by existing weapons of mass destruction and the efficiency of the global communication network, it is conceivable that some new anti-war movement might sweep through the interconnected media of the modern world and lead to dramatic changes in the world system. Such an event is perhaps most likely after a nuclear catastrophe.

But should it occur, it will not usher in the promised millennium because the fundamental offer held out by millennial movements is a sociological impossibility. That offer involves the abolition of social conflict in favor of universal cooperation. But conflict and cooperation are not separable processes: in-group cooperation implies inter-group conflict and vice versa. A social system without conflict is a contradiction in terms.

On the other hand, a significant modification of the war system in a response to a millennial movement is easily imaginable. In some of the world's most advanced industrial countries—notably the Scandinavian countries and New Zealand—public opinion is totally intolerant of nuclear weapons. When and if a few of the thousands of existing nuclear weapons are fired in anger, the threat they pose may come to be viewed in the same way worldwide. But the organizational means to bring about that result are not yet in place.

Peace through Revolution

In the aftermath of the collapse of Marxism-Leninism as a secular faith, it has been almost forgotten that it promised the total abolition of war, as an inevitable consequence of the disappearance of the bourgeois state. As Marx and Engels wrote in the *Communist Manifesto:*

> To the extent that the exploitation of one individual by another is put to an end, the exploitation of one nation by another will also be put to an end. To the extent that the antagonism between classes within the nation vanishes, the hostility of one nation to another will come to an end ([1848] 1961, 31).

Pending the disappearance of the state, which would make war impossible, Marxist theory held that proletarians of all nationalities had common interests; their mobilization against each other was a form of bourgeois oppression. Moreover, existing states were driven to war by the dynamics of capitalist exploitation; when capitalism was overthrown, there would be no motives for international war.

> The more capitalism develops, the more the need for raw materials arises; the more bitter competition becomes and the more feverishly the hunt for raw materials proceeds throughout the whole world, the more desperate becomes the struggle for the acquisition of colonies (Lenin [1916] 1929, 66).

With the appearance of a communist national government in 1917, it became axiomatic for communists that future communist governments would be natural allies, if not dependents, of the Soviet Union and that war between communist governments was inconceivable. These beliefs were held with equal fervor by anti-communists, especially in the United States; they viewed communism as a monolithic evil even after the repudiation of Soviet influence by Yugoslavia and China in the 1950s, and the active hostilities that later developed between the Soviet Union and China, Bulgaria and Albania, and China and Vietnam. In practice, communist governments turned out to deal with each other in much the same way as other governments and to make the same claims to absolute sovereignty.

Peace Through Democracy

Towards the end of the eighteenth century, Immanuel Kant proposed that perpetual peace could be achieved by a shift from monarchic to republican government because public opinion would restrain the rulers of republics from going to war. Towards the end of the twentieth century, American scholars noted the recent absence of wars *between* democratic states (Russett 1993) although the same states had been extensively involved in wars with non-democratic regimes. The assumption that pairs of democracies were somehow inoculated against mutual hostilities became part of U.S. foreign policy during the Clinton administration and still enjoys a large following.

Critics of peace through democracy dismiss the phenomenon as a coincidence based on the accident that the democracies were on the same side, or neutral, in the major conflicts of the twentieth century (Gowa 1999). They argue that no plausible mechanism had been proposed to explain it otherwise. It could hardly be the restraining influence of public opinion since no such restraint had inhibited democracies from going to war with non-democracies. When the inquiry is pushed back into earlier centuries and even into the Greco-Roman world, the problem of identifying democracies and republics becomes much more challenging and students of the question are forced to introduce fine distinctions among different types of republic (Weart 1998). For the time being, the prospect of a world made peaceable by universal democratization remains intriguing but highly uncertain.

Rational Pacifism

Since the rise of the European state, there have been innumerable attempts to undermine the war system by rational argument. Three principal arguments have been advanced in the past: that the war system is incompatible with Christian or natural morality; that its costs greatly exceed its benefits; and that it does not serve the interests of those who do the fighting.[2]

Since the advent of nuclear weapons, a new argument has been convincingly advanced: that the short-term political goals of nuclear deterrence are not worth the long-term risks (Schell 1982, 2000; Bundy, et al. 1993; and many others). Typically, such arguments are convincing but unavailing. The reasonable opinions of individuals exert very little leverage on the institutionalized practices of national governments, and war fever is remarkably effective in dissolving reasonable objections. Charles Sumner, the most eloquent American pacifist of the nineteenth century, became the leading Union hawk during the Civil War. In August 1914, the French and German socialists, totally committed to pacifism only a few weeks earlier, unanimously voted for war in their respective parliaments. The powerful "nuclear freeze" movement of the 1970s in the U.S. stopped the development of nuclear power plants but had no perceptible effect on the continued development of nuclear weapons.

World Empires

We know much more about world empires than about other forms of supranational government because history presents numerous examples of empires founded on military conquest that encompassed "known worlds" that were far more extensive, in terms of travel and communication time and cultural diversity than the entire planet is today. The empires of Alexander, Hadrian, Mohammed, Charlemagne, Genghis Khan, and Charles V were all on that scale.

The Pax Romana was the most durable of these arrangements. Its elements included dual citizenship, strong garrisons posted throughout the empire, systems of imperial justice and imperial taxation superimposed on local systems, effective means of long-distance travel and communication, and a universal coinage.

Describing Rome in the second century A.D., Edward Gibbon wrote:

> Domestic peace and union were the natural consequences of the moderate and comprehensive policies embraced by the Romans

. . . the obedience of the Roman world was uniform, voluntary and permanent. The vanquished nations, blended into one great people, resigned the hope, nay even the wish, of resuming their independence and scarcely considered their own existence as distinct from the existence of Rome. The established authority of the emperors pervaded without an effort the wide extent of their dominions, and was exercised with the same facility on the banks of the Thames, or of the Nile, as those of the Tiber . . . the civil magistrate seldom required the aid of military force ([1776] 1932, 38).

A thousand years later, an Italian traveler described the even larger Chinese empire ruled by Kublai Khan in somewhat similar terms:

Quarrels, blows, combats, and bloodshed, then so frequent in Europe, were not witnessed, even among their deepest potations. Honesty was everywhere conspicuous; their wagons and other property were secure without locks or guards; and if any of their cattle strayed, arrangements were made by which they were speedily recovered. Notwithstanding the frequent scarcity of victuals, they were generous in relieving those in greater want than themselves (Rubroquis, quoted by Komroff 1953, xvi).

In modern times, there have been three serious attempts to create a world empire: those of Napoleon Bonaparte, Adolf Hitler, and Josef Stalin. Napoleon had the advantages of a patriotic mass army; a rational administrative structure; the powerful appeal of Liberty, Equality and Fraternity; a skillfully adapted Roman model; and his own military genius. But having gained effective control of most of Europe, Napoleon was checked by his inability to match British sea power. This put a stop to his overseas ambitions. He was then defeated in his ill-advised invasion of Russia.

Yet the Napoleonic formula for conquest followed by pacification was so effective that in the 100 days that followed his return from exile in Elba, he was able to retake power in France and might have regained control of Europe if the battle of Waterloo had gone the other way.

The Napoleonic empire, despite its prefects and legions and eagles, was only partly designed on the Roman model, and that may explain its failure. The division of power between the imperial government and the subordinate kingdoms ruled by the emperor's relatives and clients was never clear. The autonomy of local institutions was only intermittently respected. Foreign contingents were never fully assimilated into the Grand Army; it remained essentially French. The separation of military and civil administration, which was so central in the Roman formula, was never achieved.

The short-lived empire of Adolf Hitler, advertised as "The Thousand-Year Reich," was the first military empire in Europe since the rise of ancient Rome that did not draw on Roman symbolism or practice. When it came to historic models, the Nazis identified themselves with the Germanic tribes that had resisted and eventually sacked Rome. But they were not much impressed with historic models or with theories of effective governance. They preferred to exalt brute force. They treated the populations of the territories they occupied so roughly that they aroused hatred and provoked armed resistance even in countries like the Netherlands and Italy where they initially had considerable support. The Nazi empire became difficult to govern as fast as it was founded but its ultimate collapse was brought about by the same factors that doomed Napoleon's empire, the inability of its naval and air forces to gain command of the English channel and protect an invasion of Britain, and the destruction of another invulnerable army by the Russian winter and Russian persistence. Yet it had acquired so much power that it took the enormous industrial and manpower resources of the United States to finally bring it down.

As the Nazi empire disappeared from the scene, the Soviet Union acquired all of its eastern provinces, either by direct military occupation or by helping the local communists to seize power under the protection of the Red Army. The three Baltic republics were absorbed into the Soviet Union. Poland, Rumania, Hungary, Czechoslovakia, East Germany, Bulgaria, Yugoslavia, Albania, China, North Korea, and North Vietnam all fell under communist rule, which meant that they were initially subservient to the Comintern in Moscow, an organization founded to direct and coordinate the communist bloc as a whole. At the same time, there were large, well-organized communist parties potentially capable of seizing power in France, Italy, India, Vietnam, Indonesia, and in a number of African and Latin American states.

It was taken for granted on both sides of the Iron Curtain around 1950 that the object of Soviet policy was the establishment of a communist world empire. In the words of Joseph Stalin himself, the USSR was "the living prototype of the future union of peoples in a single world economic system" (Mendel 1961, 267). It was also taken for granted that the Comintern would be able to control all the communist states from Moscow. Stalin and others spoke of "the voluntary amalgamation of socialist nations."

The defection of Yugoslavia and China from the communist bloc towards the end of the 1950s began to raise some doubts about the feasibility of this project of world empire. But there was still the disquieting fact that no state had ever adopted communism and then abandoned it. That condition lasted for another thirty years and then ended overnight.

During the brief period when the United States had a monopoly of the atomic bomb, there was a flurry of discussion about using it to impose world order, but the idea was never taken seriously, and could not have been, given the countervailing power of the Soviet Union.

For the time being, the project of world empire is in abeyance. No state or combination of states has either the military means or the ideological basis to embark on world conquest, and the wide dissemination of nuclear weapons makes its achievement inconceivable, except as the outcome of a large-scale nuclear war. But if such a war occurred, the project might revive in one form or another.

World Federation

The idea that a voluntary union of states under a federal government could be capable of suppressing war has a long history and a number of federations have actually been formed and endured, including the Swiss Confederation, the United Provinces of the Netherlands, and the United States of America.

The necessary features of an effective federation, as set forth by Alexander Hamilton, James Madison, and John Jay in the Federalist Papers ([1787] 1952), are:

- a single military establishment under unified command;
- courts of law with jurisdiction over individuals and officials of member states;
- the power to tax without the consent of member states;
- an unequivocal commitment to protect member states against rebellion;
- a representative assembly to make laws; and
- an executive to enforce the laws and to command the armed forces.

For practical political reasons, they failed to mention that it must be indissoluble, and the failure to clarify that point led to a difference of opinion between North and South that was very costly to resolve.

It is not easy to visualize how these conditions could be met in an association of states that did not share the same political values. In the three instances of successful federation mentioned above, the founding states shared a common history, occupied contiguous territories, and sought protection against their common enemies. But even with all these advantages, they were not completely successful in suppressing internal war. And out of more than a dozen federations of states founded since 1945, only the tiny United Arab Emirates and the tinier Federated States of Micronesia have survived intact.[3]

There is strong reason to believe that war will remain endemic until the groups that wage it are brought under a common authority.

> The final outcome [of advancing civilization] should be a rule of law that applies to which all . . . have contributed by a sacrifice of their instincts, and which leaves no one . . . at the mercy of brute force (Freud [1930] 1961, 85).

Many of the delegates to the Versailles peace congress in 1919 thought that they *had* established a world federation when they voted for the League of Nations. Indeed, the U.S. Senate's rejection of the Versailles treaty was based on the widespread belief that it put American armed forces under foreign control. There were similar illusions when the United Nations Organization was formed at San Francisco in 1945. But it became obvious almost immediately that neither of these international organizations had *any* of the essential features of a real federation.

Weak middle-class movements favoring world federation have been active in western Europe and North America since the early nineteenth century. They have never made much headway against nationalism on the one side and radical internationalism on the other. The difficulty of finding a broad constituency is compounded by large, unanswered questions in the federalist program—whether the proposed federation would guarantee the regimes, however brutal, and the boundaries, however unjust, of member states, and how it would respond to insurrections and coups. The advocates of world federation have focused their attention on the disadvantages of war and given relatively little attention to the problem of devising a workable constitution. The constitutions that have been proposed include elaborate schemes of representation, but ignore these unanswered questions (see Clark and Sohn 1966).

It appears axiomatic that a world government capable of repressing international war would have to limit the armed forces of its member states and to deploy massive armed forces of its own (Caplow 1977). None of the world's current military powers has indicated any willingness to accept these conditions.

Such consent might be forthcoming, however, under other circumstances: in the aftermath of another world war, or as part of a general reorganization of the international system jointly sponsored by five or six of the world's most powerful governments. The slow but continuing progress of the European Union towards a federal structure can be viewed as a possible model of how that might occur.

Another possibility is the development of a partial federal authority, limited to the regulation of weapons of mass destruction, along the lines of the International Atomic Energy Agency but with much greater powers. This too would require the joint sponsorship of the major nuclear weapons states but it might be much easier to achieve.

For Further Reading

Edward Bellamy, *Looking Backward*, New York: Dover, 1996. Originally published in 1888.

Murray Forsyth, *Unions of States: The Theory and Practice of Confederation*, New York: Holmes and Meier, 1981.

Notes

[1] From the book of Revelations in the New Testament whose author had a vision of how the thousand-year reign of Christ on earth would be followed by a new heaven and a new earth, where "there shall be no more death, neither sorrow, nor crying, neither shall there be any more pain" (21:4).

[2] See, among many other classics in the vast literature of rational pacifism, Desiderius Erasmus [1517] 1946, Jean-Jacques Rousseau [1756] 1962, Charles Sumner 1850, Edward Bellamy [1888] 1996, and George Bernard Shaw [1894] 1969.

[3] The failures include the Federation of Rhodesia and Nyasaland, the United Arab Republic, the United Arab States, the United States of Africa, the Federation of South Arabia, the Malaysian Federation, the Federation of the West Indies.

13

Peacekeeping Organizations

The central problem of military organizations, as we have seen, is how to persuade or coerce their members into risking death or disfigurement for the benefit of the collectivity they serve. Formal military organizations solve this problem by methods that are more coercive than persuasive. They bring enormous pressures to bear on recalcitrant members.

The central problem of peacekeeping organizations is how to persuade or coerce their member states into risking some of their own interests for the benefit of a larger collectivity. Most peacekeeping organizations have tried to solve this problem by methods that are more persuasive than coercive. They have not been able to exert much pressure on recalcitrant members, and that may be why the long history of peacekeeping organizations shows so few successes.

Leagues of Princes

An early proposal for a peacekeeping league of Christian princes was written in 1306 by Pierre Dubois and sent to King Philip of France. Dubois proposed a league that remarkably resembled the twentieth-century League of Nations. Its council would arbitrate quarrels among its members and impose settlements, but without much machinery for accomplishing these purposes. Dubois' theme was that the wars of the previous century between Christian princes had been wasteful and unprofitable and accounted for their defeat by the Saracens in the later crusades. Moreover, he argued that if the king of France were to organize such a league, it would strengthen him against the Pope and the Emperor. We will find this theme in almost every later plan of this type, right down to the United Nations Charter. Nearly always, the goal is to prevent war *and* to give some advantage to the state or states that take the initiative.

A much more elaborate peace plan was drafted by another Frenchman in 1461 and circulated as a draft treaty by King George of Bohemia. The fundamental idea was the same as Dubois' but it was worked out in much more detail. There was to be a council of princes that seldom or never met, an assembly of delegates that stayed in permanent session but moved to a different capital every five years, an international court of justice and even a secretariat. It would have an army of its own, and receive a fixed proportion of the revenues of member states. It would settle disputes by mediation whenever possible and by force as a last resort. A few princes signed up but most demurred and the project was abandoned (Vanecek 1964).

Other efforts followed. Half a century later, England's Cardinal Wolsey worked out a peacekeeping treaty that was actually signed by the rulers of England, France, and Spain and by the Pope, but the league thus formed had virtually no structure and soon fell apart.

At the end of the sixteenth century, a similar project called the Grand Design was attributed to Henry IV of France. It envisaged a league of fifteen European powers—five hereditary monarchs, three elected monarchs, four republics, the Pope, and the Holy Roman Emperor. There was to be a supreme council and a number of regional councils, controlling a huge army. The formation of the league was to be accompanied by a large-scale redistribution of territories and populations which, not surprisingly, would benefit France at the expense of Austria.

A little later, an interesting plan by an obscure writer named Emeric Cruce was published in Paris. His peacekeeping league would have a council permanently seated in Venice. What makes it interesting is that besides the usual roster of European powers,

Cruce wanted to include the rulers of China, Japan, Tartary, Muscovy, Mongolia, and Morocco. This was the first proposal for a global peacekeeping league.

Another seventeenth-century author whose work drew some attention was William Penn, the founder of Pennsylvania. His peacekeeping league centered around a European Parliament with limited powers, not unlike the European Parliament that sits in Brussels today. Penn's leading idea was that the relationship among sovereigns ought to be governed by the same type of social contract as the relationship among their subjects.

Dozens of new proposals for peacekeeping leagues saw print in the eighteenth century. The most impressive was the work of the Abbé de St. Pierre, a huge tome called *A Project for Perpetual Peace in Europe*, published in 1713. St. Pierre approached the design of an effective peacekeeping league as a problem in social mechanics, and in the long line of such projects, his is the first that seems to make sociological sense. His league—limited to the European powers of his time—would be indissoluble and heavily armed. Member states would be taxed according to their wealth, but each would contribute the same number of soldiers to the common army. The league would have representatives in each capital city and every sizable province to report preparations for war or other breaches of the peace. Its own courts would adjudicate international disputes, commercial as well as political. Its council would have the authority to enact binding laws, levy taxes, regulate markets, and set trade standards. St. Pierre's peacekeeping league had two features that all previous, and many later ones lacked: it would guarantee the boundaries and the constitution of every member state, and it would exercise authority over individuals as well as governments. As these features imply, it would undertake to suppress civil wars as well as international wars.

St. Pierre's plan was widely circulated. Frederick the Great commented on it in a letter to a friend, saying, "All that it would take to make it work would be the consent of Europe and other such trifles." Jean-Jacques Rousseau wrote a synopsis of the project ([1756] 1962) which was ultimately even more influential. One of his comments seems to echo King Frederick: "If the league could be established for a single day," he said, "it might last forever." But he did not expect that to happen.

Nevertheless, most of the essential elements of St. Pierre's project found their way into one important eighteenth-century document: the Constitution of the United States. The only missing element was that it said nothing about the union being indissoluble and that omission, as we know, led to serious trouble about seventy years later.

The Holy Alliance and the Concert of Europe

The network of alliances that developed around the Congress of Vienna in 1815 included (in the original form of the Holy Alliance) a peacekeeping league modeled on St. Pierre's *Project of Perpetual Peace*[1] and including its essential elements: protection for the regimes and borders of member states, a common military force, the compulsory adjudication of international disputes, and a jurisdiction extending beyond member states to individuals. The project was quickly overwhelmed by political considerations, especially the resistance of Britain and Austria to the threat of Russian domination that they perceived in an organization founded by the Tsar, and the Holy Alliance eventually acquired quite different purposes—the defense of absolutism and the suppression of dissent. But the amorphous league that survived, variously known as the European Confederation or the Concert of Europe, acting through periodic conferences rather than a fixed organization, did keep Europe relatively peaceful from 1815 to 1914.

The League of Nations

In the following century, another group of victorious allies met in Paris to decide the future of Europe and the world. This time, the campaign for a peacekeeping league was led by Woodrow Wilson, the president who had brought the United States into World War I and given the war a new set of purposes in his Fourteen Points.

At his insistence, the Covenant of the League of Nations was included in the peace treaty ending World War I that was signed at Versailles in 1919. The League was intended to put a permanent stop to international war, and to exercise much more authority than it ever achieved. Indeed, the principal reason why the U.S. Senate failed to ratify the treaty was that it supposedly allowed League officials to call up the armed forces of the United States without the authorization of Congress.

But the League lacked the necessary organs for effective peace-keeping. It had no autonomous power to tax member states or to raise military forces. Membership was voluntary and withdrawal easy. The decisions of the League's Council had to be unanimous, which meant that it was helpless when defied by a state that held a Council seat. Moreover, the organization relied on international public opinion to enforce its decisions. The clause in the Covenant that called for general disarmament under the League's supervision became an instant dead letter. The impotence of the League was apparent almost from the start. Most of the significant peacekeeping initiatives of the 1920s, like the Washington Naval Conference and the Locarno Pact, took place under other auspices, and the League's inability to cope with clear violations of the Covenant when in the 1930s Japan invaded Manchuria and then China; Italy invaded and annexed Abyssinia; Germany defied the provisions of the Versailles treaty; and the Soviet Union invaded Finland, hastening the onset of World War II.

The United Nations

The founders of the United Nations (UN) wanted to avoid repli-cating the familiar defects of the League of Nations, but were constrained by the political circumstances of 1945, and the developing conflict between the U.S. and the USSR to create an organization that was essentially the League under a new name. Like its predecessor, it had no coercive power, whether fiscal, political or military, and was hampered by the requirement of unanimity (achieved in this case by giving each of the permanent members of the Security Council an absolute veto). The peacekeeping achievements of the UN have been meager but for various reasons; it has had a far more salient role in international affairs than the League and has accumulated numerous functions not foreseen by its founders.

During the first half century of its existence, the UN was involved in scores of international conflicts and recently, it has increasingly become involved in internal conflicts as well, but its peacekeeping efforts have been successful only on those rare occasions (e.g., the Suez crisis, the Yom Kippur War, and the expulsion of Iraq from Kuwait) when Washington and Moscow adopted a common policy in a crisis. The veto enjoyed by the permanent members of the Security Council and the ludicrous overrepresentation of mini-states in the General Assembly, have so far prevented the UN from evolving into an effective peace-keeping league, although it provides a useful forum for negoti-ation. With three significant exceptions—the Korean War, the Katanga War, and the Gulf War—the collective security activities of the UN were until very recently limited to truce observation by tiny, multinational forces. About 200 interstate and internecine wars involving UN members, some of them very bloody, have been fought since 1945.

Since the end of the Cold War and the proclamation of a "New World Order" by the United States during the first Bush admin-istration, the United Nations has assumed a new prominence in international affairs. Numerous conflicts have drawn UN political involvement and UN peacekeeping forces have been deployed around the world on an unprecedented scale. Moreover, the character of UN units has changed from token infantry forces from tiny nations like Fiji to much heavier units from Western nations, such as the allied contingents in Bosnia.

It seems clear that since the end of the Cold War the functions of the UN have changed in a way not contemplated by its Charter so that it has recently been more concerned with the internal conflicts of its member states than with their external relations. In the early 1990s, the UN intervened in the Yugoslavian civil wars, in Iraq's repression of its civilian population, in a continuing crisis in Haiti, in the Liberian civil war, in the anarchic situation in Somalia and in the political reconstruction of Cambodia. In the late 1990s, it became heavily involved in African refugee and development problems. More recently, it has functioned as the de facto government of Kosovo and of East Timor. The results have been mixed but seem to have enhanced the influence of the organization (Damrosch 1993 and Traub 2000).

The future effectiveness of the United Nations in preventing large-scale war remains quite unpredictable. It probably depends upon:

- the willingness of the major powers at some future time to commit significant armed forces to operations over which they have no direct control or alternatively, the recruitment of a UN army;

- a reform of the structure of the UN to reflect political and economic realities, so that, for example, Japan and Germany acquire permanent seats on the Security Council, and voting rights in the General Assembly are adjusted to take some reasonable account of population, perhaps by combining the least significant states into regional blocs for purposes of representation;

- the establishment, by treaty or otherwise, of mandatory jurisdiction for the International Court of Justice, which for want of that necessary attribute, is almost completely inactive; and

- development of a regular tax base that would release the UN from dependence on the voluntary contributions of members.

The Lessons Learned

After each of the three great wars of the past two centuries, in 1815, 1919, and 1945, there was a serious attempt to create a league of sovereign states that would impose perpetual peace upon its members: the alliances that emerged from the Congress of Vienna in 1815, the League of Nations created by the Treaty of Versailles in 1919, and the United Nations founded at San Francisco in 1945. In each case, the most powerful of the victorious allies—Russia in 1815, France in 1919, the United

States in 1945—proposed to equip the new league with some of the stronger options and in each case these proposals were successfully resisted by other states. Each of the three leagues lacked the means to carry out its peacekeeping objectives. The European Confederation degenerated into a balance of power that opposed Russia and Prussia to France, Austria, and Britain. The League of Nations collapsed when it proved unable to restrain Japan from invading China in 1931 and Italy from conquering Abyssinia in 1936. The United Nations survived, but only by changing its function from the prevention of war to the negotiation and monitoring of truces.

There were some remarkable parallels in the three foregoing attempts to establish an association of sovereign states capable of suppressing war. Some of the same issues, like the boundaries of Poland, the representation of compound states, and the acceptability of regional alliances, were hotly debated on each occasion. Each of the three organizations ultimately abandoned its initial purpose of enforcing collective security and developed into a facility for diplomatic negotiations and for the performance of auxiliary tasks.

For Further Reading

Inis L. Claude, *Swords into Ploughshares: The Problems and Progress of International Organization*, 4th ed., New York: Random House, 1971.

Michael Howard, *The Invention of Peace: Reflections on War and International Order,* New Haven: Yale University Press, 2001.

Notes

[1] The resemblance of the Holy Alliance in its original form to St. Pierre's project was not accidental. The architect of the Alliance, Alexander I of Russia, had a Swiss tutor who was a disciple of Rousseau and thereby indirectly of St. Pierre.

14

Arms Control

Arms control is a relatively new activity. It has three interconnected branches: disarmament, the regulation of arms races, and
the prohibition of atrocious weapons.

Disarmament

Although the disarming of the vanquished is as old as war, the
first attempt to promote general disarmament was made at the
Hague conference of 1899. It led nowhere, but since that time
the concept of disarmament has been part of the conventional
rhetoric of war-and-peace. Disarmament appeared again as one of
President Wilson's Fourteen Points, which called for the reduction
of armaments to "the lowest point consistent with national safety."
This wording was included in the Covenant of the League of
Nations and linked to collective security. Article 8 of the Covenant
read in part:

1. The Members of the League recognize that the maintenance
   of peace requires the reduction of national armaments to
   the lowest point consistent with national safety and the
   enforcement by common action of international obligations.

2. The Council, taking account of the geographical situation
   and circumstances of each State, shall formulate plans

for such reduction for the consideration and action of the several Governments.

3.   Such plans shall be subject to reconsideration and revision at least every ten years.

4.   After these plans shall have been adopted by the several Governments, the limits of armaments therein fixed shall not be exceeded without the concurrence of the Council.

In conferences held over the next 15 years, the League sought and failed to find a disarmament formula acceptable to its members. France, which had the largest army, was unwilling to disarm without guarantees from Britain and the United States that they would participate in a possible future war against Germany— guarantees which they were unwilling to give. Germany, which had been disarmed by the Versailles treaty as a "first step" towards general disarmament, eventually used the failure of the Allies to disarm as an excuse to repudiate the Versailles treaty and rebuild its military machine.

The Regulation of Arms Races

Meanwhile, a competitive effort was proceeding on a parallel track. Some of the U.S. senators who had opposed the League, came forward with what they regarded as a more promising project—the reduction of naval power. At the Washington Naval Conference of 1921, the owners of the world's important navies—Great Britain, the U.S., France, Italy, and Japan—agreed to suspend the construction of battleships for ten years, to limit their size and equipment and to adjust their numbers so that the British and American navies would be equal, the French navy a little smaller, and the Italian and Japanese navies equal and smaller still. The parties did not agree to end their arms race but wrote new rules for it. No sooner had the Conference adjourned than all five navies set about constructing and upgrading aircraft carriers, cruisers, destroyers, and submarines, which were not covered by the agreement. Before long, they were building cruisers more powerful than the restricted battleships. At subsequent conferences in 1921, 1927, and 1935, the rules of the race were repeatedly rewritten and eventually nullified by an escalator clause that allowed any signatory to exceed the agreed limits if it judged its security to be threatened.

The disarmament effort began all over again when the United Nations Charter was adopted in 1944. It included (and still includes) Article 26:

> In order to promote the establishment and maintenance of international peace and security with the least diversion for armaments of the world's human and economic resources, the Security Council shall be responsible for formulating, with the assistance of the Military Staff Committee referred to in article 47, plans to be submitted to the Members of the United Nations for the establishment of a system for the regulation of armaments.

At its very first session in 1946, the United Nations General Assembly unanimously passed a resolution that established a commission to plan for the elimination "of atomic weapons and all other weapons adaptable to mass destruction." Later in that year, the U.S. submitted to that commission a proposal, generally known as the Baruch Plan, which called for the creation of an international Authority to control uranium and thorium in the ground or in stockpiles, to inspect and license all atomic activities, to have rights of access and inspection everywhere, and to punish atomic offenders.

Since the United States still had a monopoly of atomic weapons, most Americans thought this was a fair and generous offer. To the Russians, who were hard at work to break the American monopoly, it looked more like a sinister plot, since the plan would have permitted the United States to set its own timetable for turning over its atomic installations and weapons, while calling for the Authority to have immediate and unlimited access to Soviet facilities. As the Cold War heated up during 1946, the effort to prevent a nuclear arms race was unceremoniously abandoned.

At international conferences during the next 30 years, there were several attempts to formulate programs for "general and complete disarmament." The term became so familiar that it was shortened to GCD. None of these efforts were meant to be taken seriously.

But there was again a parallel track. After years of intense negotiation, the United States and the Soviet Union announced the Strategic Arms Limitation Treaty of 1972 (SALT I). Like the naval agreements of the 1920s, it was designed to regulate the ongoing arms race, not to end it. SALT I set a five year ceiling on the number of intercontinental ballistic missiles that each government might deploy, but did not put any limits on submarine-launched or short-range missiles. Both sides immediately rearranged their research and development efforts to take advantage of the new loopholes. The SALT II agreement of 1978 (never ratified but obeyed anyway) fixed the number of long-range delivery vehicles for nuclear warheads without limiting the number of warheads. Almost overnight the U.S. developed a system for putting multiple warheads on a single missile,[1] and the USSR caught up a few months later.

Another U.S.-Soviet agreement in 1987 called for the removal of the entire class of intermediate range nuclear missiles from their deployed positions in Europe, the actual destruction of the removed missiles, and the inactivation of production facilities, all in the presence of inspectors from the other side. Research and development immediately shifted to the upgrading of the short range nuclear missiles and cruise missiles not covered by the treaty, until these efforts were interrupted by the collapse of the Soviet Union.

The regulation of an ongoing arms race by mutual agreement is clearly advantageous for all concerned. It permits the parties to concentrate on the development of advanced weapons and provides more accurate information for strategic planning. But the agreement breaks down as soon as one of the parties achieves the superiority within the rules that all of them are trying to achieve, or is thought to be doing so.

The case is a little different for the series of agreements entered into by the United States with the Soviet Union in its last days, and then with Russia and other successor states, which represent the winding down of an arms race whose terms have changed beyond recognition.

In the Strategic Arms Reduction Treaty of 1991 (START I), the U.S. and the USSR agreed upon a reduction of their respective nuclear arsenals to approximately 7,000 strategic warheads on each side, with full access and inspection by both sides. After the disappearance of the Soviet Union in August 1991, negotiations with Russia led to the START II treaty signed in January 1993. It called for the reduction by each side of its strategic arsenal to 3,000–3,500 warheads (less than half of the number allowed under START I) and the elimination of land-based missiles with multiple warheads. Other agreements involved technical and financial assistance to Russia and other successor states for the destruction of nuclear warheads, the suspension of underground testing and, in 1994, the de-targeting of the missiles that for decades had threatened the instant destruction of every city on both sides.

This movement back from the brink is an enormous accomplishment, but it does not come anywhere close to nuclear disarmament. The number of nuclear warheads remaining in the American and Russian arsenals is more than sufficient to destroy every city and sizable town.

The Prohibition of Atrocious Weapons

The regulation by multilateral treaty of weapons considered atrocious began with the Declaration of St. Petersburg in 1868, which prohibited the military use of explosive rifle bullets that made untreatable wounds. "Poisoned weapons" were banned by the Hague Convention of 1899; noxious gases by a multilateral treaty among the victorious Allies in 1922; and "asphyxiating and poisonous gases," and bacteriological agents by the Geneva Protocol of 1925, signed by most of the world's governments. The latter prohibition was respected, with a few exceptions (notoriously, the Italian campaign against Abyssinia) until the Iran-Iraq War of the 1980s.

These treaties prohibited the use, but not the manufacture of chemical and biological weapons, and were generally interpreted to permit reprisal in kind. Consequently, the principal military powers, including especially the U.S. and the former Soviet Union, continued to manufacture and store chemical weapons in huge quantities. But the manufacture and stockpiling of biological weapons was banned by a multilateral treaty in 1972, subsequently ratified by 110 nations. Research on biological weapons was not prohibited at all and continues to this day. The 1993 Chemical Weapons Convention, which was signed by 110 nations, including the United States and entered into force in 1997, required the signatories to destroy their existing chemical weapons stockpiles.

One arms control effort that has been partially successful is the nuclear non-proliferation regime. The multilateral Non-Proliferation Treaty of 1968 was a joint project of the U.S. and the USSR, whereby non-nuclear weapons states agreed not to acquire nuclear weapons in return for a commitment by the superpowers to reduce their own nuclear arsenals. The superpowers proceeded instead to increase their nuclear arsenals to unimagined levels but the non-proliferation regime, administered by the International Atomic Energy Agency (IAEA) in Vienna, nevertheless had some moderating effect on the spread of nuclear weapons. Although the IAEA is undermanned and has only limited authority over the production, shipment and use of nuclear weapons material, the number of states voluntarily subjecting themselves to its jurisdiction has grown steadily, to 182 signatory nations today. Only four states remain outside. The IAEA has retarded, although not prevented, the acquisition of nuclear weapons by non-nuclear weapons states and facilitated the diffusion of peaceful nuclear technology.

The IAEA has no compulsory power; it cannot inspect any installation without the consent of the government to which the installation belongs, so that it is extremely easy for a government with a clandestine nuclear program to conceal it by denying access to the Agency's inspectors. Two episodes in the early 1990s highlighted the lack of fit between the meager resources and powers of the IAEA and the critical tasks which it is supposed to perform. Iraq, although subject to the non-proliferation regime, was able to conceal an ambitious program of nuclear weapons development so well that even after defeat in the Gulf War of 1991 had opened the country to compulsory inspection, it took more than two years to locate the parts and pieces of its nuclear program and probably not all of them. North Korea, another member of the non-proliferation regime, may have gone further and actually developed a few nuclear weapons. Although IAEA inspection of North Korea was resumed in 1994 on the basis of an agreement negotiated with the United States, the level of North Korea's nuclear development remains uncertain to this day.

Aside from the weakness of the IAEA's control measures, adherence to the non-proliferation regime is voluntary. Although there are some inducements for membership, such as easier availability of nuclear materials and technology for peaceful purposes, there is nothing to prevent states that do not want to be constrained from remaining outside and nothing to prevent a member state from withdrawing.

For Further Reading

McGeorge Bundy, William J. Crowe, Jr., and Sidney D. Drell, *Reducing Nuclear Danger: The Road Away from the Brink*, New York: Council of Foreign Relations Press, 1993.

Jonathan Schell, "The Folly of Arms Control," *Foreign Affairs*, September–October, 2000.

Notes

[1] This was called MIRVing, from the acronym for Multiple Independent Reentry Vehicles.

15

Postscript

The Cold War, as we saw, divided the war system into two blocs and nuclear deterrence prevented any general conflict between them, although it provoked and sustained limited local conflicts between forces supported by the two blocs.

With the disintegration of the Warsaw Pact (disbanded as a military alliance in 1991), the rise of German and Japanese power, the slow movement of the European Union towards federation, the fragmentation of the Soviet Union and of Yugoslavia, the continued instability in the Middle East and Indonesia, and the interruption of economic progress in Africa, the configuration of the war system has become more complex and potential conflicts more numerous and unpredictable.

There are clearly identifiable perils in the chaos of the post-Cold War era:

The enormous nuclear arsenals accumulated by the United States and the Soviet Union during their long confrontation are still in place, and indeed are still being modernized and improved, although they have lost their strategic rationale.

Nuclear proliferation, although slowed by the non-proliferation regime, continues nevertheless. It is virtually certain that "irresponsible" military dictators and terrorist factions will eventually acquire nuclear capabilities. Acts of nuclear terrorism, either state-sponsored or factional, will then occur. Adequate measures for coping with such events are not in place.

The war system is growing in all of its non-nuclear aspects: the number of armed states, the size and cost of their armed forces, the sophistication and lethality of their military equipment, and the frequency of conflict. Meanwhile, war grows more damaging to the combatants and non-combatants directly involved and more dangerous for third parties as well, since every local conflict carries some risk, however small, of sparking off a more general conflict and eventually a nuclear exchange.

The presence of strong military establishments in weak, developing countries encourages and supports despotic forms of government, genocidal modes of conflict resolution, the export of terrorism and the growth of violent and fanatical social movements.

Workable solutions can be imagined, however. It lies within the power of a handful of strong states to inhibit the military development of weaker states, since it is the strong states that provide them with credits, weapons, training, and technology. But to do that without arousing excessive resistance, the strong states will have to reduce their own commitments to the war system, and refuse to conduct their own conflicts through proxies. Under today's conditions, such measures appear potentially feasible and much less dangerous to the national security of the strong states than the preservation of the war system in its existing form.

Appendix

An Outline for the
Analysis of Particular Wars

There are two parts to this appendix, the outline for analyzing wars, and an example of the application of the outline to a particular war, in this case, the Soviet-German war of 1941–1945.

The Outline

I. Introduction

II. Chronology

    A.   Previous relations of the parties
    B.   Precipitating incidents
    C.   Identity of decision-makers
    D.   War aims
    E.   Principal engagements and outcomes of the war
    F.   Reasons for ending war

III. Roles of Third Party States

    A.   Mediation
    B.   Incitement
    C.   Assistance

IV. Logistics

A. Number of troops involved on each side
B. Principal weapons used
C. Casualty rates: killed, died, wounded, missing
D. Prisoners and deserters
E. Civilian casualties and non-military damage

V. Societal Support

A. Population, total and military age
B. Distribution of the population by status, ethnicity, occupation, religion, and region
C. Comparative wealth and resources of belligerents
D. Transportation and communication network
E. Organization and motivation of the armed forces
F. Relative preparedness
G. Political system of each belligerent, and wartime modifications
H. Attitudes favoring and opposing the war
I. Changes in public opinion regarding the war
J. Military reorganization during the war
K. Political reorganization during the war

VI. The Return to Peace

A. Negotiations during and after hostilities
B. Terms of final settlement
C. Short-term social, political, and economic consequences
D. Long-term social, political, and economic consequences
E. Relation to subsequent wars

Application of the Outline
for the Analysis of the
Soviet-German War of 1941–1945

Introduction

The war between Germany and the Soviet Union was the bloodiest and most destructive part of World War II, the largest-scale conflict in human history. How such a war could begin and continue for four long years is a subject worthy of study. The effects of this war are with us today: the German state still shows the effects of 45 years of dismemberment; and the superpower confrontation that grew out of World War II has only recently been suspended. Under new threats, the U.S. must confront long-ignored questions about the military's role in society and America's role in the world.

Chronology

Previous relations of the parties

The German-Slav pan-tribal conflict, of which the German-Russian war of 1940–1945 was but a part, dates back thousands of years. War has swept across the plains of what is now Russia, Poland and Ukraine countless times, as various Slavic peoples were buffeted by steppe nomads, Scandinavian princes and European invaders. "Charles XII preferred the road through Poltava," said the Tsar's minister to Napoleon when the Emperor asked about the best invasion route into Russia.

Throughout the 1920s, Germany and Russia collaborated in a number of odd ways, including the maintenance of close ties between the Reichswehr and the Red Army. Largely, this was a consequence of Lenin's separate peace that ended Russian involvement in World War I and the Soviet Union's consequent exclusion from the Paris peace conference. Internationally ostracized, the Soviet Union did what pariah states do: take up with other pariah states, in this case, humiliated Germany. Such arrangements of necessity can place together peculiar bedfellows (such as South Africa and Israel). Russia supplied Germany with huge quantities of raw materials. As both countries grew stronger and more militant during the 1930s, they began to decouple and to eye one another with increasing suspicion. In 1934, the close military collaboration ended, although the shipments of raw materials continued right up to the German invasion (Craig 1980, 682).

The Ribbentrop-Molotov non-aggression pact culminated a decade of increasing tension between the Third Reich and the Union of Soviet Socialist Republics. The pact marked the meeting of two expanding spheres of influence along a line from the Baltic to the Balkans. Ribbentrop and Molotov sought to negotiate a halt to their respective eastward and westward expansions by dividing the spoils of eastern Europe. As an alternative to further expansion at each other's expense, Hitler offered Stalin a share of the British empire in return for help in destroying it. The offer was accepted.

Precipitating incidents

At the end of 1940, Hitler was at a strategic crossroads: his logical target, Britain, lay beyond reach and he needed a substitute. Emboldened by the poor showing of the Red Army against the Finns, like a shark watching a weakened fish, he began to take intense interest. The friction point on the edge of the Soviet and German spheres of influence was Romania, which was pressured by both sides to cede various territories to various other countries. There were no provocative moves by the Russians prior to hostilities. German reconnaissance flights deep into Russia were ignored. Stalin desperately sought to avoid war, going so far as to order his own troops not to defend themselves during the early hours of the German advance. The Germans staged border "incidents," as they had before their invasion of Poland, but these were entirely pro forma.

The Decision-makers

Adolf Hitler, art school dropout, wallpaper hanger, decorated corporal, and political madman, was from a lower-middle class family in Austria. His tiny group of fanatic nationalists, anti-communists and anti-Semites, was active throughout the 1920s in Munich, as the economic dislocations that followed the Versailles treaty produced resentment against the Weimar Republic (Kolb 1988). The collapse of speculative bubbles in various stock markets, coupled with incompetent monetary and tariff policies, triggered a world-wide depression that hit hardest in Germany. Economic disaster bred political chaos which allowed the Nazis to do well in one semi-free national election and to seize dictatorial power soon afterwards. Economic problems were alleviated by restarting the German industrial sector with large military orders for new equipment and an ambitious program of civilian projects including the autobahn system. Unemployment fell from 30.1 percent in 1932, to 14.9 percent in 1934, to 8.3 percent in 1936 (Mitchell 1981, 178). Inflation had been halted with a new currency in 1924 and reparations were ended.

If Hitler created a totalitarian regime, Josef Dzhugashvili, who took the name Stalin as a young Bolshevik revolutionary, inherited one. Lenin had intended the reins to go to someone more intellectually capable, and left instructions to this effect, but when push came to shove, Stalin's years of controlling the Party secretariat paid off. The party rank-and-file found Stalin more familiar than various theorists such as Trotsky and Kamenev. Stalin drenched the Party in bloody purges to insure his own supreme authority, killed millions of troublesome landowning peasants (kulaks) during the forced collectivization of agriculture, and brought about the fastest industrialization in history by deporting and enslaving millions of his own people (Solzhenitsyn 1973). In the 1930s,

Stalin had Trotsky, Kamenev, most of the original Bolsheviks, and most of the military leadership murdered (Medvedev 1984, 13).

War aims

It had been Hitler's intention to reduce, invade, and subdue Britain as he had France, before turning his attention to the Soviet Union. However, as would happen again at Stalingrad, Goering's failure to deliver on promises of the Luftwaffe's abilities led to strategic misfortune. The German Air Force failed to secure air superiority over the English Channel. The German surface navy failed to distract, much less destroy, the British home fleet based at Scapa Flow and German submarines failed to find British cruisers on the high seas. In view of these unpleasant realities, the military leadership of Germany advised Hitler that a cross-channel invasion attempt carried an unacceptably high likelihood of devastating British naval attack (Churchill [1949] 1983, 2: 576). Thus, Hitler had to be content with the U-boat strategy of starving the British out. Shortly after this decision, Hitler ordered the preparation of Operation Barbarossa, announcing to his staff that leaving Britain battered but unbroken was a risky but justifiable proposition. It is unclear exactly when Hitler came to this conclusion but it is plain that he did not want to cease land operations after the fall of France, Norway, and everything between him and the Russians. With the Continent conquered or cowed and England temporarily out of reach, Hitler turned east. It was his strategic intention that the Soviet Union's destruction would allow the Japanese to pressure the Americans so hard that they could not aid Britain when her turn came.

Hitler thought that the conquest of the Soviet Union would alleviate two problems pressing on the Reich by providing it with food from Ukraine and oil from the Caucasus. The German High Command agreed with these aims but argued that sweeping the plain clean of Russian resistance as far as the Ural mountains was the first priority.

Principal engagements and outcomes of the war

The Germans attacked Russia in late June 1941, along a thousand-mile front, and achieved complete tactical surprise. They conquered more than 100,000 square miles of territory, inflicted enormous material losses, and captured huge numbers of prisoners, some of whom joined "liberation armies" to fight the Soviets. The German Army "took 150,000 prisoners, 1,200 tanks, and 600 artillery pieces in the first ten days" (Craig 1980, 730). The Luftwaffe destroyed 2,000 Russian aircraft. The devastation of the Soviet armed forces was nearly total: probably no modern war has been won by a state so badly trounced at the outset. After vanishing for several days when news of the German betrayal reached him, Stalin reappeared and delivered a stirring address that roused the Russians against the invaders. Within months, German forces were outside Moscow and Leningrad. Continuing until winter reduced their mobility, German troops shelled the outskirts of Moscow, encircled Leningrad, and spread through the Volga basin, the breadbasket of Russia.

During the following year, the front swept back and forth as both armies fought to the limits allowed by the arrival of new troops, weapons, equipment, food, ammunition, and spare parts. A front that shifted back and forth over the countryside replaced the trenches of World War I. After an agonizingly long struggle, the Soviets began to get the upper hand. Their population was larger and more dispersed; factory output was reestablished in the Urals after being knocked out in Russia proper; more and more aid came from Russia's new allies, Britain and America; and Hitler was forced to divert ever greater assets to other fronts. The high water mark came at Stalingrad at the end of 1942. The German Sixth Army under von Paulus captured most of the city in hideous house-to-house fighting but large Russian forces remained along the riverbank and across the river. The winter turned nasty, the tactical situation of the river turned the city into a trap, and von Paulus requested permission to withdraw. It was denied by Hitler personally. Again Goering overestimated the Luftwaffe's capacity, this time wildly. Given the task of resupplying von Paulus by air, the planes never achieved 10 percent of the weekly minimum of fuel, parts, food, and ammunition requested by the Sixth Army staff. By December 1942 the Soviets had encircled the Sixth Army with strong forces and a German armored relief column failed to breakthrough. Over 200,000 Germans were killed and 90,000 captured.

From this point on, throughout 1943 and 1944, the German tactical situation deteriorated. Soviet attacks against prepared German positions began with assaults by savage gangs brought directly from the gulag camps to the battlefield by cattle car. An attempt by Hitler to trap a large Soviet force turned into a debacle at Kursk, the largest tank battle ever fought.

The later phase of the war was a series of maneuver battles involving large armored forces and aggregations of artillery and rockets, supported by ground attack aircraft. Decisive engagements between enormous tank armies took place on the plains and between massed divisions of infantry in or around cities. In 1945 the Soviets crushed what was left of the German Army on the eastern front. The Red Army occupied Berlin, all of eastern Europe, and that part of Germany that became the German Democratic Republic.

Reasons for ending the war

The manner of Nazi Germany's defeat had been settled earlier by Roosevelt, Stalin, and Churchill. They had agreed that there would be no negotiated peace. Stalin had insisted on this clause out of his fear of a separate peace between the Anglo-Americans and the Germans. When the Soviet and Western armies met on a line dividing Germany, the war ended with the unconditional surrender of all German forces by Admiral Donitz, who came to be in charge because the entire Nazi leadership above him had committed suicide, surrendered separately, or gone into hiding. By this time, virtually every able-bodied male in Germany had been expended; famine was beginning; and industry had collapsed from lack of energy, raw materials, bombardment of factories, and the destruction of German railroads. The war ended with the literal exhaustion of Germany, the occupation of the entire country, and the dismantling of Germany's political and economic institutions.

Roles of Third Party States

Mediation

Mediation between Germany and the Soviet Union was not attempted after the start of hostilities. Both leaders saw the war as a personal battle to the death. Hitler planned the extermination of "not only the leadership cadres of the Soviet state . . . but the whole Russian intelligentsia" (Craig 1980, 730). Stalin's men harbored similar sentiments toward the Nazis. The principal third parties had agreed to "unconditional surrender" as part of a program of reassurances to Stalin that he was not being played for a fool by Roosevelt and Churchill.

Incitement

"If Hitler invaded Hell I would make at least a favorable reference to the Devil in the House of Commons." Thus spoke Winston Churchill ([1949] 1983, 3: 370), the most powerful political leader in Great Britain, upon hearing of Hitler's attack on Stalin. Britain's foreign policy had long sought to avoid a Russian-German alliance, the one virtue of Bolshevism in British eyes was its incompatibility with German fascism. Churchill had personally courted the Russians and had been mortified by the Molotov negotiations in Berlin (Churchill [1949] 1983, 3: 388). But Hitler needed no incitement to kill Slavs and the Soviets quite realistically feared for their lives.

Assistance to Germany

Direct military assistance to Germany by other Axis countries was limited to the furnishing of conscript divisions whose combat ability was low. Large German forces were tied down in Italy and elsewhere, which probably more than offset the gain of reluctant foreign soldiers on the eastern front. Germany did benefit from a huge war industry dispersed through conquered lands that was manned largely by captured peoples reduced to varying degrees of slavery based on various ethnic, religious, and national criteria. These plants did not typically provide the actual implements of war (with the Skoda works in Czechoslovakia being an important exception), but produced blankets, messkits, trucks, rations, and medicine; and freed up German industry to concentrate skilled labor on howitzers, aircraft, ammunition, and so forth. Germany's ally, Japan, was too far away to send effective help across oceans still dominated by the British Royal Navy. Some of Stalin's forces were tied down in the Far East, but even this pressure began to subside in late 1942 and divisions that Stalin had sent hurrying west on the Trans-Siberian railroad provided the crucial reinforcements for Zhukov's forces at Stalingrad in early 1943.

Hitler had counted on yet another lightning victory over Russia like those he had enjoyed with France and Poland. When this did not happen, the German armies exhausted their fuel reserves and became dependent for mobility on Romanian oil, which was more or less freely provided (Craig 1980, 737).

In the early days of the German invasion, various lands that had chafed under the Russian yoke, especially White Russia, Ukraine and the Baltic states, were happy to see the Soviets beaten and would have willingly helped the Nazis. The Ukrainians declared independence and formed an army of their own. Other units were formed elsewhere in the Soviet Union. In one of the most egregious blunders of the war, an initial sympathy toward the Germans among the peoples liberated from Soviet tyranny was reversed as Nazi anti-Slav ideologies led to policies in the occupied countries that generated non-cooperation and non-compliance. When German rear units began to loot and enslave, fanatic partisan bands sprang up and attacked the Germans. Savage reprisals followed, with the eventual result that German supplies had to pass through hundreds of miles of thinly patrolled and hostile territory behind the actual front.

Assistance to the Soviet Union

Allied assistance to Stalin's forces, on the other hand, was continuous and massive, and may have been the decisive factor in the eventual success of the Red Army. This assistance involved weapons, explosives, trucks, aircraft, spare parts, food, technical assistance, intelligence, and huge piles of miscellaneous supplies. From the start of the war, Roosevelt and Churchill had independently decided that Stalin had to be kept fighting at all cost. Despite enormous early losses, convoys to Russia sailed continually from Allied ports through very hazardous waters to Murmansk. Parts of the British Royal Navy were put at risk periodically to assist this effort. Overland supplies began to flow through Iran.

None of this support (very costly for Britain) was a matter of disinterested charity, of course. Stalin may have been a disagreeable fellow but he had the manpower and was both willing and compelled to use it against Germany and Japan. Roosevelt and Churchill accurately surmised that their democracies were simply incapable of sustaining the casualties necessary to beat Hitler's forces on the ground in Europe, even supposing that a way could be found to transport the Allies unmolested into Europe.

There were limits to this aid. The Russians were not offered truly secret materials such as Ultra intelligence (derived from decoded German radio traffic), radar, and the Norden bombsight. Nor were the Russians invited to collaborate on the atomic bomb. Nevertheless, priceless cargo ships sailed for Russia carrying more mundane items that were desperately needed in Britain.

Logistics

Number of troops involved on both sides

The armies of Hitler and Stalin constituted the largest organized combat forces ever assembled before or since. In 1941, Stalin estimated that the German army had 175 divisions at the outbreak of war, which rose to 232 divisions in six weeks, and could reach 300 divisions. Stalin estimated his own forces' potential mobilization at 350 divisions (Sherwood 1948, 333). Stalin was not far off: for Operation Barbarossa, the German High Command allocated 148 divisions (3,050,000 men) equipped with 3,350 tanks, 7,184 artillery pieces, 2,500 aircraft and 200,000 trucks. At the start of the war, the Soviet Union had 203 divisions (including 33 in the Far East). Soviet divisions were smaller so only 2,300,000 troops were on hand to face the German onslaught. These troops, however, were armed with three times as many aircraft as the Germans (many of which were destroyed on the ground), and 10,000 tanks. The German failure to eliminate enough of these tanks in the early stages would have grave consequences for them.

At its zenith, the Wehrmacht deployed some 10 million men. The Soviet army eventually swelled to perhaps 12.5 million. In January 1944, the Russian combat troop advantage on the German frontline was 5,700,000 to 3,000,000 (Craig 1980, 757). The advantage grew rapidly as the Russians bore down on the Fatherland.

Weapons

The armies of Hitler and Stalin employed the full panoply of modern industrial weapon systems in numbers never seen before or since: thousands of tanks and aircraft, tens of thousands of artillery pieces and rockets and uncounted millions of mines, mortars, and machine guns. Both forces were partly mechanized (requiring huge quantities of fuel) and fully interconnected by redundant and sometimes secure radio and wire communications.

Contrary to popular opinion, German weapons were not, on balance, markedly superior to Soviet versions. The 1930s had been a time of immense technological advancement in the Soviet armed forces, with pioneering efforts in aircraft design, paratroop drops, and infantry weapons (by Kalashnikov). The Soviets' initial catastrophic losses can be traced almost entirely to strategic paralysis, tactical incompetence, and the German perfection of the blitzkrieg operation. In contrast to their experience in Poland and in France against armies little changed since World War I, the

German army began to sustain serious losses as soon as the front stabilized.

Casualties, prisoners, and deserters

By the winter of 1942–1943, the Russians had sustained some 4.2 million casualties, a rate of almost 250,000 per month. In the same period, the Germans suffered 3.1 million casualties. In the next year, the Russians had another 5.7 million casualties, while the Germans lost another 3 million. Total combat deaths were 7.5 million Soviets and 3.5 million Germans. Prisoners and deserters were in the millions on both sides. Available figures are estimates.

Civilian casualties and non-military damage

The civilian casualties and non-military damages of the Russian-German war exceeded any conflict in human history. Estimates vary as to the number of civilians (mostly Slavs) killed, but they start at 11 million and climb from there. In contrast to World War I, with its static trenches and set piece artillery duels, World War II was a fluid battle of tanks, bombers, and mobile artillery. The front line moved back and forth as battle swept through city after city and back again. Some cities were conquered and liberated, house by house, several times. By 1945, few civilian structures remained undamaged across hundreds of thousands of square miles from Germany to the middle of Russia.

Typical estimates of losses are: for the Soviet Union, 15–20 million civilian deaths and hundreds of billions of rubles in damage; for Germany, 6 million civilian deaths, and 90 percent of civilian housing destroyed. Paul Kennedy quotes a recapitulation of the scene in the German-occupied parts of Russia:

> Of the 11.6 million horses in occupied territory, 7 million were killed or taken away, as were 20 out of 23 million pigs. 137,000 tractors, 49,000 grain combines and large numbers of cow sheds and other farm buildings were destroyed. Transport was hit by the destruction of 65,000 kilometers of railway track, loss of or damage

to 15,800 locomotives, 428,000 goods wagons, 4,280 river boats, and half of all the railway bridges in the occupied territory. Almost 50 percent of all urban living space in this territory, 1.2 million houses, were destroyed, as well as 3.5 million houses in rural areas. . . Many towns lay in ruins. Thousands of villages were smashed. People lived in holes in the ground (1987, 362).

Societal Support

In demographic terms, the fight was hardly fair. Russia was more than twice Germany's size. According to censuses taken in the late 1930s, Russia had a total population of 170 million to Germany's 70 million. Russia had 39 million men aged 15–44, while Germany had only 17 million (Mitchell 1981, 47, 57).

Comparative wealth and resources of belligerents

It was certainly true that Germany was more involved in the world trade and financial markets. However, until the late 1930s this involvement was governed under the ruinous Versailles arrangements that made German currency worthless for letter-of-credit purposes. Thus, Germany was in a position not unlike that of Japan, condemned to rely on international trade that was being strangled by others. Conversely, Russian credit was good, better even than British, because after repudiating the Tsar's bonds and debts, the Soviets had taken an almost quaint approach to international finance, paying in gold or in kind and never reneging on contracts. Thus, when Roosevelt devised plans like Lend-Lease to aid the British, it was easy to extend them to include the Soviet Union.

German coal (anthracite and bituminous) production reached 400 million metric tons in 1938 and held that level throughout the war. Russian coal production reached 165 million metric tons in 1940 and was 148 million tons in 1945 (Mitchell 1981, 387–389). Output during the middle years of the war cannot be accurately estimated, but probably fell somewhat, perhaps to 100 million tons. However, coal is a much less important war material than liquid petroleum, in which Russia had a great advantage. Before the war, Germany had traded coal for oil. With hostilities, this was no longer possible, nor could the coal be spared.

German domestic crude oil production was only 1 million tons in 1940 and declined to half that level by 1945 (Mitchell 1981, 397). Production in conquered territories (Romania, France, Hungary, and Czechoslovakia) peaked at 6.2 million tons in 1943, but not all of this was available for the war effort. Russian oil production (mostly from the Baku region, far from German tanks), on the other hand, was 31.1 million tons in 1940, more than four times as much. Figures for the middle years of the war are unreliable, but Russian production was still 19 million tons in 1945, indicating a huge wartime advantage. Moreover, the Russians were not using oil for ships at sea. Russian natural gas outpaced German supplies by about 2:1. The Germans attempted to acquire Russian oil directly—von Paulus's Army at Stalingrad was covering the flank of a strategic push into the Caucasus region to seize the Baku fields. Advance units reached the area but could not hold it. This was the farthest point reached by the German invasion.

Germany had a modest advantage in steel production. In 1932, both Germany and Russia were producing about 6 million tons of steel per year. The steel industries of both countries grew enormously during the 1930s. By 1940, steel production had risen to 21 million tons in Germany versus 18 million tons in Russia (Mitchell 1981, 421–422). It is clear that, contrary to popular views, Russia was not an industrially backward country when the Germans attacked. Eighteen million tons of steel represents an enormous quantity of tanks, trucks, rifles and locomotives. It is remarkable that German output remained steady throughout the war (up to the actual invasion of the Reich in 1945). Allied strategic bombing of German heavy industry did not reduce output, though it may have prevented further growth in capacity.

Transportation and communication network

The story of the two sides' transportation and communication networks is one of paradox. Germany possessed a very efficient railroad network that was compromised by the diversion of rolling stock to the concentration camp system; a large and potentially useful transport aircraft fleet that was completely mismanaged; and the world's best secure radio net, which was nevertheless cracked on a grand scale by Polish foresight and British mathematical genius. European Russia's internal transportation then, as now, relied on roads (then made of dirt or mud) and rivers. The seasonally changing utility of these means worked to the Russians' advantage once the German lines extended beyond the railroad tracks. Where they needed railroads, to and from the Urals and beyond, the Russians had them (with sufficient rolling stock) and were able to move their industrial plants largely beyond German reach. As has been noted, the German General Staff was not prepared for the logistical difficulties of a protracted war at the end of very long, unreliable lines while Russian resources, production, and manpower could, over time, be called up from the Urals and beyond. It was almost a thousand miles from Berlin to the German front lines and more than a thousand miles farther to the factories in Sverdlovsk. Russia's sheer size would save it.

Organization and motivation of the armed forces

Despite provisions of the Treaty of Versailles, the German army—especially its General Staff—did not evaporate after World War I. Throughout the turbulent interwar period, they continued to plan and train for another war. German military activities started again in the 1920s under various guises: Gymnasium "drill" units, "veterans' units," "self-protection units," police auxiliaries, etc. The General Staff secretly coordinated and controlled these activities, providing a qualified officer to supervise and instruct each one. By 1933, it was possible for the Wehrmacht to spring into being almost overnight and to begin a sustained drive for greater size and power.

The senior general of the German High Command reported directly to Hitler, a figure with complete dictatorial authority. In the beginning of Hitler's aggressions, the generals simply could not believe that he could get away with such blatant treaty violations and provocations of the other powers. As each incident failed to provoke resistance from the democracies, the generals divided into two groups: those who resigned rather than be associated with risks they deemed unwise; and those who stayed on, with their credibility weakened by each demonstration of Hitler's political acumen. By the time Hitler attacked Poland, the High Command had been intimidated into submission. By the time Hitler attacked Russia, no one was left who could counsel against the move. As the war against Russia dragged on past the General Staff's planning timetables, Hitler grew progressively more involved in eastern front operations. By now fancying himself as a military genius and facing generals who had run out of plans and reserve forces, Hitler made a series of operational decisions that divided his forces, isolated combat units, and exposed strategic flanks. Tempting targets began to appear before an exhausted and desperate Red Army. Hitler decided to concentrate on taking Leningrad and Moscow after initial efforts failed, instead of seeking out and destroying the nearby Red Army forces under Timonshenko, as the General Staff prudently counseled. This crucial decision prompted the resignation of the top German military figure, Brauchitsch, and the assumption of direct operational control by Hitler himself (Craig 1980, 731).

Later, Hitler decided to push south into the Caucasus, leaving a gigantic hole in the line and exposing the Sixth Army at Stalingrad to encirclement. These decisions led to disasters that shook the confidence of the soldiers and caused periodic reorganizations of the top military leadership as blame was apportioned among the generals. As the Russians gained the upper hand, Hitler became more irrational and in 1944, with the war clearly lost, a group of aristocratic officers tried to kill him. They failed and there were wide, savage reprisals. From that point on, there was no resistance to Hitler's leadership until Germany was completely invaded and subdued.

The German army was probably the best military force in the world in 1940. Fresh from walk-over victories in France and Poland, the Wehrmacht had gained invaluable combat experience that built on the base of gigantic training exercises held in the 1930s (many with the Russians). Its soldiers possessed relevant technical skills in abundance, and were obedient to officers who represented a tradition stretching back for centuries.

The Red Army was more diverse, with language and nationality problems. The average level of technical skill was lower. Training was less realistic and conducted on the cheap. Political commissars played havoc with military activities. Suspected officers and men disappeared into labor camps, or worse. Most of the military leadership down to brigade level had been liquidated in the terror of the 1930s. On the other hand, Russian soldiers were inured to virtually any hardship, as their pattern of attacking after the Germans had dug-in for the winter would demonstrate.

Relative preparedness

In 1940, German readiness for a protracted war was not nearly what it could have been. Nazi fear of the political repercussions of reduced consumer goods production, and Hitler's ideological objection to the use of women in industry (fearing impairment of their motherly abilities), led to a military effort that, while substantial, was far short of total. This was in part a result of the easy German victories in France and Poland, which had "paid for themselves" (Craig 1980, 733). Even after the failure to subdue Russia quickly, German war production did not expand dramatically. Throughout the war, Albert Speer and others urged the drafting of women into factories, putting more pressure on France, and, most important, abandonment of consumer production. These calls went unheeded until far too late.

The situation in Russia was much different. Russian industry was forcibly developed at a frantic pace and the Russian "consumer" was not a political force.

Political systems

At the beginning of the war, Adolf Hitler governed Germany without organized opposition, but still had to rely on arm-twisting, cajolery, politicking, and the mobilization of public opinion to take actions that disturbed powerful interests such as the industrialists, the military, and the aristocracy. As the war progressed, the Nazi party became increasingly isolated from other leading elements in Germany. The Nazis centralized decision-making, increased censorship and ruled with more and more reliance on command, intimidation, and violence. Numerous prominent Germans resigned or retired over this or that Nazi plan or policy. So long as they did not speak openly against the Nazis, this was tolerated and most of them suffered no harm. Hitler was a demagogue who held the masses in thrall but who was regarded with suspicion and alarm in the ruling circles that had promoted him, profited by him, and now were powerless to stop him.

In Russia, Stalin ruled absolutely and those around him lived in constant physical fear. The communists had been killers from early on and the tradition continued. Russia was far more thoroughly a police state than Germany had time to become. The NKVD was more bloodthirsty than the Gestapo, and had been operating longer.[1] Hardly a whiff of democracy or republicanism touched Russian life. During Stalin's rise to power, millions of people were shot for political reasons. At one point, Stalin was killing more people *per day* than the entire toll of the French Revolution.

Public opinion

It did not occur to the terrified survivors of ten years of purges in the Soviet Union to express opinions on foreign policy. Among the Moscow intelligentsia, it was clear that loss to Hitler would be worse, if possible, than life under Stalin. After the German attack, Stalin skillfully blended familiar communist rhetoric with nationalistic themes and rehabilitated the Russian Orthodox Church to help mobilize the populace. Soviet propagandists successfully remade Stalin the Butcher into Stalin the General and Statesman.

German public opinion was a real force, however, and Hitler took it very seriously. Indeed, the mobilization of masses was the source of Hitler's power over the aristocracy, the businessmen and the military. Redress of Versailles grievances and explanations of Germany's betrayal in World War I had been the platform from which Hitler climbed to power. His deputy for propaganda, Goebbels, "was well aware that the German people had gone to war without enthusiasm and that from that time on their mood varied . . . between brief periods of exultation when victories were announced and relapses into depression when they were not followed by a return to peace" (Craig 1980, 737). Hitler's unilateral declaration of war against America worsened matters, since the German people recalled that the entry of the Americans into World War I was followed closely by German defeat. As the war with Russia dragged on, the German civilian situation worsened quickly and public opinion turned down.

Military reorganization during the war

As the blitzkrieg failed, the senior German general resigned over the failure to designate Moscow as the main target. His replacement, Halder, lasted until he stood up to Hitler in September 1942, suggesting that it was time to fall back and regroup. German field commanders remained effective throughout the war although Hitler periodically harassed them. The Berlin staff toward the end of the war was dominated by Keitel and Jodl, sycophants who simulated appreciation for Hitler's military genius.

In contrast, the Soviet Union eventually had excellent generalship. Stalin repented his earlier decimation of the military leadership and instituted a promotion-by-merit program. He was intensely interested in details, but issued only general directions and gave few absolute orders. There ensued a kind of survival of the fittest, as German units ground up the lesser Soviet commanders. The survivors were sharp, smart, and very brave. Marshal Zhukov, the hero of Moscow and Stalingrad, became the central front commander and eventually took Berlin.

Political reorganization during the war

The National Socialist party had originally been a band of bizarre characters like Himmler, Goebbels, Bormann, Hess, and Goering. With the accession of Hitler to power, more bourgeois types, such as Albert Speer, moved into the Nazi hierarchy. In 1940, key sectors of Germany were being run on reasonably rational principles by men who were at least sane. As the war inflicted progressively greater hardship on the German people, there was a return to earlier patterns. As the tide turned and total mobilization was ordered, Goebbels' propaganda machine and Himmler's police and armies dominated the country. The failed assassination attempt of 1944 revealed widespread dissatisfaction with the Nazis. One by one, the holdovers from institutions that had been co-opted by the Nazis resigned, retired, committed suicide, or were imprisoned.

In the Soviet Union, the German invasion worked a miracle of cohesion in the Soviet government. Many jobs were reshuffled early in the war, but then relative stability prevailed. Molotov served as Foreign Commissar during the entire conflict. Most other key jobs were held for the duration.

The Return to Peace

Negotiations and terms of settlement

Negotiations during the hostilities were essentially non-existent, due to the Allies' mutual suspicions of each others' motives. After hostilities concluded, the terms of peace were settled at Potsdam and dictated to the defeated Germans. Germany was to be occupied; de-militarized; de-nazified; dismembered into four zones of occupation by France, Britain, the United States, and the Soviet Union; stripped of remaining colonies; ordered to make reparations; and de-industrialized so as no longer to pose a threat to peace. Complete de-nazification proved impossible; eventually mere membership was forgiven. Reparations were structured to allow recovery of the German economy and were soon reduced further. De-industrialization never really began, and German industry came roaring back in the 1950s.

Short-term social, political, and economic consequences

German institutions were thoroughly discredited (Craig 1980, 759). The business class, in especially the industrial houses of Krupp and I.G. Farben, were blamed for not stopping Hitler. The aristocracy was blamed for promoting him in the first place. The military was discredited for slavishly following a madman into ruin. Educators were shamed by Heidegger's *Rektoratsrede* and devastated by the loss of intellectuals to America and to the Holocaust. The craven judiciary and churches had little reason to be proud.

The industrial plant of the Soviet Union was very badly damaged and that of Germany was almost completely destroyed. What little in Germany was not destroyed was hauled back to Russia as booty. However, raw materials remained abundant in the Soviet Union, and a stable system of international payments dictated by the United States allowed Germany to develop an export economy. Many young men had been killed or disabled, but not all. The return to prewar production levels was startlingly rapid in both societies. Prewar steel production was surpassed in the Soviet Union in 1948, doubled in 1954, doubled again in 1963 and in 1971, the USSR was the world leader in steel production. In West Germany, steel production rebounded to prewar levels by 1957, and doubled by the 1970s (Mitchell 1981, 423).

The survivors in the parts of Germany controlled by France, Britain, and the U.S. created a largely new country called the Federal Republic of Germany. The Soviet Union created a new country for the rest of Germany, the German Democratic Republic.

Stalin took personal credit for the victory over the Nazi invaders and assumed the role of savior of Russia. Stalinism was reinforced as a governing style and as an economic system. The gulag continued in earnest, with some camps having new missions, such as uranium mining, but there was never a return to the wholesale slaughter of the 1930s. Stalin was busy fomenting trouble outside the Soviet Union, especially in Eastern Europe. The Soviet apparatus evolved from its wartime pattern to a more finely articulated one.

Long-term social, political, and economic consequences

Defeat in World War II destroyed the Germany that had been unified by Bismarck in the 1860s and 1870s. The physical destruction took decades to rebuild. The population never regained its demographic momentum and eventually began to decline. Shame and guilt pervaded German cultural life. German poets pointed out that even the German language was forever polluted because common words like "transport" and "shower" could not be uttered without inescapable allusion to Nazi horrors. Germany was garrisoned by hundreds of thousands of foreign troops and thousands of nuclear warheads and uttered no complaint. The Bonn government gave billions of dollars in reparations to the survivors of the Nazis. Germany regained its technological sophistication but remained a distinctly subdued society. Only recently, with the rise to power of a generation with no recollection of the war, has this begun to change.

The long-term demographic consequences of the war included a dearth of men in certain age groups, which continued for many years. As of January 1, 1961, in the Soviet Union there were 1,209 females for every 1,000 males—the highest such ratio ever measured (McWhirter 1968, 271). In West Germany in 1961, there were 1.69 million women aged 40–44 but only 1.22 million men of the same age (Mitchell 1981, 48).

Victory further legitimated the Communist Party and ended rule by terror. The social influence of the military was strengthened, which added a counterweight to the Party-KGB system.[2] Political paranoia contributed to the subjugation of eastern Europe, the nuclear arms race and the Cold War. The Soviet economy concentrated on large-scale mass production in heavy industry and sought to achieve economic independence. Forced integration of the economy under war planning agencies laid the groundwork for

GOSPLAN (the overall Soviet economic planning agency) and its bureaucratic labyrinth of forms, targets and directives. This structure functioned until the collapse of the Soviet Union in 1991.

Relation to subsequent wars

The outcome of the Russian-German war determined the distribution of power in Europe for the next forty-five years. The USSR was by far the greatest power on the Eurasian continent and was prevented from conquering all of it only by the intervention of the United States on behalf of the democracies of Western Europe. This resulted in the Cold War, which consumed enormous resources, but resulted in almost no loss of life. At the same time, the entire continent of Europe enjoyed an amazingly long stretch of international peace. So peaceful was Europe that a few shots between minor naval vessels of Britain and Iceland over the right to fish for cod were considered a "war" (Hartman and Mitchell 1985, 8). Other warlike incidents included civil war in Greece from 1943–1949; insurrections in Hungary in 1956 and Czechoslovakia in 1968; the invasion of Cyprus by Turkey in 1974; and "troubles" in Northern Ireland. The violent ethnic and religious rivalries of Eastern Europe and the Soviet Union were almost entirely stifled.

With the American victory over Japan, there were only two powers of consequence left in the world: the United States and the Soviet Union. Both had an interest in the energetic dismantling of the European colonial empires. In the United States, ideological and economic reasons were paramount: the "self-determination" of peoples was held to be a universal good and the end of colonialism meant vast new markets for U.S. companies. The Soviet Union saw colonial regimes as "imperialism, the highest stage of capitalism" and opposed them as a matter of communist doctrine. The practical political opportunity for the USSR involved the creation of Marxist parties in scores of new countries and the acquisition of outright allies, such as Cuba. This bipolar world was the stage for a great number of regional wars in which the U.S. supported one side and the USSR the other.

Notes

[1] Russian acronym for the secret police.

[2] KGB: Komitet Gosudarstvennoi Bezopastnosti (The Committee for State Security). The KGB was a reorganization of the NKVD.

References

Allen, Thomas B. 1987. *War Games*. New York: McGraw-Hill.

Allison, Graham T. 1971. *Essence of Decision: Explaining the Cuban Missile Crisis*. Boston: Little, Brown.

Ardrey, Robert. 1966. *The Territorial Imperative: A Personal Inquiry into the Animal Origins of Property and Nations*. New York: Atheneum.

Ashworth, Tony. 1980. *Trench Warfare 1914–1918: The Live and Let Live System*. London: Macmillan.

Axinn, Sidney. 1989. *A Moral Military*. Philadelphia: Temple University Press.

Babington, Anthony. 1983. *For the Sake of Example*. New York: St. Martin's Press.

Barbera, Henry. 1973. *Rich Nations and Poor Nations in Peace and War*. Lexington, Mass.: Lexington Books.

———. 1998. *The Military Factor in Social Change*. New Brunswick, New Jersey: Transaction Press.

Baskir, Lawrence M. and William A. Strauss. 1978. *Chance and Circumstance*. New York: Vintage Books.

Bearman, Peter S. 1991. "Desertion as Localism: Army Unit Solidarity and Group Norms in the U.S. Civil War." *Social Forces* 70:321–342.

Bellamy, Edward. [1888] 1996. *Looking Backward*. New York: Dover.

Benét, Stephen Vincent. [1922] 1970. *John Brown's Body*. London: David Bruce & Watson Ltd.

Bertaud, Jean-Paul. 1979. *La Revolution Armée: Les soldats-citoyens et la Revolution Francaise*. Paris: Robert

Laffont.

———. 1985. *La vie quotidienne des soldats de la Revolution 1789–1799*. Paris: Hachette.

Binkin, Martin. 1986. *Military Technology and Defense Manpower*. Washington: Brookings Institution.

Black, Donald. 1998. *The Social Structure of Right and Wrong*. Revised edition. San Diego: Academic Press.

Boëne, Bernard. 2000. "Social Science Research, War and the Military in the United States: An Outsider's View of the Field's Dominant National Tradition." Pages 149–254 in *Military Sociology*, Gerhard Kümmel and Andreas D. Prüfert, eds. Baden-Baden: Nomos Verlagsgesellschaft

Boëne, Bernard and Christopher Dandeker, eds. 1998. *Les Armées en Europe*. Paris: Editions La Decouverte.

Booth, Bradford, Meyer Kestnbaum, and David R. Segal. 2001. "Are Post-Cold War Militaries Postmodern? *Armed Forces and Society* 27:319–342.

Borg, Marian. 1992. "Conflict Management in the Modern World-System." *Sociological Forum* 7(2): 261–282.

Bowden, Mark. 2000. *Black Hawk Down: A Story of Modern War*. Thorndike, Me.: G.K. Hall.

Bracken, Paul. 1983. *The Command and Control of Nuclear Forces*. New Haven: Yale University Press.

Brierly, James. [1928] 1963. *The Law of Nations: An Introduction to the International Law of Peace*. Oxford: Clarendon Press, 6th edition.

Brogan, Patrick. 1990. *The Fighting Never Stopped; A Comprehensive Guide to World Conflict Since 1945*. New York: Vintage Books.

Brown, Michael and others, eds. 1998. *Theories of War and Peace: An International Security Reader*. Cambridge: MIT Press.

Brubaker, William Rogers. 1990. *Citizenship and Nationhood in France and Germany*. Ph.D. dissertation, Columbia University.

Bueno de Mesquita, Bruce. 1981. *The War Trap*. New Haven:

Yale University Press.

Bundy, McGeorge, William J. Crowe, Jr.. and Sidney D. Drell. 1993. *Reducing Nuclear Danger: The Road Away from the Brink.* New York: Council on Foreign Relations Press.

Burchett, Bruce M. 1984. *Race and AWOL Offender: The Effect of the Defendant's Race on the Outcome of Courts-Martial Involving Absence Without Leave.* Ph.D. dissertation, Carleton University.

Burk, James, ed. 1998. *The Adaptive Military: Armed Forces in a Turbulent World.* New Brunswick, New Jersey: Transaction Publishers.

Caplow, Theodore. 1964. *Principles of Organization.* New York: Harcourt Brace.

———. 1968. *Two Against One: Coalitions in Triads.* Englewood Cliffs, New Jersey: Prentice-Hall.

———. 1977. *A Feasibility Study of World Government.* Muscatine, Iowa: Stanley Foundation.

———. 1989. *Peace Games.* Middletown, Conn.: Wesleyan University Press.

Caplow, Theodore, Louis Hicks, and Ben J. Wattenberg. 2001. *The First Measured Century: An Illustrated Guide to Trends in America, 1900–2000.* Washington: AEI Press.

Carlton, Eric. 1990. *War and Ideology.* London: Routledge.

Chang, Iris. 1997. *The Rape of Nanking.* New York: Basic Books.

Christopher, Paul. 1994. *The Ethics of War and Peace: An Introduction to Legal and Moral Issues.* Englewood Cliffs, New Jersey: Prentice-Hall.

Churchill, Winston. [1949] 1983. *The Second World War* (six volumes). New York: Houghton Mifflin.

Cipolla, Carlos. 1965. *Guns and Sails in the Early Phase of European Expansion 1400–1700.* London: Collins.

Clark, Grenville and Louis B. Sohn. 1966. *World Peace through World Law.* Cambridge: Harvard University Press.

Clark, Ian. 1985. *Nuclear Past, Nuclear Present: Hiroshima, Nagasaki and Contemporary Strategy.* Boulder: Westview Press.

Claude, Inis L., Jr. 1971. *Swords into Ploughshares: The Problems and Progress of International Organization*. 4th edition. New York: Random House.

Clausewitz, Carl von. [1832–1834] 1976. *On War*. Princeton: Princeton University Press.

Collins, Randall. 1981. *Sociology Since Midcentury: Essays in Theory Cumulation*. New York: Academic Press.

———. 1986. *Weberian Sociological Theory*. Cambridge: Cambridge University Press.

Corbett, Percy E. 1968. International Law. In *International Encyclopedia of the Social Sciences*, Volume 7. New York: Macmillan.

Coser, Ruth Laub. 1961. "Insulation from Observability and Types of Social Conformity." *American Sociological Review* 26(1):28–39.

Cowley, Robert. 1992a. "The Tunnels of Hill 60." In *Experience of War*, edited by Robert Cowley. New York: Norton.

———, ed. 1992b. *Experience of War: An Anthology of Articles from MHQ, The Quarterly Journal of Military History*. New York: Norton.

Craig, Gordon A. 1980. *Germany 1866–1945*. New York: Oxford University Press.

Crosby, Alfred. 1972. *The Columbian Exchange; Biological and Cultural Consequences of 1492*. Westport, Conn.: Greenwood Press.

Damrosch, Lori Fisler, ed. 1993. *Enforcing Restraint: Collective Intervention in Internal Conflicts*. New York: Council on Foreign Relations Press.

de Landa, Manuel. 1991. *War in the Age of Intelligent Machines*, New York: Zone.

Demchak, Chris C. 1991. *Military Organizations, Complex Machines: Modernization in the U.S. Armed Services*. Ithaca, New York: Cornell University Press.

Diamond, Jared. 1999. *Guns, Germs, and Steel: The Fates of Human Societies*. New York: Norton.

Diehl, Charles. 1957. *Byzantium: Greatness and Decline.* Trans. by Naomi Walford. New Brunswick, New Jersey: Rutgers University Press.

Dozier, Edward P. 1967. *The Kalinga of Northern Luzon, Philippines.* New York: Holt, Rinehart and Winston.

Dreisziger, N. F., with R. A. Preston. 1990. "Polyethnicity and Armed Forces: An Introduction." In *Ethnic Armies; Polyethnic Armed Forces from the Time of the Habsburgs to the Age of the Superpowers.* Waterloo, Ontario: Wilfrid Laurier University Press.

Dubois, Pierre. [1306] 1972. *The Recovery of the Holy Land,* translated by W. I. Brandt. New York: Columbia University Press.

Dunnigan, James F. 1993. *How to Make War: A Comprehensive Guide to Modern Warfare for the Post-Cold War Era,* 3rd ed. New York: William Morrow.

Dupuy, R. Ernest and Trevor N. Dupuy. 1986. *The Encyclopedia of Military History: From 3500 B. C. to the Present.* Second revised edition. Philadelphia: Harper and Row.

Durkheim, Émile. [1915] 1965. *The Elementary Forms of the Religious Life.* Translated by Joseph Ward Swain. New York: The Free Press.

Ehrenreich, Barbara. 1998. *Blood Rites: Origins and History of the Passions of War.* New York: Henry Holt.

Eisenhower, Dwight D. 1948. *Crusade in Europe.* Garden City, New York: Doubleday.

Eisler, Riene Tennenhaus. 1987. *The Chalice and the Blade.* Cambridge: Harper and Row.

Enloe, Cynthia. 1989. *Bananas, Beaches and Bases: Making Feminist Sense of International Politics.* London: Pandora.

Erasmus, Desiderius. [1517] 1946. *Querela Pacis: The Complaint of Peace.* New York: Scholars' Facsimiles and Reprints.

Etzioni, Amitai. 1961. *A Comparative Analysis of Complex Organizations.* New York: Free Press.

Finer, S. E. 1988. *The Man on Horseback: The Role of the Military in Politics.* 2nd, enlarged ed. Boulder: Westview Press.

Foner, Jack D. 1970. *The United States Soldier Between Two Wars: Army Life and Reforms, 1865–1898.* New York: Humanities Press.

Forsyth, Murray. 1981. *Unions of States: The Theory and Practice of Confederation.* New York: Holmes and Meier.

Foy, David A. 1984. *For You the War Is Over: American Prisoners of War in Nazi Germany.* New York: Stein and Day.

Freud, Sigmund. [1930] 1961. Civilization and Its Discontents. In *The Standard Edition of the Complete Psychological Works of Sigmund Freud.* Edited by James Strachey. London: The Hogarth Press.

Friedman, Leon, ed. 1972. *The Laws of War: A Documentary History.* 2 vols. New York: Random House.

Gabriel, Richard A. 1987. *No More Heroes: Madness and Psychiatry in War.* New York: Hill and Wang.

Gabriel, Richard A. and Paul L. Savage. 1978. *Crisis in Command.* New York: Hill and Wang.

Galvin, John R. 1996. *The Minute Men, The First Fight: Myths and Realities of the American Revolution.* Washington: Brassey's.

Gibbon, Edward. [1776] 1932. *The Decline and Fall of the Roman Empire.* New York: Modern Library edition.

Gilbert, Felix. 1986. "Machiavelli: The Renaissance of the Art of War." In *Makers of Modern Strategy*, edited by Peter Paret. Princeton: Princeton University Press.

Goodall, Jane. 1986. *The Chimpanzees of Gombe; Patterns of Behavior.* Cambridge: Harvard University Press.

Gowa, Joanne. 1999. *Ballots and Bullets: The Elusive Democratic Peace.* Princeton: Princeton University Press.

Grotius, Hugo. [1625] 1901. *The Law of War and Peace*, translated by A. C. Campbell. Washington: M. Walter Dunne.

Hamilton, Alexander, James Madison and John Jay. [1787] 1952. The Federalist. In *American State Papers.* Chicago: William Benton.

Hartman, Tom and John Mitchell. 1985. *A World Atlas of Military History, 1945–1984.* New York: De Capo Press.

Hicks, Louis. 1993. "Normal Accidents in Combat Operations." *Sociological Perspectives* 36(4): 377–391.

Higginbotham, Don, ed. 1978. *Reconsiderations on the Revolutionary War.* Westport, Conn.: Greenwood Press.

Hobson, J. A. [1902] 1993. *Imperialism.* Ann Arbor: University of Michigan Press.

Howard, Michael. 2001. *The Invention of Peace: Reflections on War and International Order.* New Haven: Yale University Press.

Huntingford, Felicity and Angela K. Turner. 1987. *Animal Conflict.* New York: Chapman and Hall.

Huntington, Samuel. 1993. "The Clash of Civilizations?" *Foreign Affairs* 72 (3):22–49.

Ingraham, Larry H. 1984. *The Boys in the Barracks; Observations on American Military Life.* Philadelphia: Institute for the Study of Human Issues.

International Institute for Strategic Studies. 2000. *The Military Balance 2000–2001.* Oxford: Oxford University Press.

James, William. 1912. The Moral Equivalent of War. In *Memories and Studies.* New York: Longmans, Green.

Janowitz, Morris. 1964. *The Military in the Development of New Nations.* Chicago: University of Chicago Press.

———. 1971. *The Professional Soldier: A Social and Political Portrait.* New York: The Free Press.

Johnson, Roger N. 1972. *Aggression in Man and Animals.* Philadelphia: W. B. Saunders.

Jones, Robert F. 1992. The Kipkororor Chronicles. In *Experience of War*, edited by Robert Cowley. New York: Norton.

Kahn, Herman. 1962. *Thinking about the Unthinkable.* New York: Horizon Press.

Kaiser, David. 2000. *Politics and War: European Conflict from Philip II to Hitler.* Cambridge: Harvard University Press.

Kant, Immanuel. [1795] 1917. *Perpetual Peace: A Philosophical*

Essay, translated by M. C. Smith. London: Allen and Unwin.

Kautsky, Karl. [1892] 1973. *The Class Struggle*. New York: The Norton Library.

Keegan, John 1977. *The Face of Battle: A Study of Agincourt, Waterloo and the Somme*. New York: Vintage Books.

———. 1987. *The Mask of Command*. New York: Viking Penguin.

———. 1993. *A History of Warfare*. New York: Alfred A. Knopf.

Keeley, Lawrence H. 1996. *War Before Civilization*. New York: Oxford University Press.

Kennedy, Paul. 1987. *Rise and Fall of the Great Powers*. New York: Random House.

Kidron, Michael and Dan Smith. 1983. *The War Atlas: Armed Conflict-Armed Peace*. London: Pan Books.

Kolb, Eberhard. 1988. *The Weimar Republic*. Translated by P. S. Falla. London: Unwin Hyman.

Komroff, Manuel. 1953. Introduction to *The Travels of Marco Polo*. New York: Liverwright, Lauterpacht.

Lapping, Brian. 1985. *End of Empire*. New York: St. Martin's Press.

Lenin, Nikolai. [1916] 1929. *Imperialism*. New York: Vanguard Press.

Lennon, Daniel. 1991. "A Communitarian Army?: Status and Role Considerations in the Use of Courts-martial in the United States Army." *Deviant Behavior* 12: 31–79.

Lesser, Charles H., ed. 1976. *The Sinews of Independence: Monthly Strength Reports of the Continental Army*. Chicago: University of Chicago Press.

Luttwak, Edward. 1976. *The Grand Strategy of the Roman Empire from the First Century A.D. to the Third*. Baltimore: Johns Hopkins University Press.

Lutz, William. 1989. *Doublespeak*. New York: Harper Perennial.

Machiavelli, Niccolo. [1521] 1965. *The Art of War*, edited by Neal Wood. Indianapolis: Bobbs-Merrill.

Malthus, Thomas. [1798] 1973. *An Essay on the Principle of*

Population. London: J. M. Dent.

Mann, Michael. 1986. *The Sources of Social Power.* Vol. 1, *From the Beginning to A.D. 1760.* Cambridge: Cambridge University Press.

Marx, Karl and Friedrich Engels. [1848] 1961. "The Communist Manifesto." In *Essential Works of Marxism*, edited by Arthur P. Mendel. New York: Bantam Books.

McNeill, William. 1974. *Venice: The Hinge of Europe, 1081–1797.* Chicago: University of Chicago Press.

———. 1982. *The Pursuit of Power: Technology, Armed Force and Society Since A.D. 1000.* Chicago: University of Chicago Press.

———. 1995. *Keeping Together in Time: Dance and Drill in Human History.* Cambridge: Harvard University Press.

McPhee, John. 1984. *La Place de la Concorde Suisse.* New York: Farrar, Straus and Giroux.

Medvedev, Roy. 1984. *All Stalin's Men.* Garden City, New York: Anchor Press.

Mendel, A. F., ed. 1961. *Essential Works of Marxism.* New York: Bantam.

Mendelsohn, Everett, Merritt Roe Smith, and Peter Weingart. 1988. *Science, Technology, and the Military.* Dordrecht: Kluwer.

Miller, Judith, Stephen Engelberg, and William Broad. 2001. *Germs: Biological Weapons and America's Secret War.* New York: Simon and Schuster.

Mitchell, B. R., ed. 1981. *European Historical Statistics 1750–1975.* New York: Facts on File.

Morris, Desmond. 1967. *The Naked Ape: A Zoologist's Study of the Human Animal.* London: Jonathan Cape.

Moskos, Charles. 1970. *The American Enlisted Man.* New York: Russell Sage Foundation.

———. 1988. "Institutional and Occupational Trends in Armed Forces." Pages 15–26 in *The Military: More than Just a Job*, edited by Charles C. Moskos and Frank R. Wood. Washington: Pergamon-Brassey's.

Moskos, Charles, John Allen Williams, and David R. Segal, eds. 2000. *The Postmodern Military: Armed Forces after the Cold War*. New York: Oxford University Press.

Mosse, George L. 1990. *Fallen Soldiers: Reshaping the Memory of the World Wars*. New York: Oxford University Press.

Moynihan. Daniel P. 1990. *On the Law of Nations*. Cambridge: Harvard University Press.

Mueller, John E. 1973. *War, Presidents and Public Opinion*. New York: John Wiley.

Murray, Williamson. 1992. "What Took the North So Long?" In *Experience of War*, edited by Robert Cowley. New York: Norton.

Nalty, Bernard C. 1986. *Strength for the Fight*. New York: Free Press.

Nef, J. U. 1950. *War and Human Progress*. Cambridge: Harvard University Press.

Noble, Douglas D. 1989. "Mental Materiel; The Militarization of Learning and Intelligence in US Education." Pages 13–41 in *Cyborg Worlds: The Military Information Society*. Edited by Les Levidow and Kevin Robins. London: Free Association Books.

_____. 1991. *The Classroom Arsenal: Military Research, Information Technology, and Public Education*. London: The Falmer Press.

Odom, William. 1998. *The Collapse of the Soviet Military*. New Haven: Yale University Press.

Orme, John. 1998. "The Utility of Force in a World of Scarcity." In *Theories of War and Peace: An International Security Reader*, edited by Brown, et al. Cambridge: MIT Press.

Paret, Peter. 1986. *Makers of Modern Strategy*. Princeton: Princeton University Press.

Parry, V. J. and M. E. Yapp, ed. 1975. *War, Technology, and Society in the Middle East*. London: Oxford University Press.

Parsons, Talcott. 1956. "Suggestions for a Sociological Approach to the Theory of Organizations." *Administrative Science*

Quarterly. Vol. 1. June and September.

Peckham, Howard H., ed. 1974. *The Toll of Independence: Engagements and Battle Casualties of the American Revolution.* Chicago: University of Chicago Press.

Penn, William. [1693] 1983. *An Essay Towards the Present and Future Peace of Europe.* Hildesheim: Georg Olms Verlag.

Peter, Laurence J. and Raymond Hull. 1969. *The Peter Principle.* New York: William Morrow.

Porch, Douglas. 1991. *The French Foreign Legion: A Complete History of the Legendary Fighting Force.* New York: Harper Collins.

Pope, Dudley. 1981. *Life in Nelson's Navy.* Annapolis: Naval Institute Press.

Putkowski, Julian and Julian Sykes. 1992. *Shot at Dawn.* Revised edition. London: Leo Cooper.

Reppy, Judith. 1983. "The United States." In *The Structure of the Defense Industry; An International Survey,* edited by Nicole Ball and Milton Leitenberg. New York: St. Martin's Press.

Riches, David. 1987. "Violence, Peace and War in Early Human Society: The Case of the Eskimo." In *The Sociology of War and Peace,* edited by Creighton and Shaw. Dobbs Ferry, New York: Sheridan House.

Ricks, Thomas E. 1998. *Making the Corps.* New York: Scribner.

Roberts, Adam, and Richard Guelff, eds. 2000. *Documents on the Laws of War.* 3rd ed. New York: Oxford University Press.

Rousseau, Jean-Jacques. [1756] 1962. *Jugement sur la Paix Perpetuelle.* Vaughan edition. New York: John Wiley.

Russell, Bertrand. 1956. *Portraits from Memory and Other Essays.* London: Allen and Unwin.

Russell, Frederick H. 1975. *The Just War in the Middle Ages.* Cambridge: Cambridge University Press.

Schaeffer, Robert K. 1990. *Warpaths: The Politics of Partition.* New York: Hill and Wang.

Schell, Jonathan. 1982. *The Fate of the Earth*. New York: Knopf.
————. 2000. "The Folly of Arms Control." *Foreign Affairs*
    79:5:22–46
Scott, Samuel F. 1978. *The Response of the Royal Army to the
    French Revolution: The Role and Development of the
    Line Army 1787–93*. Oxford: Clarendon Press.
Segal, David. 1983. "Military Studies." In *Applied Sociology*,
    edited by Howard E. Freeman, et al. San Francisco:
    Jossey-Bass.
Segal, Mady Wechsler. 1988. "The Military and the Family as
    Greedy Institutions." In *The Military—More Than Just a
    Job?* Edited by Charles C. Moskos and Frank R. Wood.
    Washington: Pergamon-Brassey's.
Shaw, George Bernard. [1894] 1969. *Arms and the Man*. India-
    napolis: Bobbs-Merrill.
Sherwood, Robert E. 1948. *Roosevelt and Hopkins*. New York:
    Harper & Brothers.
Shils, Edward, and Morris Janowitz. 1948. "Cohesion and Disin-
    tegration in the Wehrmacht." *Public Opinion Quarterly*
    2:280–315.
Simmel, Georg. [1908] 1955. *Conflict and the Web of Group
    Affiliation*. Translated by Kurt H. Wolff and Reinhard
    Bendix. Glencoe, Ill.: The Free Press.
Simons, Anna. 1997. *The Company They Keep: Life Inside the
    U.S. Army Special Forces*. New York: Free Press.
Skocpol, Theda. 1979. *States and Social Revolutions*. New York:
    Cambridge University Press.
Smith, Adam. [1776] 1937. *The Wealth of Nations*. New York:
    Random House.
Smith, Merritt Roe, ed. 1985. *Military Enterprise and Techno-
    logical Change*. Cambridge: MIT Press.
Solzhenitsyn, Aleksandr I. 1973. *The Gulag Archipelago*. New
    York: Harper & Row.
Sombart, Werner. [1937] 1969. *A New Social Philosophy*. Trans.
    and ed. by Karl F. Geiser. New York: Greenwood Press.
Sorokin, Pitirim A. 1928. *Contemporary Sociological Theories*.

New York: Harper and Row.

———. [1937] 1962. *Fluctuations of Social Relationships, War and Revolutions.* Vol. 3 of *Social and Cultural Dynamics.* Reprint, New York: Bedminster Press.

Spector, Ronald H. 1992. "A Very Long Night at Cam Lo." In *Experience of War,* edited by Robert Cowley. New York: Norton.

Spencer, Herbert. [1892] 1914. *Social Statics, together with The Man* versus *the State.* New York: Appleton.

Spengler, Oswald. [1926–1928] 1961. *The Decline of the West.* Trans. Charles Francis Atkinson. New York: Knopf.

St. Pierre, Charles Irene Castel de. [1713] 1981. *Project pour rendre la paix perpetuelle en Europe.* Edited by Simone Goyard-Fabre. Paris: Garnier.

Starr, Harvey. 1972. *War Coalitions: The Distribution of Payoffs and Losses.* Lexington, Mass.: Lexington Books.

Stein, Arthur. 1980. *The Nation at War.* Baltimore: Johns Hopkins University Press.

Stein, Jeff. 1992. *A Murder in Wartime: The Untold Spy Story That Changed the Course of the Vietnam War.* New York: St. Martin's Press.

Stinchcombe, Arthur. 1971. "Social Structure and Organizations." In *Structures, Symbols, and Systems,* edited by Marshall W. Meyer. Boston: Little, Brown.

Stouffer, Samuel A., et al. 1949–1950. *The American Soldier.* 3 vols. Princeton: Princeton University Press.

Straus, Murray A. 1992. "Sociological Research and Social Policy: The Case of Family Violence." *Sociological Forum* 7:211–237

Strang, David. 1991. "Global Patterns of Decolonization, 1500–1987." *International Studies Quarterly* 35:429–454.

Stromberg, Roland N. 1982. *Redemption by War: The Intellectuals and 1914.* Lawrence: Regents Press of Kansas.

Sumner, Charles. 1850. "The War System of the Commonwealth of Nations." In *Orations and Speeches,* 2 vols. Boston:

Ticknor, Reed and Fields.

Sun Tzu. [ca. 500 B.C.] 1963. *The Art of War*. Translated by S. B. Griffith. New York: Oxford University Press.

Teachman, Jay D., Vaughn R. A. Call, and Mady Wechsler Segal. 1993. "Family, Work, and School Influences on the Decision to Enter the Military." *Journal of Family Issues* 14: 291–313.

Theweleit, Klaus. 1987. *Male Fantasies*. Vol. 1, *Women, Floods, Bodies, History*. Translated by Stephen Conway. Minneapolis: University of Minnesota Press.

Tiger, Lionel and Robin Fox. 1971. *The Imperial Animal*. New York: Holt, Rinehart, Winston.

Toynbee, Arnold. 1961. *A Study of History*. London: Oxford University Press.

Traub, James. 2000. "Inventing East Timor." *Foreign Affairs* 79:4:74–89.

Tuchman, Barbara. 1962. *The Guns of August*. New York: Macmillan.

U.S. Bureau of the Census. 2000. *Statistical Abstract of the United States: 2000*. Washington: Government Printing Office.

U.S. Congress, Office of Technology Assessment. 1993. *Proliferation of Weapons of Mass Destruction: Assessing the Risks*. Washington: Government Printing Office.

Valle, James E. 1980. *Rocks and Shoals: Order and Discipline in the Old Navy*. Annapolis: Naval Institute Press.

Van Creveld, Martin. 1991. *The Transformation of War*. New York: The Free Press.

Vanecek, Vaclav. 1964. *The Historical Significance of the Project of King George of Bohemia and the Research Problems Involved*. Prague: Czechoslovak Academy of Science.

von Luck, Hans. 1992. "The End in North Africa." In *Experience of War*, edited by Robert Cowley. New York: Norton.

Wallerstein, Immanuel. 1974. *The Modern World-System*. Vol 1. *Capitalist Agriculture and the Origins of the European World-Economy in the Sixteenth Century*. San Diego:

Harcourt, Brace, Jovanovich.

Warf, James C. 1989. *All Things Nuclear*. Los Angeles: The Southern California Federation of Scientists.

Weart, Spencer R. 1998. *Never at War: Why Democracies Will Not Fight Each Other*. New Haven: Yale University Press.

Weber, Max. [1905] 1958. *The Protestant Ethic and the Spirit of Capitalism*. New York: Scribner's.

———. [1921] 1978. *Economy and Society: An Outline of Interpretive Sociology*. Translated and edited by Guenther Roth, Claus Wittich, et al. New York: Bedminister Press, 1968. Reprint, Berkeley: University of California Press.

Weber, Marianne. [1926] 1975. *Max Weber: A Biography*. New York: Wiley.

White, Lynn. 1962. *Medieval Technology and Social Change*. Oxford: Clarendon.

Winsor, Justin, ed. 1972. *The American Revolution: A Narrative Critical and Bibliographical History*. New York: Sons of Liberty.

Wright, Quincy. 1965. *A Study of War*. 2d edition. Chicago: University of Chicago Press.

Zurcher, Louis A., Milton L. Boykin, and Hardy L. Merritt, ed. 1986. *Citizen-Sailors in a Changing Society; Policy Issues for Manning the United States Naval Reserve*. New York: Greenwood Press.

Index

25, 88–89, 162n, 175
conflict resolution, 36–37, 210
conformity, and observability,
    112
Congo, 18, 26, 92
Congress (U.S.), 49, 87, 197
Congress of Vienna, 25, 29, 196,
    199
conscription, 83, 85, 106, 126,
    137–138
Constitution of the United States,
    89, 196
contraband, 54
Continental Congress, 84, 85, 87
conventional war, 18, 20n, 64
    advantage of the attack, 146
    affected by nuclear weapons,
        30–31
conventional weapons, 147,
    149–150
Cortez, Hernando, 91, 142, 157
Costa Rica, 21
cost-benefit ratio, 46
counter-escalation, 6–8
coups d'état, 33, 70, 166
courts-martial, 4, 109–112
    command influence in,
        110–111
Coventry, 59
Crimean War, 46
Croatia, 27, 33, 76
crossbow, 144, 159
Cruce, Emeric, 194–195
cruise missiles, 149, 151, 204
Crusades, 18, 19n–20n, 130, 144,
    194
Cuba, 34, 47–48, 64, 69, 234
Cuban missile crisis, 47–48
Cyprus, 27, 234
Czech Republic, 27

Czechoslovakia, 25, 27, 187, 220,
    225, 234

D

Declaration of Paris, 56
Declaration of St. Petersburg,
    205
decolonization, 17, 28, 90–92,
    234
defeat in war
    causes of, 153–161
    effects of, 163, 164, 166, 168,
        170–171, 177n
Denmark, 27, 138
Desert Storm, 147
desertion, 85, 106, 109, 212, 223
deterrence, 30, 32, 77, 160, 185,
    209
Diplomatic Corps, 33
diplomatic network, 33–35
diplomatic recognition, 33, 34
disarmament, 197, 201–207
discipline, 157–159, 165–167
    in the Roman legion, 14, 77,
        158
    in the phalanx, 14, 158
    incompatibility with chivalry,
        80
    invented by war, 158, 165
    lacking in the Dark Ages, 78
    Maurice of Nassau and, 83
    observability and, 112
    part of the definition of war, 3
    punishment and, 105, 109–112
    sexuality and, 134–135
disease
    analogue of war, 51
    crucial battlefield factor,
        160–161

sexually-transmitted, 134, 172
"Don't ask; don't tell," 135
Dresden, 23, 59, 149
drill, 117–119
  in Islamic cavalry, 158
  in the Roman legion, 75, 78
  Maurice of Nassau and, 82–84
due process, 110
Duke of Wellington, 109
Durkheim, Émile, 118

E

economy
  costs of World War I, 58
  Germany and Russia in World
    War II, 231–233
  war and, 174–175
education
  in the U.S. military, 124, 133,
    171–172
Egypt, 13, 25, 26, 64, 76, 143
Ehrenreich, Barbara, 12
electromagnetic pulse, 148
emotional arousal
  in social conflict, 4–5
enemy
  fraternization with, 129
  in coalitions in triads, 44–45
  perceptions of, 130, 133
  sex with, 134
  treatment of 54, 55, 57, 59,
    60–61
Engels, Friedrich, 163, 183
England, 14, 40, 216
  at Agincourt, 127–128,
  early peacekeeping treaty, 194
  Norman invasion of, 160
enlisted personnel, 131–133, 137
  compensation of, 107–108

lacking honor, 81, 101, 123,
  127
mobility of, 104
ranks in U.S. armed forces,
  96–101
selecting officers, 85
status gap and, 101, 121,
  123–125
entrenchment, 83, 90, 92n, 146
episodic conflict
  defined, 8
  tribal warfare as, 12–13
equipment, 159, 174–175, 210
  as military advantage, 141–142
  borrowing, 120
  inspection of, 119–120
  modification of, 120–121, 182
  nomenclature, 122
  observability and, 112
  of Roman legion, 76–77
  personnel needs of, 104,
  tables of, 75, 103, 143
Eritrea, 26, 27
escalation, 6–9
espionage, 33
Essex, 23
Estonia, 25, 27
Ethiopia, 26, 27, 37, 64, 69, 150
ethology, 10
Etzioni, Amitai, 106–108
European Community, 36, 45
European Confederation, 196,
  200
European Parliament, 195
European Union, 28, 190, 209
expected utility theory, 46–47
explosive shells, 58, 88, 146

166
Medal of Honor, 107
mediation, 36–37, 194
Meinertzhagen, Richard,
    105–106
mercenaries, 79, 81–83, 108
Mesopotamia, 143
Mexico, 36, 66
  conquest of, 142, 157
  pre-Colombian, 13,
Micronesia, 26
Middle East, 91, 209
Midway, Battle of, 142
migration, 35, 169
Milan, 82
military culture, 117–139
military etiquette, 121
military language, 121–122
military law, 109–112, 135, 175
military leadership, 113–114,
    159–160
military medicine, 173–174
military occupational specialties,
    102
military organization
  modern, 95–116
  origins of, 75–93
  modes of, 155
  victory and, 159
military planning, 153, 170–171,
    204
military police, 106, 118
military revolution, 164
military rituals, 117–121
military sociology, 113–116, 160
military success and failure,
    153–162
military technology, 141–151,
    173–174
military units, 96, 102, 103,

millennial movements, 181–182
milspec, 174
mines, 56, 90
mobilization
  in social conflict, 6–7
Mohammed, 185
Moldova, 27
Mongols, 130
Monroe Doctrine, 32
Montenegro, 25, 64
morale, 130, 157–158
  in advanced militaries, 111
  in World War II, 113
  inspection of, 119
Moscow, 187, 188, 198, 217,
    227, 229, 230
multimedia, 172
multinational corporations, 35
multinational forces, 198
multinational institutions, 35–36
Munich, 215
Murmansk, 221
Myanmar, 18, 66, 68
mythmaking
  in social conflict, 5

N

Nagasaki, 23, 49, 59
Napoleon, 42, 87, 159, 186–187
  Russian campaign of, 16, 47,
    213
Napoleonic Wars, 15, 176
national fusion and fission, 23–29
National Guard, 85, 176
  National Security Agency, 173
NATO, 7, 31, 37, 138, 142
  as peacekeeping organization,
    32, 38n
navies, 107, 216

Paris Commune, 58
Pax Romana (Roman peace), 75, 78, 185
peace
  by balance of power, 29–30
  by democracy, 184
  by deterrence, 30–32
  by diplomacy, 33–34
  by empire, 185–188
  by national fusion, 23–29
  by rationality, 184–185
  by revolution, 183
  by socialism, 50, 52, 58, 183, 187–188
  by world federation, 188–191
  defined, 21
  King's, 21–22
  religious, 22, 181–182
peace projects, 181–191
peacekeeping organizations, 32, 193–200
Pearl Harbor, 157
Pemba, 26
Penn, William, 39, 195
Pentagon, 113, 173
perceptual distortion, 5
Permanent Court of International Justice, 37
Peru, 142
Peter Principle, 105
phalanx, 14, 141, 158
Philippines, 18, 41, 133
  tribal war in, 12–13
"phoenix effect," 170
Piedmont, 24
poison gas, 17, 59, 90, 146, 150
Poland, 25, 187, 200
  in Soviet-German war, 213, 215, 220, 222, 227, 228
Poltava, 213

Ponape, 26
population
  as cause of war, 19, 50–51
  as strategic resource, 28
  government and, 40–41, 49, 71, 198
  war and, 168–169
positivism, 182
power
  in military organizations, 106–109, 158
  military, distribution of, 65–66
  See also balance of power, coalitions.
Presley, Elvis, 126
prisoners of war, 5, 60
Prohibition, 22
protocol, diplomatic, 34, 53
psycho–analytic explanation of war, 50
public opinion, 88, 184, 197
  in Soviet-German war, 229–230
  manipulation of, in war, 23, 70–71
  military law and, 110

Q

Al Qaeda, 66

R

radar, 65, 90, 159, 174, 175, 221
radiation, 148,
Rational Actor Model, 47–48
rational pacifism, 191
Reconstruction, 89
Red Army, 187
  Berlin and, 134,
  World War II and, 214, 217,

caused by third party intervention, 37
caused by possible domination, 45
demographic effects of, 169
defense, primacy of, 170–171
disarmament after, 201–203, 205
executions in, 108, 119
German Revolution and, 170
moral costs of, 58
number killed, 16
number mobilized, 16
number of casualties, 16
poison gas in, 17, 150
Russian Revolution and, 166
technical conditions of, 58, 90, 103, 146, 174
U.S. home front in, 168
U.S. recruiting in, 133
U.S. troops in, 109, 111
unofficial truces in, 129
violations of laws of war in, 59, 60
See also Versailles treaty, League of Nations.
World War II
  as second part of the Great War, 15, 89
  as terminal conflict, 9
  atomic bomb in, 147
  balance of power after, 45, 63
  bombing in, 149
  decolonization and, 28, 91
  demographic effects of, 169
  domestic politics and, 128
  GI Bill, 172
  internment of Japanese-Americans, 4
  League of Nations and onset

of, 37
military law and, 110
military sociology during, 113, 130
number killed, 17
number mobilized, 17
number of casualties, 17
offense, primacy of, 90, 146
sex in, 134
Soviet-German war, 213–235
technical conditions of, 90, 103, 146, 174
U.S. conscription in, 138
U.S. home front in, 168
U.S. industrial might in, 141–142, 157
unofficial truces in, 129
violations of laws of war in, 59, 60
Wright, Quincy, 13–15, 19n

Y

Yap, 26
Yemen, 25, 26, 27, 28
Yom Kippur War, 198
Ypres, 103
Yugoslavia, 25, 33, 187
  fission of, 27, 64, 209
  intervention in, 31,
  split from Soviet Union, 183, 188

Z

Zambia, 26
Zanzibar, 26
Zimbabwe, 26
Zulu, 130

About the Authors

Theodore Caplow is the Commonwealth Professor of Sociology at the University of Virginia. Among his many books, *Principles of Organization* (1964) and *Peace Games* (1989) are the closest in theme to *Systems of War and Peace*. He saw combat as an amphibian engineer in New Guinea and the Philippines in World War II and holds the Purple Heart.

Louis Hicks is an associate professor of sociology at St. Mary's College of Maryland. He is a coauthor of *The First Measured Century: An Illustrated Guide to Trends in America, 1900–2000.* He is a Fellow of the Inter-University Seminar on Armed Forces and Society. During the waning years of the Cold War, he served in the U.S. Army as a Russian linguist.